MIND OVER MONEY

The PSYCHOLOGY OF MONEY and HOW TO USE IT BETTER

CLAUDIA HAMMOND

CANONGATE
Edinburgh · London

Published in Great Britain in 2016
by Canongate Books Ltd,
14 High Street, Edinburgh EH1 1TE

www.canongate.tv

1

British Library Cataloguing-in-Publication Data
A catalogue record for this book is available on
request from the British Library

ISBN 978 1 78211 205 1

Typeset in Plantin Light by Palimpsest Book Production Ltd,
Falkirk, Stirlingshire

Printed and bound in Great Britain by Clays Ltd, St Ives plc.

For my sister Antonia
and my nieces Florence and Matilda

CONTENTS

INTRODUCTION

ON THE EVENING of 23 August 1994, in a small abandoned barn on the island of Jura in the Scottish Inner Hebrides, a fire was burning. Had you stepped inside you might have thought that a newspaper archive was being destroyed. Great bundles of printed paper were alight, sending smoke and ash billowing up into the air.

You'd also have noticed that there was something a little odd about the way the paper ignited. It took a while to catch and then burned sluggishly. Eventually you'd have realised that the paper was denser than the fine stock used for newsprint – and the sheets were much smaller than newspaper pages. Then a torn corner dancing past in a hot air current might have caught your eye. Wasn't that a picture of the Queen's tiara? Indeed, weren't those £50 notes on the fire? And not just a few, but hundreds?

In fact, what you'd have witnessed on that August night more than twenty years ago was the destruction by fire of £1 million. A million pounds in £50 notes. It took just over an hour – 67 minutes, to be precise – to complete the task. A fat hour to burn the stuff of every lottery player's dreams.

The two men behind the fire were from the band KLF. They had made the money with dance tracks from the early 1990s such as 'Justified and Ancient' and '3 a.m. Eternal'. Tired of the music scene, they'd moved on to making art. For them, the burning of the million pounds was a work of conceptual art. Their first idea was to make a sculpture from bundles of notes nailed to a wooden frame. But as a sign of the taboo they were dealing with, they couldn't find a gallery willing to exhibit such a sculpture. So they had another idea.

Just burn the money.

The whole process was videoed. You can watch it on YouTube today. The two members of KLF are dressed, rather predictably, in black. At first, they peel £50 notes from a wad one at a time, feeding them casually to the fire, almost as if they're throwing bread to ducks. Jimmy Cauty screws up every note before consigning it to the flames; Bill Drummond frisbees them into the blaze. The notes burn slowly. Some drift out of the fire and have to be gathered up and thrown back in again. After a while the K Foundation, as they called themselves by then, realise that at the rate they are going, the process will take hours. So they speed things up: chucking in armfuls of notes at a time.

Despite the video evidence, there were suspicions afterwards that the whole thing was a stunt. Would anyone really burn so much real money? To prove the doubters wrong the K Foundation had the remains of the fire tested in a laboratory. There it was confirmed that the ashes were the genuine remains of a very large quantity of banknotes.

The performance went to plan, but nothing prepared the band members for the hostility the act would induce.

People *hated* them for it, saying if they didn't want the money why not give it to charity? People called them selfish and stupid.

After a few minutes of seeing the money burn on the video we all want to know *why* Cauty and Drummond did it. Okay, it was some sort of art work, but signifying what?

Surprisingly, in the many interviews they've given over the years (you can watch these on YouTube too) the two men struggle to answer this question – seeming incoherent, inconsistent, and not even convincing to their own ears.

In the official documentary Jimmy Cauty admits that what they did was possibly meaningless, that its status as a work of art is highly disputable. 'You can get into this whole area where it's pretty black.' You hear him fumbling for an explanation, falling into despair.

In one TV interview, Bill Drummond says: 'We could have done with the money.' Cauty and he had six children between them. Only to add: 'but we wanted to burn it more.' Then when asked what it was like to throw the notes onto the fire he says he felt numb, that the only way to do it was to operate on autopilot. 'If you're thinking about every fifty quid or every bundle . . . ' and his voice fades almost as though he can't bear to think about it.[1]

Yet Drummond also insists they hadn't really destroyed anything. 'The only thing that's less is a pile of paper. There's no less bread or apples in the world.'[2]

It is this apparently unarguable statement that gets to the heart of the matter – and explains why so many people were so angry and upset by what Cauty and Drummond did. For although it's true that no actual bread or apples were destroyed in the fire, something *was* destroyed. The *possibility* of bread and apples. A million pounds worth. Food that could have fed people.

What was also destroyed was the possibility of planting trees to grow apples or building a bakery to make bread – or employing others to do so. Which might have resulted in *many* millions of pounds worth of produce over the years.

And it doesn't stop there either. Everyone who watches the film of the burning cash thinks about what they could have done with the money. A new house. A new car. Freedom from debt. The option to set up a new business. The opportunity to help family and friends. The chance to travel the world. Aid for thousands of children in a poor country. Help for a project to save the rainforest.

It would have been a different situation if Cauty and Drummond had set fire to an object worth a million pounds. In that case *only* that particular object – a painting, a yacht, a precious jewel – would have been destroyed. And not everybody would even have valued what was lost.

Had they frittered the money away in traditional rock star fashion – trashing a hotel or snorting it up their noses – people would doubtless have deplored the waste and excess, but there wouldn't have been such an outcry. And if they had just hoarded the money or put it in a high interest account or invested (and perhaps lost it) on the stock market, few people would have cared. While if they had given it away, they would of course have been applauded.

The issue is not that two men had a million pounds and then they didn't. It is that *nothing* came of this vast sum. All the possibilities inherent in the money – for them, but also for the rest of us – were lost.

Herein lies the extraordinary power that money has over our minds. We have invested in bits of paper, lumps of metal and figures on a screen (all worthless in themselves) the promise of so many things we value. More than that, the promise, and our confidence in it, actually summons those myriad things we value into existence. If there is magic in our world this is surely it. Something abstract and virtual, a product of our minds, helps us to create the things we need and want.

It is this property of money that made Cauty and Drummond's act so transgressive, so sacrilegious: such a taboo. To strike at money is to strike not just at the foundations of modern human society but almost at what it means to be a contemporary human being.

For we are profoundly psychological beings – it is our minds that make us what we are – and money is a mental construct, that doesn't exist beyond our idea of it, but on which we now depend for most of the things we need to live.

And yet most of us affect to despise money. We would do away with it if we could and are drawn to societies, both real and imagined, which apparently have no need of it. Take this passage from Herman Melville's early travelogue-cum-novel *Typee* published in 1846. Who wouldn't want to live in this earthly paradise?

> There were none of those thousand sources of irritation that the ingenuity of civilised man has created to mar his own felicity. There were no foreclosures of mortgages, no protested notes, no bills payable, no debts of honour in Typee; no unreasonable tailors and shoemakers, perversely bent on being paid; no duns of any description; no assault and battery attorneys, to foment

discord, backing their clients up to a quarrel, and then knocking their heads together; no poor relations everlastingly occupying the spare bed-chamber, and diminishing the elbow room at the family table; no destitute widows with their children starving on the cold charities of the world; no beggars; no debtor's prisons; no proud and hard hearted nabobs in Typee; or to sum it all up in one word – no Money!

Melville ended up in Typee, a real place on a South Sea Island, after jumping ship. But for all its charms so fondly recalled and re-imagined by Melville – the book is a blend of fact and fiction – he constantly longed to escape, back to civilisation, back to the society he knew, and back, by implication, to money.

This is how it is for us. We've cast ourselves out of money-free supposed Edens like Typee. And yearning to go back to them or trying to recreate them (as my old friend Dylan Evans tried to do recently when he set up a self-sufficient society in Scotland, where things didn't quite go to plan)[3] is to miss the point. The ills of our society are not caused by money itself, but the way we use it. So how can we all do a better job of using money for good rather than ill?

This book is called *Mind Over Money*. It's a play on words, of course. But there's more to it than that. My starting point is that too often we are prone to the opposite. We let money control our thinking, sometimes in counterproductive and even destructive ways. To stop that happening, to allow money to help us lead a good life and create a good society (which it can do), we need a better understanding of our psychological relationship with the stuff. There are lots of books about what to do with money or how to make it. This isn't one of those books. Nor is this a book about the evils of money, consumerism and capitalism. They undoubtedly bring their problems, but currently this is the way we live. I'm not arguing that money necessarily sullies us. It is more complex than that, but in this book I will be disentangling the links between money and our minds.

Inevitably different disciplines approach the topic of money from different perspectives. The political economist Karl Polanyi defined money in the broader sense as a semantic system, in the way that language or weights and measures might be thought of, or in a narrower sense as the items used for 'payment, standard, hoarding and exchange'.[4] Freud compared money with faeces, saying children are initially interested in playing with their waste products before they move onto mud, then stones and eventually money. The nineteenth-century philosopher and psychologist William James considered money to be part of our extended self. 'Our self,' he says, 'is all that a man' – and he did just refer to men – 'can call theirs which includes your body, your psychic powers, your clothes, house, wife and children, ancestors, friends, lands, horses, yacht and bank account.'[5]

The key psychological feature of the idea of money for me is trust. The historian Yuval Noah Harari calls money the 'most universal and most efficient system of mutual trust ever devised'.[6] Money provides us with an abstract way of freezing trust. To stay safe and to prosper we need to co-operate with each other. This is easy if you know someone well, but co-operation with strangers requires a means of quantifying and exchanging that trust. This is what money can provide. No wonder that no society that has begun to use money has reverted to doing without.[7] But this is not a book about the history of money. It is a book about what money does to us today, how it changes our thinking, our feelings and our behaviour, and how when it's scarce, it can have even more of a hold over us.

We constantly make assumptions: that big bonuses encourage chief executives to try harder, that we can bribe our children to do their homework, or that faced with a set of deals we know exactly how to choose the one that is the best value. But as I'll show, the evidence demonstrates that we're not always right. Along the way we'll meet the people who find thinking about money eases their fear of death, the man who gambled away more than four million pounds, and the people of Tamil Nadu who freeze when faced with life-changing amounts of cash.

Once you've finished this book, I trust you'll think there's a better response to the problems of money than burning £50 notes or escaping to your own Typee. That instead of feeling you're controlled by money you control it. In other words you will have achieved *Mind Over Money*.

1

FROM CRADLE TO GRAVE

Where our relationship with money starts, why money is both a drug and a tool, why we hate to see money destroyed and how it wards off our fear of death

If you are like me and enjoy the occasional bar of chocolate or the odd glass of wine, every time you indulge, your neurological reward system responds. A pathway is activated in your brain. You experience a spike of dopamine. Which gives you pleasure. *Do it again*, your brain seems to be saying. *Do it again and you'll get another reward.*

It's easy to see how parts of your brain might become active in these circumstances. A chemical and neurological chain reaction takes place. Yet the same thing has been shown to happen when people are given money.[1] In one study winning money and having tasty apple juice squirted into the mouth produced similar responses in the brain.[2] And the reward doesn't even have to be a coin or banknote as long as it represents money. When neuroscientists put people in a brain scanner and gave them vouchers as prizes when they won in a quiz, the brain's limbic system released dopamine.[3]

Dopamine is all about immediate reward rather than delayed gratification. And what's remarkable here of course is that there's no direct link between consumption and reward. Money and vouchers are promissory. They promise you can do something in the future. Okay, you could rush down to the corner shop to buy wine or chocolate (maybe even with the vouchers) but the gratification still isn't instant.

Money is acting like a drug, not chemically but psychologically. Money hasn't existed for long enough in evolutionary terms for humans to develop a specific neural system to deal with it. So it seems as though a system usually associated with immediate rewards has been co-opted to deal with money. Sometimes neuroscientific studies can feel as though they simply reflect in the brain what we already know to be true from our experiences. Here neuroscience can tell us something more curious.

For a *promise* of money – someone merely saying they're going to give you money but not handing over notes or a voucher – doesn't have the same effect. When this happens, different regions of the brain are activated. We don't view the prospect of money in the same way as actual money (or even vouchers), despite the fact that the latter can't be spent immediately either.

So it appears we desire money for its own sake. It's a kind of drug. Of course money isn't physically addictive as such, but as I'll show in Chapter 2, we're all drawn, to varying degrees, to the thing itself.

Yet, at the same time, we desire money because it helps us to accomplish what we want in life. In other words, money is a tool: a way of getting the things we want.

Psychological research on our attitudes to money has tended to concentrate either on money as a drug *or* as a tool. But the British psychologists Stephen Lea and Paul Webley surely echo common sense in suggesting it's both. Sometimes money seems to control us – money over mind; sometimes we are able to use money in the way we want – mind over money.

But of course it's more complex than that too. Money affects our attitudes, our feelings and our behaviour. And these three dimensions interlink, merge and decouple in fascinating and downright strange ways.

Yet to complicate things even further, when money is destroyed our brains revert to seeing simply it as a tool.

Time to think back to that night on Jura, when the K Foundation burnt a million pounds. What was it that upset people so much about the destruction of cash?

In 2011, the husband-and-wife cognitive neuroscientists Chris and Uta Frith conducted a study that might shed some light on it.[4] They slowly reversed prone volunteers into a brain scanner, where a mirror angled at 45° allowed them to watch a series of short videos on a screen. Each film lasted 6.5 seconds and every one featured the same woman wearing a black jumper and sitting at a shiny white table.

The people watching the video never saw the woman's face, but they could see her torso and also her hands, which held a banknote. Sometimes the banknote was real, but worth a lot (the Danish krone equivalent of £60); sometimes it was real but worth a lot less (the equivalent of £12); and sometimes it was the same shape and size as a banknote, but featured scrambled-up pictures (making it obvious that the note was worthless).

As the people lying in scanners watched, the woman held up one of the notes, slowly moved her fingers to the centre of the top of the note and then ripped it very deliberately – from top to bottom. The reactions were what one might expect. When the woman was tearing up the obviously fake notes, people were fine about it. But when real money was destroyed they felt uncomfortable, particularly with the higher denominations. But when real money was destroyed they responded to a questionnaire saying they felt uncomfortable, particularly with the higher denominations.

In many countries, it's illegal to deface or destroy money. In Australia, such action lays you open to a fine of up to A\$5,000 or a two-year prison sentence.[5] These were punishments that some felt the prime minister of the country should have faced back in 1992. Paul Keating was visiting the Townsville Oceanarium in North Queensland when a local artist asked him to autograph two A\$5 banknotes. He did so, was filmed in the act and a storm of outrage followed.

It turned out the artist was protesting at the new design of the A\$5 note, on which a portrait of Queen Elizabeth II had replaced that of the nineteenth-century human-rights campaigner Caroline Chisholm. (As we'll see in the next chapter such changes can stoke strong feelings.) But to add fuel to the flames, it was a time when the future of the Queen as Australia's head of state was the subject of much controversy, and Keating was also known to have reservations about the change. Angry royalists pointed out that another man who had stamped a protest message on banknotes had been convicted, so why not this artist and the prime minister?[6]

Another Australian, Philip Turner, discovered that defaced banknotes were rendered worthless when he was handed a A\$20 note in his change at a petrol station. Written in felt tip pen on one side was the message: 'Happy birthday.' (Nice – though it wasn't Mr Turner's birthday.) While on the other it said: 'Suck it. Now you can't buy anything.' (Not so nice.) The unknown author of this two-faced foolery was right, though. Shops wouldn't accept the defaced note, the garage refused to take it back and not even the bank would exchange it.[7]

Writing on money is nothing new. What better way of literally getting your message into people's pockets? In Britain the suffragettes did it. On display in the British Museum is a penny minted in 1903 and subsequently stamped with the slogan 'Votes for women'.[8] It was a clever method of protest, as such a low-value coin was likely to be passed around a lot before being taken out of circulation. But whoever stamped the coin took a big risk – at the time, defacing money could result in a prison sentence.

What of going a step further and trying to destroy money altogether? In the United States the seriousness with which the burning of banknotes is taken is clear from the language used in Title 18 of the United States code that prohibits it under the heading 'Mutilation of national bank obligations'. In practice, convictions seem to be rare. Desecrating flags is taken far more seriously. Across the border in Canada, the melting down of coins is banned, but for some reason notes aren't mentioned. While in Europe, the European Commission recommended in 2010 that member states must not encourage 'the mutilation of euro notes or coins for artistic purposes, but they are required to tolerate it'.[9]

But these are the rules set by institutions. How about our personal feelings about the act of destroying money? We return to the Friths and their colleague, Cristina Becchio, who together measured the reactions of people watching as Danish banknotes were torn up. The experimenters did not fear prosecution as they'd obtained permission from the Danske Bank to go ahead with the study. Even so, this destruction of money was clearly a transgressive act in the minds of most people.

As I mentioned earlier, the volunteers in the brain scanners described their distress as they watched the real notes being torn in half, but what was of real interest were the areas of the brain which were stimulated. It was not the regions usually associated with loss or distress that saw raised activity, but two small areas of the brain, the left fusiform gyrus and the left posterior precuneus. The first of these areas has been found in the past to have an involvement in the identification of pen-knives, fountain pens and nut-crackers; in other words, tools with a purpose. This suggests that the idea of money as a tool is not just descriptive. The association we make between printed sheets of paper and their usefulness is so strong that our brains appear to respond to them as if they were actual tools.

And this of course fits with the reasons many people have given over the years for feeling so upset about the K Foundation's actions. They tend to emphasise all the useful things that could have been done with that money. They're not, in other words, distressed at the destruction of the physical artefact (though in the next chapter I'll show we are also attached to money's concrete forms) but at the idea of the loss of its potential.

I'm wary of reading too much into one study, and the authors concede that the changes in brain activity could have been caused by the sheer distress of watching the money get torn up. Previous studies have found that people with damage to a part of the brain called the amygdala stop minding so much about losing money. [10] The amygdala is a walnut-shaped area deep inside the brain associated with some, but not all emotions. Such studies suggest an emotional connection with money. What's so fascinating about the Friths' study is that it hints at the *symbolic* nature of money: that we know that it can be used as a tool. It goes to show – as I'll demonstrate again and again in this book – that when we look at, handle, or even just think about a sum of money, powerful reactions are stirred. Some good, some bad, some downright weird. But before that we need to look back to where our relationship with money all starts.

MONEY-MINDED CHILDREN

When small children first encounter money, they see it as something to value for itself. They handle a sparkly coin or a nice, crisp banknote and take pleasure in that. They quickly grasp that these pieces of metal or paper are to be treasured and not discarded, that when a grandparent sneaks a coin into their hand (it's probably a note these days) it is something special, magical even. I'm not sure that feeling ever stops. Certainly the novelist Henry Miller, in his non-fiction book, *Money and How It Gets That Way*, didn't think so. 'To have money in the pocket is one of the small but inestimable pleasures of life. To have money in the bank is not quite the same thing, but to take money out of the bank is indisputably a great joy.'[11]

Recently I was in a park with my friend's four-year-old daughter, Tilly. She'd just been given a sparkly, beaded purse that contained a few coins she'd saved. Every time a stranger passed, she waved her purse and shouted delightedly: 'Look – I've got lots of money!' When I asked her what the loose change might buy her, she had no idea. That was not the point. She had money, and money was magnificent.

How strongly she wanted to hold onto it was shown when, after half an hour on the swings and slides, she refused to return home with us. We tried leaving her behind and telling her she'd be there on her own. We tried threatening to report her to her mum when we got back to the house. We tried playing a chasing game. Nothing worked. She wouldn't budge from the playground. Then the little girl's aunt had an idea. She grabbed Tilly's purse when she wasn't looking and ran off with it. She'd only get her purse back if she came with us, Tilly was told. That did the trick. Tilly didn't know how much money she'd lost, still less what it would buy her, but it was *her* money and she valued it for its own sake. She was starting her life-long relationship with money.

It's a relationship that becomes richer and more complex quite quickly.

When I was at junior school, my sister and I had savings accounts at the local building society. Occasionally, we would go in to deposit a pound in our accounts and come out proudly with our updated passbooks. One year, the building society held a competition to create a piece of art depicting their office, a Victorian villa situated on the roundabout just off the high street of the little town where we lived.

My entry was a collage. I made the walls of the building from pale yellow hessian. I cut out pieces of paper to look like people and placed them so that they were leaning out of the upstairs windows waving their passbooks. Looking back, I've no doubt it was these cut-out people who helped me to win the competition. But it was not because my artistic efforts so delighted the judges – one of whom was the building society manager. More likely it was down to my massive overestimation of interest rates.

I'd filled in the little cardboard passbooks held by my paper people with figures such as: 'Deposit: £600, Interest: £300. Balance: £900'. Admittedly interest rates were running high in those days, but definitely not that high! Still, it showed that even as a little girl I had some understanding of how money works, even if I was sketchy on the detail. I'd already been introduced to the concepts of saving, interest, deposits and balances. I knew that money wasn't just a matter of handing over a certain number of coins in order to get a certain number of sweets.

One study I particularly like about our early grasp of money involves a group of six-year-olds in a Finnish nursery school. It's 2008, and they sit on a carpet to create their own theatrical production. Adult producers are there to help them, but the point is for the children to make as many decisions about the play as possible – everything from the set design to the plot and the wording of the script.

After some discussion, they invent a story they call 'Six Million Lions'. They select parts for themselves, with one boy insisting that he would play a table made from potatoes, a role that sounds as though it would stretch most actors, but which – in the spirit of self-determinism – is permitted. The whole idea of this project is for the children to be in control. The adults don't mention money, but that doesn't stop the children.

Marleena Stolp from the University of Jyväskylä in Finland spent six weeks watching the theatre production, recording the children's conversations and then analysing them.[12] She soon found one topic that predominated – money. The children knew they were creating something with a market value; they discussed ticket prices and the possibility of filming the performance in order to sell the DVD in shops. They were only six years old, but far from viewing the play as simply an entertaining experience, they were already thinking about how to market and monetise it. There was no doubt that they loved the idea of making money. They even discussed how to select a ticket price that people would be prepared to pay, well aware that the market would not allow them to overcharge and that they risked having no paying audience if they did.

So these children already had some comprehension of money, pricing and the idea of the market. Where does this understanding of the value of money come from?

SAVING FOR A LUTE

In a study conducted in Hong Kong, a group of five- and six-year-olds were given the word 'money' and asked to free associate. They had plenty to say on the subject. Not surprisingly, they mainly associated it with the ability to buy things they wanted (similar studies in the US and Europe have found the same). They didn't tend to have views on the virtue or otherwise of money.

Which is not the case with adults. When the same researchers gave adults questionnaires about whether money was good or bad, different groups took different stances. Students in particular had negative views about it. They believed it to be less good, less interesting and, strikingly, less powerful than business people did.[13] By contrast the young children hadn't developed ethical positions on money. It was just there, and they knew it was something desirable and useful, something you wanted to have, ready to spend. The notion of saving is something children learn about and appreciate even when they're quite little. That said, before going to school, when children do save, the main motivation is usually the pleasure of collecting money, piling it up and counting it. It's only as children get a bit older that they begin to save for a particular item they want to buy.

In my case, the cherished item was, rather bizarrely, a lute. I'd seen one at a craft fair at Hatfield House, the Tudor mansion in Hertfordshire where Elizabeth I was supposedly sitting under an oak tree in 1558 when she was given the news that she was to become queen. More than half a millennium later I became determined to save up enough to buy a lute. In order to track my progress, I carefully drew one of those fundraising thermometers. I also opened a special savings account at my favorite building society. I was extraordinarily, and rather sweetly, tenacious about my saving. After five years I had accumulated £187. Which was a good effort, but not nearly enough loot to buy a lute. The one I had my eye on cost £1,400.

Still, if I hadn't been so set on the unobtainable lute I might never have saved that much. By the end of the five years, I was at the age where children realise that saving is useful more generally. Money doesn't just have to be earmarked for a particular purchase. It represents choice. It's worth having even when you're not sure what you want to buy with it. Some time in the future you'll want or need something, and if you have savings you might be able to afford that something.

Sadly, I rather frittered my lute money away. Having grown out of my Elizabethan phase, I spent my savings on records by Billy Idol, The Sisters of Mercy and U2. (Though, thinking about it, vinyl of that vintage might not be such a bad investment after all.)

This illustrates how hard it is to define 'good' saving among children. You could measure their saving as a proportion of any money they have received over a certain period of time, whether that's regular pocket money or birthday money from their grandparents. But is saving up some of that money for several months or years and then buying an expensive toy really worthy of praise? If an adult did something similar – a fifty-year-old man spending all his savings on a pricey motorbike, for example – we might see him as extravagant. He might have saved up for some time, but then he blew the cash all in one go.

But then is it really better to save a little less for shorter periods and to spend that money on, say, books? If you really like books, this sort of saving is really just another form of indulgence. And what of saving a large sum with no great object in mind? It might seem responsible. You never know when you might need the money. But in an adult, such saving might seem stingy or even miserly.

Taking everything into account, adults generally applaud

the regular saving of a proportion of income. We need to save in order to afford a deposit on a home. It's a form of insurance for spells of unemployment or a bout of illness. And of course, we have to think about retirement. I'll come back to how adults can trick themselves into saving more in Chapter 13. But children struggle with the concept of a 'rainy day' – the umbrella in these situations is provided by their parents, their very own 'nanny state'. And the self-restraint that saving requires is a real trial for children who live much more in the moment.

This was nicely demonstrated in a study that created a so-called 'play economy'.[14] Each child was told that to start them off they had an imaginary bank account containing 30 tokens. Then they were told that time in this imagined world was speeded up. Each 'day' lasted just 10 minutes and every 'day' they'd be given an additional 10 tokens. So, for instance, after the first hour – '6 days' – if they'd spent none of the tokens in the meantime, they would have 'saved' 90 tokens.

Next, the children were shown around a set of rooms. Some activities were free. Others cost tokens. In the library, there was no charge for reading books, but they had to pay if they wanted to watch a film. In the room next door, video games attracted a charge, as did items in the café and the sweetshop, but borrowing pencils and paper for drawing was free. The decisions the children made about their spending would affect their activity in the final room – the toyshop – where they could buy real toys to take home, but only if a child still had 70 tokens left. You can see the excruciating calculations the children had to make. In order to get a toy in the toyshop, they would have to spend time, but very little money in the different rooms. It would mean forgoing computer games, food, drink and sweets for 40 minutes in order to accumulate those 70 tokens. They would be left with nothing to do but boring old reading or drawing.

Children tend to take experiments like this very seriously, but find them hard. Part of the reason is that for children such tests involve real sacrifice. This was demonstrated by Walter Mischel, the psychologist who invented the famous marshmallow test.[15] As you may know, the marshmallow test offers children the choice between eating one marshmallow straight away or waiting 10 minutes to get two. An adult taking part would know they could show restraint during the test because they could always buy a whole bagful of marshmallows on the way home if they felt like it. The small child has no such get-out.

The children in the 'play economy' faced the same struggles, and very few had the willpower to save up enough tokens for a toy, however much they wanted it. They had already learnt that savings were a good thing, but when faced with more immediate temptations in the other rooms, they couldn't restrain themselves. By the end of the experiment, only half the children had saved enough tokens for a toy and a quarter hadn't saved any tokens at all. For those who worked out quite early on they were going to be a long way short of being able to 'buy' the toy, their overall behaviour was actually very rational. After all, they couldn't take their play savings out of the play economy. Certainly they felt their 'savings' were money lost, rather than something useful.

BANKS, SHOPKEEPERS, ROBBERS AND TOOTH FAIRIES

Back in the 1980s, the influential Italian psychologists Anna Berti and Anna Bombi followed a group of three- to eight-year-olds in order to track how their ideas about money changed as they grew up.

What the two psychologists found was that children of about four or five usually had no idea where money came from. They had little concept of paid work and tended to assume that everybody was given money, often by the bank.[16] It was an assumption a group of five- and six-year-olds also made when questioned by New Zealand's 'fourth most popular musical comedy band' Flight of the Conchords. The duo was looking for ideas for lyrics for a song to raise money for sick children for Red Nose Day in 2012. They asked a group of children in a school where money comes from. 'Banks,' came the answer. And where do the banks get the money? 'The prime minister.' And where does the prime minister get the money? 'The Queen.' And where does she get the money? 'Banks.'

Given the complex circularity of modern economies, maybe it's a fair enough answer. Money does sort of begin and end with banks. And until you are yourself working, it's easy to forget that the wealth stored in money has to be created somewhere. Indeed in the UK, our economy is based on a financial sector, rather than manufacturing.

The children helping Flight of the Conchords with their Red Nose Day song also had some good ideas about raising money for ill children, which a chancellor struggling to find funds for the NHS might wish to take note of. Among their suggestions were trapping robbers and taking the money out of their pockets, and asking children to save up their teeth and then collecting them in one big bowl so that they could get lots of money from the tooth fairy.

Anyway, you can watch the resulting song online.[17] It's

very funny, and you might argue it's as good a guide to our financial system as some economics text books.

But back to Berti and Bombi's research: they found that children a little older than four or five often had the rather sweet idea that money came from shopkeepers. They had seen staff in shops giving their parents change, while seemingly missing the fact that their parents had handed over rather more money in the first place. It was only when children were about seven or eight, Berti and Bombi concluded, that they properly understood that their parents had money not because banks or shopkeepers gave it to them, but because they were paid for their work.[18]

However, more recent research on children's understanding of money would appear to contradict – or perhaps bring up to date – the seminal work of Berti and Bombi. This research, conducted in 2010, is by the Finnish social anthropologist Minna Ruckenstein and it involves group discussions with young children at nurseries in Helsinki.[19] Ruckenstein admits that she and other facilitators often have no idea what the children are talking about until they carefully study the transcripts afterwards. But what those transcripts reveal is that these days pre-schoolers seem well aware that you get money through working and then you exchange it for food and other items in shops. Indeed when a few children in the groups suggested that you could obtain money by buying things, others soon corrected them.

Generally these young children were also able to explain the purpose of piggy banks, cash machines and high-street banks. What they really liked was finding what they called 'free money' around the house, but even then they knew it hadn't just appeared magically, that it must belong to someone. The children in Ruckenstein's study knew so much about the idea of saving money, of only buying what they could afford, and not wasting money on things they didn't need, that they were annoyed when they were asked about it. One child even refused to respond to questions about saving because the answers were so obvious, saying: 'Do you have some other questions?'

Not surprisingly, the main source of the children's information on money was their parents. Ruckenstein found that some parents actively taught their children how *not* to spend – in other words to exercise the self-restraint the children in the play economy had found so difficult. The huge influence of parents might explain why the young children in Ruckenstein's study seemed more clued up about the source of money than the kids in Berti and Bombi's studies. Remember the latter pair was doing their research in Italy back in the 1980s, when fewer women would have been out at work and more would have been caring for children at home. These days, both parents (especially in a country like Finland) are likely to work. And when little children ask the question: 'Why do you have to go out to work, Mummy?' the answer is very likely to be: 'To earn the money we need to live.'

So children acquire most of their knowledge from their parents. But how exactly? Mostly through observation. They see the frequency with which their parents buy or deny themselves the things they want. They repeatedly witness their parents selecting certain brands, or going to different shops for bargains. They watch the way they weigh up price and value.

This process of acquiring financial knowledge and developing attitudes toward money is known as financial socialisation. Active discussion of money matters is much rarer. Research shows that many children reach adulthood without any idea what their parents earn or what savings they might have. Some therapists have found that couples would rather discuss their sex lives or even their infidelities than discuss their finances.[20] And if people won't discuss money with their partners, they're even less likely to discuss it with their children.

THE POWER OF POCKET MONEY

For most of us, our first introduction to the concept of having our own money to manage is through pocket money. In the UK, for example, research has shown that most children get some sort of pocket money or allowance, however poor their parents might be. Indeed a study by the influential London-based psychologist Adrian Furnham has found that low-income families tend to give their children proportionately more money than middle-income families. His study also found that pocket money rises fastest between the ages of seven and ten, and slowest between the ages of 15 and 18.[21]

Furnham's study also showed that middle-income parents were more likely to make their children work for their allowance, an interesting finding given that these parents could afford to be more generous without expecting any help around the house in return. Though maybe parents in households where there is more money available feel that it is more important to emphasise the message that money doesn't grow on trees.

There is no definitive proof on whether the middle-income parents are taking the right approach. Some studies suggest that a contingent approach, where pocket money has to be earned through completing homework or doing chores, is the best way for children to learn about money. Others find that a consistent allowance gives the child more responsibility for planning how to manage their own cash.

Then there's the risk that once you monetise housework, your children won't ever volunteer to help. (We'll learn more about this issue, which affects adults too, when I turn to intrinsic motivation in Chapter 7.) Then there's the problem that when it comes to exam time, you might prefer it if your children revised rather than washed up to earn their pocket money.

Some researchers in the field suggest it's a good idea to explain the family budget to children as they get older, so that they can see where their allowance fits in to the bigger picture and how, if they want more money, it will have an impact elsewhere. Neale Godfrey, the author of parents' money guides such as *Money Doesn't Grow on Trees*, goes as far as to suggest that children's pocket money should be treated in the same way as an adult's income. She recommends 15 per cent should be taken away in tax and put into a general family fund. A family vote would then decide how it was spent. Another 10 per cent of a child's pocket money should go to charity, she says. The child gets no choice about the amount assigned, but does get to choose the good cause. In this way children learn to become 'citizens of the household', Godfrey argues.

Not everyone will want to go to such extremes. What all parents should do, however, is be open and consistent about where pocket money comes from and what children can expect to get. And they should be able to ask for similar transparency from their children in return. Indeed there are even experts who have made the rather extraordinary suggestion that parents should ask their children to provide a yearly review of their spending so that they can see how this fits in the context of the family budget.

That said, in a study of 1,500 families living across the United States, almost two-thirds of young people between the ages of 12 and 18 said that their parents usually or almost always knew what they spent their money on. The study also found that those children who had to work to get their allowance were almost twice as likely to donate to charity. Surprisingly, family income didn't make a difference to how much children saved or gave away. It was emotional warmth that mattered, with those children living in a warm family more likely to save up their cash, sometimes for their own college fees.[22]

Of course, as well as knowing how much you have, successful money management also requires you to know what it will buy you. Minna Ruckenstein's research suggests nursery-school-aged children know the former, but not the latter. The kids she studied all knew the total amount of money they had and were very keen to tell her, even though she didn't ask them. What they couldn't work out was how their cash converted into spending power. When one child said they had $200, the others all agreed that this was a lot, but none of them knew what that sum might buy.

It is as children that we learn about the maths of money. There is evidence that a good conceptual grasp of maths leads to better financial management in adult life, and in the American study of families referred to above, children who were not good at maths were more likely to exhibit financial anxiety. By contrast, those who were best at calculation were more likely to donate to charity and to save for the future.

It all means that just as parents should talk about money more with their children, so they should also encourage them to master maths. It will help their children grow into adults who know how to handle money more wisely and to have a healthier relationship with it. What it won't do is allow them to enjoy total control over money. Mind over money is always a matter of degree.

We've seen where our relationship with money starts. But where does it end? Money is more tied up with our thoughts about death than you might ever imagine.

THE ANTI-DEATH DRUG

Here's a statement: 'I am very much afraid to die.' Would you say that was true for you, or false? Here's another: 'The thought of death seldom enters my mind.' Again: true or false?

If you were to take part in one of the experiments run by psychologist Tomasz Zaleskiewicz in the Polish capital Warsaw, a further ten questions measuring your anxiety about death would follow. But Zaleskiewicz is not really interested in your attitudes to death. He's interested in your attachment to money.

Before he starts quizzing people on their mortality, he sets them an exercise. Half the participants are given a stack of banknotes to count, while the other half get a pile of pieces of paper of the same dimensions as the banknotes, with numbers printed on them. The task is the same for both groups: to add up all the numbers. The result: people who count the money are less afraid of death. [23] Their fear is reduced by almost a fifth.

This isn't what Victorian morality tales teach us, is it? In those stories, the old miser counting his piles of dusty coins is usually portrayed as wracked with mortal terror. It is the hero living in poverty who cares nothing for worldly goods who has no fear of the end.

Hanging in the National Gallery in Washington, DC, there's a gruesome painting by Hieronymus Bosch in which a miser on his death bed reaches for a bag of gold proffered by a demon, even as death – in the form of a shrouded skeleton – appears at his door. Meanwhile an angel puts a hand on the miser's shoulder, hoping to lead him down the route to salvation instead. To the medieval mind, this painting was not suggesting that counting money was a way to ward off fear of death. Rather it was the road to damnation.

Fewer of us fear hell these days. A more common fear is of nothingness, a great void. Perhaps that's why we find it comforting to reach for something concrete; something measurable; something we like to think is reliable; something that will live on – money.

That at least is the idea.

Zaleskiewicz argues that money in general is an 'existential drug', by which he means a drug that relieves our existential angst. So that is why we seek to accumulate money, he says: it serves as a buffer against our greatest fear.

This may all sound unlikely. We've been told, most famously by Benjamin Franklin, that only two things are certain: death and taxes. Yet we know that however much we pay of the second we are not going to escape the first.

'You can't take it with you' applies as much to money as our other material possessions. But of course you can pass it on, provided it's not taken from you in tax. Perhaps that's why some people object so passionately to inheritance tax. You have gone, but your children live on, and if your money doesn't go in tax they will have it to comfort them – which is some comfort for you.

Zaleskiewicz and his team have also conducted their study the other way round: putting death before money, as it were. This time half the participants were asked to fill in the questionnaire about death anxiety at the start of the experiment. Then they were shown a series of coins and banknotes and asked to estimate their physical size. This group over-estimated the size of the coins by more than the control group, who had filled in a questionnaire about the fear of going to the dentist. There were other differences too.

How much money does a person need to qualify as rich? The death group named a higher sum than the dental torture group.

A small sum of money now, or a slightly larger sum in the future? The death group were more inclined to take the money straight away.

Now there is some debate surrounding studies of this kind, which employ a technique called 'priming', and I'll come back to that in Chapter 11. Having said that, this last finding in particular does make some sense. If you are contemplating your own death – which as we all know can come at any time – it is best to cash in now. But an important point in Zaleskiewicz's studies is that people dwelling on death seem to be comforted by *having* money, not spending it. In the 'small sum now or a larger sum later' question, it wasn't that people were considering one final blow out. And in a further study by Zaleskiewicz and his team, when people were asked to fill in the death anxiety questionnaire and then imagine how they would deal with a surprise windfall, they allocated more to saving than spending.[24]

These studies all involved real banknotes, and there is nothing we like better. Numbers on a screen or figures on a bank statement don't compare. And it is to the curious power of physical money that I turn next.

2

HOLDING FOLDING

*Why we're so attached to familiar forms of money,
why we think coins are bigger than they are, why
it's good to be grumpy if you don't want to get
ripped off and why paying with cash might be
better than credit.*

AT ONE TIME, money was really worth something. That is
to say, its physical form – coinage – was valuable in and of
itself. Yet we've long known that isn't really the point. The
point is that money represents a store of value. Its worth lies
in the fact that we can exchange it for something valuable.
But even though we know that, we're still strongly attached
to the forms money takes, and we're sensitive, and sometimes
even distressed, when those forms change.

Anthropologists such as David Graeber have shown that
money existed in early human societies living 5,000 years
ago.[1] And what's really interesting is that its existence as a
virtual concept – in the forms of debt and credit – long
predated its appearance in physical form as coinage. In

other words, money was in our minds long before we could hold it in our hands. Contrary to popular belief, earlier societies did not use to rely entirely on bartering – that is to say, the direct and immediate exchange of goods or services: 'I'll mend your wall if you give me right now something we agree is equivalent – say, ten eggs.' Instead, people have always recognised that a form of abstract exchange is necessary: 'For mending that wall, I'm willing to accept something that can be redeemed at some stage in the future for goods and services we agree are equivalent to the mending of the wall.'

Immediately we can see that this is a complex mental concept, requiring imagination, the ability to inhabit a mind other than our own, the capacity to conceive of a number of futures and – crucially – notions of trust, honour and confidence. We think that contactless payments, chip and pin, and all the rest are signs of twenty-first-century sophistication, but in a sense they are simply a return to money as it started out. Before it became a coin, for example, the Mesopotamian shekel was a unit of weight representing the amount of barley a worker received for his labour in the fields. A shekel was therefore a promise, an IOU. It was only over time that it became a stamped coin.

That said, coinage soon established a firm grip over human imagination; a grip it exerted for many centuries. And although actual currency is less and less important in our monetary transactions these days, when we think of money we still tend to see it as a physical thing.

To this day a British £10 note is printed with the words 'I promise to pay the bearer on demand the sum of ten pounds' – a promise which used to mean you could exchange it in a bank for gold to the same value, literally ten gold sovereigns. It was long thought that without that written guarantee there would be no confidence in national currencies.

Indeed the 'gold standard', as it came to be known, under-pinned even advanced economic systems until well into the twentieth century, with the United States only abandoning it altogether as recently as 1971. But there was a big problem with the gold standard. It was too rigid for complex, dynamic economies – and strict adherence to it led to the miseries of the Great Depression of the 1920s and '30s.

Even so, coming off gold proved to be a protracted busi-ness, and to this day central banks retain large stocks of gold as a bulwark to other confidence measures.

Assuming you were able to succeed in exchanging the money in your bank account for gold, would you know what to do with it? You can't eat gold after all. And as a metal, it's not even one of the most useful. Its value lies partly in its relative rarity and the fact that we like the look of it, but largely because we have collectively invested it with a sense of preciousness. Again, it is essentially a psych-ological thing. If we all decided that gold was dross, it would become so.

We imbue money with its value. The Pacific island of Yap is famous for its huge stone discs – as large as 4 metres in diameter with holes in the middle – which were used as currency back in the 1900s. Mined from limestone on another island hundreds of miles away, the stones were traded for goods. When sold, they remained in the same place, but with a new owner. Economists such as Milton Friedman have used these stone discs as an example of how money can still be seen as valuable if it is declared to be so, despite not being made from a material as useful as metal (fiat money as some economists call it).[2] And as he points out, it's the money we've grown up with which feels most real to us. Foreign notes can feel like toy money. But in fact these stones did have an intrinsic value to the islanders. They were considered both to be aesthetically beautiful and to have a religious significance. The story goes that when a storm caused one of these vast stones to fall overboard on a boat journey back to the island, it was decided that the money was not lost, even though it now lay at the bottom of the sea. Mentally it was still money.[3] They still believed in it, just as we believe in the value of our £10 notes.

Of course these days if you went into a bank to redeem the promise to pay the bearer the sum of ten pounds, there is nothing they can give you apart from other notes to the same value also bearing promises. More than that, your money in the bank comes in the form of a figure listed on your statement, and you can only have the banknotes as long as lots of other people don't want to do the same thing at the same time. If that happens – as it did in Britain in 2007 when there was a run on the Northern Rock bank – it quickly becomes evident that banks don't hold sufficient quantities of cash to pay everyone their money back at once.

In the case of Northern Rock, and the financial crisis that ensued, the Bank of England and the British government had to intervene to prevent the complete collapse of our economic system. How did they do this exactly? Psychology again. The various actions of the Bank and the Treasury somehow 'restored confidence'. In ways we don't really understand, we all decided that we would continue to believe in money so that economic life could be maintained.

It's essentially a confidence trick. As the Bank of England website drily puts it: 'Public trust in the pound is now maintained by the operation of monetary policy, the objective of which is price stability.'[4] The Bank is exerting its mind over money.

No wonder that the stuff itself, in its various physical manifestations, fascinates us and exerts a power over the mind. As we'll see, we even consider money of the same value differently, depending on its form.

THE POUND IN YOUR POCKET

In the 1980s the psychologists Stephen Lea and Paul Webley developed a psychological theory of money that shows we value cash, cheques, gift vouchers and bank account balances differently.[5] One of the things they discovered was that we are particularly attached to physical forms of money.

A crisp new banknote is very satisfying to have and hold, particularly a rarely seen pink £50 note. To be 'holding folding', as the old British expression describes the possession of cash, gives us a visceral pleasure. When a lottery winner finds out they've won a few million they often say they can't really imagine that much money. To make it feel more real, they might be presented with one of those giant cardboard cheques. But just imagine how much more thrilling it would be if the National Lottery handed the money over as stacks of bills in sleek leather brief cases. Far more exciting than an electronic money transfer.

Somewhat in the same way, we all enjoy a pile of coins. When I was little, my grandparents used to save particular pennies and halfpennies and give them to me to stack in satisfying piles. The ones they saved were the bright and shiny coins, which they called 'new money'. A stack would have been worth less than twenty pence, but given the condition of the coins, we all considered my pennies a little bit special.

Most of us like wads of notes too, of course. But as notes get older and dirtier we actually spend them faster. Research has shown that their 'dwell time' – the time a particular note spends in a wallet – is shorter than for newer, cleaner notes.[6] Ten pounds is ten pounds is ten pounds. But the fact is we regard different notes differently.

At the moment, the Bank of England is replacing paper £5 and £10 notes with stronger material made from polymer, which will last two-and-a-half times as long. Every day 2 million notes are removed from circulation, with high-speed sorting machines identifying those that are too dirty or torn, or have impaired security features. There are good, practical arguments for making this switch, but if history is anything to go by, the new notes are likely to excite comment and divide opinion.

We take the design, as well as the form of our money, very seriously. So seriously, in fact, that a change in design can spark outrage and even death threats. That's what happened in Britain in 2013, when the Bank of England announced it was removing the picture of the social campaigner Elizabeth Fry from £5 notes and replacing it with an image of Winston Churchill, meaning there would be no women, other than the Queen, left on Sterling notes. Feminist campaigner Caroline Criado-Perez led calls for another notable woman, Jane Austen, to appear on £10 notes – and for her pains was threatened with rape and murder.

No doubt much of the vile abuse heaped on her through social media was simply down to misogyny. Even in this day and age, some men are unhappy that women speak out publicly. But the hatred directed at Criado-Perez was much worse than the harassment received by many other women who've campaigned for women's achievements to be recognised. Why is that? When I met Caroline Criado-Perez at Cheltenham Science Festival, where she was speaking on a panel I was chairing about feminism and bringing up girls today, she told me she wonders whether the reason is that money is seen to emanate from the establishment, and so to have women demanding recognition *on* that money represents a particular threat to the 'natural' order of things.

Banknotes are both ubiquitous and somehow sacred. They're a strong projection of nationhood and economic power. A banknote isn't just a store of value; it is a symbol. One of the most powerful a country has. The choice of person featured on banknotes matters: kings and queens, independence leaders, military heroes, social reformers, writers and composers. Do governments hope that a reminder of power or influence in the form of a portrait on a note might add to our confidence in its currency? The implication is that this note, just a bit of paper (or soon, polymer) and of no intrinsic value, can be trusted because it is issued by the central bank of a country that produces such monumental figures.

Happily Criado-Perez eventually won her battle, and Jane Austen will feature on the new British £10 note.

HOW NOT JUST GRANNY STRUGGLED TO GET THE POINT

In 1971, Britain's whole system of currency was overhauled. To aid the country's accession to the European Economic Community, now the European Union, Britain changed to a decimal system to match the other countries involved.

Under the old system, a penny was one twelfth of a shilling, and there were twenty shillings in a pound. Under the new system, a penny was one tenth of the new 10 pence coin (effectively the replacement for the shilling) and ten 10 pences added up to a new pound.

Decimalisation was introduced only three months after I was born, so I've known nothing else. But for those who had grown up with the 'old' money, the change caused considerable confusion, as well as provoking strong reactions. Some saw it as a surrender of British uniqueness to European uniformity; others were suspicious they were in some way being swindled. Most were at the very least uneasy about such a big change to something as foundational as the currency.

The Government was concerned enough to commission a 5-minute public information film explaining the benefits of the new money. It was called, rather patronisingly, 'Granny Gets the Point'. (They'd never get away with such ageism and sexism now.) My own grandmother could see the logic of the change well enough, but it didn't stop her from feeling some mistrust. And that was an entirely rational reaction. For a start, for quite some time, whenever she bought something with the new money, she had to mentally calculate what it would have cost in the old money just to be sure she was getting a fair deal. It was like being abroad and having to work out whether two francs for a cup of coffee was a rip off.

It didn't help that decimalisation coincided with an era of high inflation. Each month, the new pound bought you a little less than it did the month before. Of course, it was nothing like those situations in countries wracked by hyper-inflation – Germany between the wars; Zimbabwe more recently. In these places, in their darkest days, it took barrow-fuls of bills to buy a loaf of bread, workers were paid as often as three times a day and 2,000 printing presses worked day and night to print higher denomination notes. Crazy numbers – 5 million marks, 500 million marks, 5 billion marks – reflected a complete collapse in economic confidence. Even so, in the 1970s British people came to see their new pounds and pence as diminished, not just in terms of what they could buy, but in their actual physical size.

Five years after the introduction of decimal coins, there was an experiment in which people were shown a series of circles of different sizes on a piece of paper and asked to guess from memory which best matched a coin of a particular value. It was true that the new decimal coins were generally smaller than the old coins, but even so people significantly overestimated the dimensions of the old coins.[7] It was as if their minds were telling them that old money bought more so it must have been bigger.

Perception of size is something we learn through experimentation as babies and toddlers. As the developmental psychologist Jean Piaget famously discovered, very young children cannot fathom how a taller, thinner beaker could possibly hold the same amount of liquid as a shorter, fatter one. At that age tall means big. Only as our cognitive abilities improve do we develop a more sophisticated understanding of volume that enables us to estimate how much differently shaped beakers will hold.

As we develop, our perceptual skills gradually improve, only for things to go awry again when money is involved. In a classic study, conducted way back in 1947, children more than old enough to understand Piaget's liquid conservation tasks were presented with a table laid out with a series of coins and cardboard discs. The discs were identical in size to the coins, but again and again the children judged them to be smaller than the real money.[8] These were children who knew the value of the coins, and this knowledge seemed to skew their perception of size. More than that, the more the coin was worth, the more their perception became skewed. An abstract concept, the store of value in coins was overtaking their sense of something more concrete – the physical size of the coins compared with the discs.

Masses of studies followed, confirming that all over the world, adults as well as children overestimate the physical size of money, regardless of the currency. And, as we've already heard in Chapter 1, people prompted to think about death are even more prone to this perceptual exaggeration. Not only that, but the size of the effect depends on whether or not the participants in studies are rich or poor. For example, the 1947 researchers tried out their experiment both with children in a settlement house in one of Boston's slums and with pupils at a school in a well-to-do area. The children living in poverty overestimated the size of the coins more than their wealthier counterparts. Echoing findings I'll discuss later in Chapter 10, their lack of money, and therefore the precious quality they attributed to it, skewed their perceptions that bit more.

MONOPOLY MONEY, THE ACCORDION EFFECT AND
WHY BEING GRUMPY LIKE JEAN-MARIE LE PEN CAN BE
USEFUL

In April 1983, Britain began the changeover from the £1
note to the £1 coin. The press was not keen on the idea.
'The Pound Britain Doesn't Want' read a headline in the
Daily Mail, dubbing the new gold-coloured pieces 'toy town
coins'.[9] The economic value of the coin was exactly the same
as the note. The problem was that people didn't see it that
way. They viewed and treated the two forms of £1 (which
for a limited period were both in circulation) differently, as
the economic psychologist Paul Webley discovered.[10]

Webley persuaded a group of people to allow him to
examine the contents of their wallets every day for a month.
He marked every note and coin with one of those invisible
detective pens that can only be seen under UV light, before
returning every penny to their wallets. This allowed him to
track the dwell time that each coin or note spent with its
temporary owner before it was passed on to someone else.

At the start of the six-month transition period, during
which notes were phased out, people obviously had fewer
£1 coins than notes. The new coins were a novelty, and were
bright and shiny, and you might think people would be keen
– for a while at least – to hang on to them. Indeed, some
people in Webley's experiment did hoard them or put them
in piggy banks, but for the most part the coins had shorter
dwell times than the notes.

What could Webley conclude from this finding? He had
some ideas, but first he wanted further evidence. The problem
with his initial experiment was that, with so few coins in

circulation, it was hard for Webley's team to collect enough data. So they tried something else. Members of the university staff were given either a pound coin or a pound note, pre-marked with the special pen, in exchange for completing a questionnaire. When the staff returned the following day for the next part of the experiment, they were asked to reveal the contents of their wallets. Half of the pound notes remained, while most of the pound coins had already been spent.

Paul Webley complains that most economists considered this finding to be of no interest.[11] Like him, I think they're wrong. Even if people were simply disposing of the relatively heavy coins weighing down their pockets, this was presumably having some impact on economic activity at the time. Pounds were being spent more readily because of their change of form.

Of more interest psychologically, the study seemed to show that people considered pounds in coin form as loose change that was more disposable. A pound note by contrast still seemed to represent a more significant sum to be used cautiously. That is surely evidence that the form money takes can change our sense of its value, which if nothing else should make central banks pause whenever they consider replacing one form of currency with another.

In the United States, feelings also ran high when an attempt was made to replace bills with coins. Dollar coins were introduced back in 2007, but the famous greenback dollar bills continued to be produced, and the use of the coins was low. By 2011, with more businesses returning than requesting them, the Federal Reserve Banks found themselves with enough dollar coins to meet the demand for the next 40 years. The Treasury ordered production to cease and now, although ticket machines occasionally spit coins out at you in change, the US is the only G8 leading economic power still using a note of such little value.

But the Dollar Coin Alliance, backed by car wash companies, vending machine firms and snack food sellers, is still campaigning for dollar bills to be replaced by coins.[12] Not surprisingly, mining and metals companies support the change too. The Alliance argues that a single coin can last 35 years, 17 times as long as a dollar bill; that coins are 100 per cent recyclable; and that when people complain about the weight of coins in their pockets, they should bear in mind that four quarters weigh three times as much as a single dollar coin. Taking all of this into account, they say, the US government could save $150 million a year if coins replaced bills.[13]

The Federal Reserve Board argues these savings are exaggerated; that the growth of debit and credit card use renders coins less relevant today than in the 1980s, when many other countries made the transition; that their notes can now last six years due to their superior production; and that coins cost more to produce and are easier to forge.[14]

So it seems there are strong economic and practical arguments on both sides, but that's not what interests me. Rather I'm struck by the strength of feeling the debate generates, which is passionate and heartfelt. It's not just a case of finding the most sensible and sustainable course of action. There are emotional attachments to consider, particularly with regard to the much-loved dollar bill. And for the moment that attachment seems to be winning out. In a Reuters poll, the complete replacement of bills with coins was not at all popular, with three-quarters of people saying they preferred their greenbacks.[15]

The world's largest-ever currency changeover, in 2002, saw 12 countries in the EU give up their individual currencies and replace them with the euro. As the change took place the European Central Bank used the slogan '*the* EURO. OUR *money*', stressing pan-European solidarity, and after the introduction of the new currency the majority of people polled in the affected countries did say they felt more European as a result.[16]

Not everyone was happy of course. On the steps of the Paris Opera House, the leader of the French far-right National Front Party, Jean-Marie Le Pen, called for a contemporary Joan of Arc to drive out the Eurocrats. 'Long live the franc, long live France, long live the French!' he cried. [17]

As a result of the currency change, 9 billion notes and 107 billion coins were withdrawn. The European Central Bank introduced 15 billion new notes and 51 billion new coins.[18]

Public information campaigns across Europe suggested simple conversion strategies to help people adjust to the new currency. Kits containing one of each of the new coins were bought by 150 million members of the public, to familiarise themselves with the coinage before it could be spent. Products were labelled with dual prices at the start of the three-year transition period. And, in a sign of the times, diskettes were handed out to householders containing information on the changeover.[19]

After that, it all happened remarkably quickly. Within two weeks of 1 January 2002, euros made up 95 per cent of the currency in circulation. In that first week of the New Year, withdrawals from ATMs were far higher than usual. But curiously robberies from security vans dropped right down. So thieves apart, most Europeans quickly got used to having euros in their pockets. Yet by the end of the first month, only 28 per cent of people said they thought in euros.[20]

Despite the extensive publicity campaigns to familiarise everyone in the Eurozone with their new currency, people still needed to do mental conversions between the old and new money.

Ireland's reaction to the euro changeover was among the most positive. 77 per cent of people said they were very or quite happy with the idea compared with a European average of 53 per cent.[21] Some Irish people did remark that it was a pity to lose the attractive designs on the Irish banknotes, but during in-depth interviews with psychologists, others liked the new notes. One said it was like being 'a child at Christmas', another that it was like having Monopoly money.

This reaction partly stemmed from the fact that of all the countries joining the single currency only Ireland had a previous currency with a unit value higher than a euro. An Irish pound was worth 1.28 euros. So people marvelled at these new high numbers on their salary slips. For a fleeting moment, they felt richer. Until, that is, they went shopping, where everything looked more expensive. Some people suspected that shopkeepers were taking the opportunity to rip them off, although in fact there was little evidence to back up this suspicion. The real problem was one most of us are familiar with if we travel overseas: it's just difficult to calculate whether prices in an unfamiliar currency are fair.

One technique that Irish people used was to learn a few reference prices along the spectrum and then guess prices in between. Another strategy – you may have used it yourself – is to learn the price of one thing, let's say a pizza, and then apply it to anything else you purchase. So, while it may be hard to calculate quickly whether the scarf you want to buy is good value just by converting x currency to y currency, you find you can compute the sums if you think to yourself, how many pizzas would that scarf set me back?

While the Irish, along with other people in the Eurozone, struggled a bit to adapt, the new coins and notes became a little more familiar every day. However the old currency still holds a nostalgic draw for some Eurozone citizens. In 2014 sales of gold and silver reproductions of the old Italian lira coins and commemorative books on the currency amounted to more than 25 million euros.[22]

In countries that hadn't adopted the euro, where of course there were no public information campaigns, dealing with the currency has not been as easy. The Swedes didn't have to use the euro on a daily basis, but the fact that many of their close European neighbours had joined the single currency meant some familiarity with the new money was important. How then would they cope with it?

The first experiment carried out by a group of researchers as part of a study in 2002 was a simple one. They asked people in the Swedish city of Gothenburg to look at a list of prices of magazines, bus fares and monthly rent expressed either in the local Swedish crown or in the euro. Then people were asked to rate each price on a five-point scale ranging from very cheap to very expensive. Now the cost of living in Sweden does tend to be higher than in most European countries. But it was not that which led the Swedish respondents given the amounts expressed in euros to say that prices were cheaper. No, they thought euro prices were lower for one simple reason: the numbers on euro notes were smaller than the numbers on Swedish crowns.[23] People were being fooled by the fact that a two-euro bus ticket sounds cheaper than a five-crown bus ticket, just because two is a smaller number than five. People were just guessing, rather than bothering to do the calculations, but would they take sums more seriously if they were asked to ponder the possibility of actually moving to a country? Or would they still be mesmerised by the numbers on the notes?

Next time round, the Gothenburg residents were asked to consider the following scenario. They had been offered a good job in another EU country known to have friendly people and a pleasant climate. It was surely an attractive prospect. But of course, before moving, people would want to consider the cost of living.

The prices of various items including a cinema ticket, a haircut, a piece of cheese, a vacuum cleaner and a queen-sized bed (yes, a rather random selection of objects) were given to the participants in various made-up currencies. Did they think these items were more expensive in these currencies than the prices they were used to in Sweden or not? With a bit of effort to calculate exchange rates, people could have worked it out for real. But instead they tended to assume that if the price was expressed in a high-number currency – something like the old Italian lira – then the item was more expensive in that country than at home.

This effect has been dubbed the 'euro illusion'.[24] (It's a variant on the broader 'money illusion', a phenomenon first noticed by the economist Irving Fisher back in 1928.) What happens is that we can't help but focus on the actual numbers printed on banknotes and this skews our attention away from real values. So why do we fall into this trap?

For a start, as we've found, thinking this way is easier

than doing complex calculations. But there's also the issue of what's known as psychological salience. This can take various forms. It might be that something stands out from the crowd, such as a single red tulip in a sea of white flowers, in which case our attention is drawn to the exceptional thing. But in another case – one angry face in a crowd of happy people – the salient thing is not that the angry face is the exception (we don't tend to notice one happy face in a crowd of angry people) it's that our minds are attuned to notice anger in particular. We do that because anger can spell danger for us. In the case of money, what is particularly salient is the big number. We've been taught since childhood to equate big numbers with more money. So – using the old Italian lira as an example again – when I visited Rome in the mid-1990s and a glass of prosecco was advertised as costing 10,000 lira, my immediate response was, 'What?!' The number in front of me dominated my thoughts. And only later, perhaps after I'd decided not to bother, did I work out that 10,000 lira was less than £3, which was reasonable enough for a glass of fizzy wine at a café in a sunny piazza.

Back among the Eurozone countries, there was another difficulty for some people. In Austria, Portugal and Italy, half of those people questioned in polls said the change was still causing them problems a year later.[25] And what they were struggling with was what's known as the accordion effect – that two prices in euros were harder to compare than two prices in their old currencies, because in the new currency the numbers were much closer together.

Think about it: the difference between one and two euros doesn't seem that big. But 20,000 lira seems a lot bigger than 10,000 lira. To revert to my example above (and this time imagine I'm Roman born and bred), the cost of a glass of prosecco expressed in euros not only seems cheaper than it was in lira, but having two glasses doesn't seem so extravagant because doubling such a small number seems pretty trifling.

Something along these lines may have happened in another country that joined the single currency in 2002. Every September, the National Collection for Mentally Handicapped Persons would go door-to-door in the Netherlands asking for donations. In a study conducted in three villages in the September after the adoption of the euro, giving rose by 11 per cent.[26] Income levels remained the same, and it's unlikely that compassion had suddenly increased, so the probable explanation was the new currency.

It seems people simply weren't prepared to put in the cognitive effort to calculate the exact amount in euros, which would equate to the amount they used to give in Dutch guilders. Instead they roughly estimated the sum, and fortunately for the charity this meant they rounded it up a bit. Incidentally, the next year donations to the charity rose again, but this time by 5 per cent. Perhaps people were getting better at their calculations.

Anyway, the picture is clear. The change to the euro messed up people's ability to exert mind over money. Unhitched from the familiar moorings of their old currency, they were, temporarily at least, at sea with their new currency, rather in the way we all are when we use foreign money. In the great scheme of things it probably didn't matter all that much. People were not so muddled as to go on wild spending sprees or demand massive pay hikes. The impacts were at the margins and in time people adapted. But even so, any change in the physical manifestation of money causes some psychological disruption.

I close this section by positing a possible strategy for coping with currency change. Be warned it involves being grumpy, so it might not appeal to all.

The basis for my idea is this: psychologists have demonstrated that when people are happy – immediately after they've watched a video of penguins slip-sliding on the ice, for example – they are better at generating creative answers, but they are less good at mental arithmetic or tasks needing thorough processing.[27] Recalling this research left me wondering whether those who were strongly opposed to the introduction of the euro (Jean-Marie Le Pen, for instance) might have had an advantage over jubilant federalists who welcomed monetary union.

The reason is obvious when you think about it. Jean and his Eurosceptic friends would have experienced a dampening of mood every time they saw a price label expressed in their new and unwanted currency. But there was an upside. Their grumpiness could allow them to make more precise calculations about prices.

Of course you may have noticed that there is a problem with the application of this stratagem. When do you need to be able to do currency conversions most often? Probably when you're on holiday. So to avoid getting ripped off abroad you might need to go to places you loathe to ensure that you're miserable. Perhaps this isn't going to work . . .

CASH OR CARD?

So far we've been considering how our minds deal with changes to coins, banknotes or types of currency. But money has changed in a more fundamental way in recent years, away from physical forms of any kind.

In your wallet it is likely you're carrying coins and banknotes, credit cards and debit cards, electronic travel cards and vouchers, as well as points on loyalty cards. But if I asked you how much money you have on you right now you'd probably only include the amount you had in cash.

We treat cash, cards and vouchers separately, so we don't tend to calculate their combined spending power. In some instances that is logical. Try going into a pub and buying a round with a combination of a supermarket loyalty card and some book tokens and you'd get short shrift. Yet increasingly we pay for drinks – or even *a* drink – with debit or credit cards.

It's convenient, but is it money-wise? Perhaps not. Only a couple of decades ago, the limit on your spending in a bar in one evening was the cash you had with you. Even if the bar staff had accepted it, you wouldn't have got out your cheque book to pay for 'one for the road'. These days the boundary between everyday money and all the money you have (in your current account at least) is increasingly blurred.

I know some people who feel that for a small purchase such as a sandwich you should always use cash. Debit cards are for bigger purchases and credit cards for luxuries and holidays. It's a way of exerting self-control over money. It doesn't seem right to borrow from a bank to buy a cheese-and-pickle sandwich with a credit card, if you can avoid it.

This might sound rather quaint and fastidious, but recent research suggests it's a sound mental strategy. Researchers in

the United States monitored the food shopping of 1,000 households for 6 months.[28] Controlling for all sorts of factors, the
researchers found that when people were paying by credit or
debit card, they tended to make more impulsive purchases of
unhealthy foods like cakes or chocolate. It seems our propensity to indulge in guilty pleasures increases when we don't
have to hand over 'real' money. So going 'contactless' might
expand our waistlines as well as slimming down our bank
accounts.

Of course it is not in the least surprising that we tend to
use a card when the price is higher. It means we don't have
to carry around large sums in cash, and – in the case of a
credit card – allows us to spend money we don't actually
have yet. But there's more to it than that.

When we use a card we are not only more likely to decide
to go ahead with a purchase, but our thinking changes. We
are less likely to remember the amount we paid,[29] and more
likely to add a bigger tip. And as this next experiment shows,
we are even prepared to spend more on the same goods.

At 1pm on Sunday 19 April 1999, the Boston Celtics
began their last basketball game of the season against the
Miami Heat. The match was crucial. If the Celtics were to
take the division title, they needed a win. Celtics games
always sold out well in advance, but MBA students at the
world-famous Massachusetts Institute of Technology (MIT)
in Boston were offered the chance to get their hands on a
pair of tickets just the week before the game by taking part
in a psychology experiment.

Psychologists who set up such experiments are notorious
for their use of subterfuge, but in this instance the tickets
were genuine and one lucky participant really would get to

see the game with a friend. Not for free, mind. This was not a giveaway exercise. The winner would have to pay the face value of the tickets. And here's where there was a bit of economy with the truth – the students didn't know that. They were told they had to bid against others in a silent auction and believed that they could pay more than the standard ticket price if they chose to.

What the researchers wanted to know was the price students were prepared to pay for these precious tickets; and in particular, whether the form of payment would make any difference.

All the students were given a sheet of paper on which to write their best offer, but half of them were told they would need to pay in cash – and would be allowed to visit an ATM if necessary – while the other half were told they could pay with a credit card. How much would they offer for the tickets?

The difference was striking. Those paying cash bid an average of $28, but the card payers were prepared to offer more than double that amount: $60.[30]

Now I say this result was striking, but even so I doubt it surprises you that much. I suspect the behaviour of the MIT students mirrors your own attitudes. It certainly does mine. Paying with cash always feels that much more *real* somehow; and parting with it, that much more painful. Paying with a card delays the pain and makes the transaction easier. Some would say too easy. With the increase in the availability of instant credit, personal debt in the UK, for example, more than tripled between 1990 and 2013.[31] There is a lesson to learn from this. Whenever you are tempted to buy something on a credit card, imagine getting the same amount out of a cash machine and spending that instead.

Perhaps the card-paying MIT students could afford $60 for the basketball tickets – and thought that was a fair price. If so, okay. But I suspect they overbid, determined to win the tickets, whatever the cost, and not worrying about how they would pay for them.

One final thought on the cash or credit question. The MIT experiment took place in 1999, when students with credit cards were a relatively new phenomenon. Indeed for us all, cash-free payment is a fairly recent thing, certainly for the majority of purchases. Now, one of the reasons why personal debt has risen is that personal finance markets have mushroomed and there are many more ways of acquiring credit. But another is surely that we are still in something of a mental transition period from cash to cashless. And during that transition our grip on 'virtual' money is not as tight as it should be. Maybe it should come as no surprise that we tend to spend it more loosely than we do 'real' money.

Perhaps children growing up now, children who will almost never see their parents pay in cash, will not make the sometimes dangerous distinction between cash and cashless – respecting the first and being cavalier with the second. Indeed cash may soon disappear altogether. For people of the near future, 'real' money will *only* be numbers on a screen. And maybe they'll soon find virtual transactions involving lots of digital noughts as daunting as we do handing over a stack of notes.

3

MENTAL ACCOUNTS

Why the more an item costs, the more careless with money we are, why we should all use psychological moneybags and how certain budget airlines could have saved themselves a lot of grief.

IMAGINE YOU ARE on a seaside holiday and you decide to hire a bike to cycle along the coast road. You walk along the promenade checking out the prices. The first hire shop you find is charging £25 a day, but then you see a sign for another shop that offers a bike for just £10 a day. The second shop is a 10-minute walk away, but with a price difference like that, maybe it's worth checking out the cheaper bikes. As long as they look reasonably roadworthy, you can hire one of those instead and congratulate yourself on saving £15, enough to pay for a second day's cycling or a nice lunch in a café on the cliffs.

Now imagine that you are back home and are buying a new car. In the first showroom you find one you like for

£10,010. You want to check you are getting a good deal, so
you go to a second showroom 10 minutes away. They have
much the same car for £10,025 (this might sound unlikely,
but for the purposes of these experiments you need to bear
with it). Is it worth going back to the first shop to save £15?
Almost certainly not. For a transaction that big, a difference
so small feels inconsequential. Yet the sum you could save
is exactly the same as with the bike hire. In the earlier
example, you are delighted with that saving. Now you dismiss
it.

Countless studies have demonstrated that we constantly
make judgements like this, viewing a saving as a proportion
of the total cost, rather than as an actual amount of money
with a determined spending power. This is called relative
thinking, and it is particularly common among people who
are comparatively affluent.[1]

This struck me forcefully when my husband and I moved
home recently. It involved the largest financial transaction of
our lives. London prices, so hundreds of thousands of
pounds: a huge commitment, and one we weighed up carefully. Yet we behaved exactly in line with the research which
shows that the bigger the purchase, the greater the likelihood
people will take little care over associated costs. Having made
such a massive outlay on the house itself, we should have
been keen to save every penny we could on other aspects
of the move. Yet we didn't check that the solicitor handling
the exchange was offering a competitive rate; we simply used
the one we'd been to last time we moved. Likewise we took
a friend's advice – 'They're not the cheapest of all, but they're
really good and it makes life a lot easier' – when it came to
hiring a firm of furniture movers. In the context of buying

a house, a few hundred pounds – which usually we would be so careful about – felt neither here nor there.

Not everyone can be so cavalier of course. The Indian economist Sendhil Mullainathan asked people in poverty attending a soup kitchen whether they would be prepared to travel for 45 minutes to save $50 on a household appliance. [2] He knew all about the research famously done by Daniel Kahneman and Amos Tversky, which showed that people tend to make decisions of this type within the context of the original price.[3] In these cases, if a household appliance cost $100 before the markdown, then a 50 per cent discount would make the journey worthwhile, but if the full cost of the item was $1,000 it wasn't worth bothering with a saving of $50. What Mullainathan showed was that the people in the soup kitchen couldn't afford to think this way. They weren't swayed by the initial price because whatever that price was, a $50 saving for them was a sum of money they couldn't afford to forgo.

On the face of it, theirs was the more rational behaviour. But does that mean that richer people are being wholly irrational? Not necessarily. We factor into our thinking not just the financial saving but the value of our time, which in some cases is more precious to us. Unlike the people at the soup kitchen, we often consider we are – to use the cliché – 'money rich, but time poor'.

Yet we don't behave entirely consistently in making these calculations. Many of us spend hours online, finding the very cheapest deal on a flight or a rail ticket and saving relatively small sums in the process. Now that might be sensible for people who can hunt for bargains in the office (without the boss seeing), in which case they're making the saving and the firm is paying for the time. But I work freelance from home a lot of the time and do the same thing. I've never calculated it, but it would almost certainly make more financial sense for me to spend the time working. Yet in this instance, the lure of a cut-price deal is irresistible. Moreover, research has shown, we aren't prepared to spend the same time to review much bigger, ongoing financial commitments.

To take one example: in the UK, people have the option to change energy suppliers to find the best deal, but research has shown only 1–10 per cent of people regularly monitor prices and save money by switching.[4] And this, despite the fact that savings on utility bills can run into hundreds of pounds a year.

So why do we make an effort in some cases and not others? Sometimes it is to do with necessity. We have to choose a train ticket because we need to get somewhere, but we don't have to bother changing electricity supplier. But there is another reason. We hate committing ourselves to future work. The first stage of switching energy supplier is easy enough to do, but it involves more of a commitment than making a one-off purchase. There will be the hassle of reading the meter at a future date, sending the information off to the new supplier, checking the direct debits are working correctly and so on. It's all a bit of a chore. And of course the reward is a saving in the future, not the instant gratification of shopping in the sales, where you've paid less than you might have done *and* got something shiny and new straight away.

What should be clear from these examples is that the idea that every pound is worth the same to every one of us – a concept that underpins our system of monetary exchange and which we all take for granted – is not true at all, psychologically speaking. Indeed each of us individually puts a different value on each pound we have, depending on the circumstances. From one moment to the next, we consider the money we have differently from the money we spend.

PSYCHOLOGICAL MONEYBAGS

Some years ago, I interviewed the Nobel prize-winning psychologist and best-selling author Daniel Kahneman.[5] He told me one of his all-time favourite thought experiments, which is something of a classic in behavioural economics. It involves a woman who has spent $160 on two theatre tickets. She is looking forward to the show, but when she arrives at the theatre she can't find the tickets. She empties out her bag. She goes through her pockets. No sign of them. She feels slightly sick as she thinks of the large sum of money she's wasted. But what about the show? Will she spend another $160 on replacement tickets, or will she just give up and go home?

When Kahneman tested this scenario with a sample of people back in the 1980s, nearly nine out of ten assumed that having lost the tickets the woman would forgo seeing the play.[6] But what if the scenario was slightly different?

This time, the woman hasn't booked in advance. Instead she has brought $160 in cash with her, ready to buy tickets at the box office. But when she gets to the theatre she opens her purse and sees that the money is somehow missing. Does she use her credit card instead?

With this scenario more than half of the people Kahneman questioned changed their answer and said yes. So why is it

okay to in effect pay twice for the tickets in the second
scenario, but not in the first?

The theory advanced by the economist Richard Thaler,
famous for the behavioural theory 'nudge', is that we have
different 'mental accounts'.[7] We assign different characteristics and purposes to different portions of our money.
'Spending money' is different from savings. Money you win
in a bet is different from money you earn. Even as an adult,
the £10 note sent by a great-aunt in a Christmas card is
more exciting than the £20 note I've just collected from a
cash machine. These mental accounts aren't generally organised like real bank accounts. We don't make precise, conscious
deposits into them or monitor the balances to avoid over-
drafts. Indeed, most of the time, most of us are barely
conscious of them. But they can nonetheless exert a powerful
influence over the way we use our money.

For Thaler, the explanation for the different attitudes above
would run as follows. The theatre tickets come from a mental
account devoted to entertainment and making a double
purchase out of that account after the tickets have been lost
feels unduly extravagant. But lost cash is different: it sits in
a 'general' mental account, and there's still money left in
there to spend. For Thaler, this explains why so many more
people said the woman would still buy tickets if she'd lost
the cash than if she'd lost the tickets.

Thaler first coined the term 'mental accounts' in the 1990s.
But other researchers also described similar ideas. In 1982,
researchers in Japan found that even within the single category
of 'spending money', women divided their cash into nine
mental accounts or 'psychological moneybags', as the
researchers termed them: daily necessities, small luxuries,

culture and education, personal fortune, security, clothes and make-up, going out, pocket money and raising the standard of living.[8] The women judged the value of an item not by comparing it with *all* the items they might wish to purchase, but by making a comparison with other items in the relevant moneybag. For example, oranges sold on the train on a family daytrip were more expensive than oranges in the local store, but the women were happy to pay the higher price because the money was coming from the 'going out' moneybag, which was used for special and therefore pricier items, rather than from the mental account for the daily necessities, so a different judgement about the cost was made.

It's pretty intuitive when you think about it. Maybe a bottle of gin is something you always have in the house, in case visitors ask for a gin and tonic. When it runs out, you get some more from the supermarket and it goes on the food and drink bill. You pay £20 for it at the very most. Yet on holiday you might agree to pay almost half that for a single gin and tonic in a bar with a great view, but you don't resent it. Why? Because the money is coming out of a different mental account.

Now you might think having these accounts would make us careless with money. But in fact we are not. We don't throw all our money into the high-end and 'fun-stuff' accounts. We assign it quite carefully, putting larger amounts of money into the more serious mental accounts, from which we spend more, but with a keener eye on the price.

Matsutake mushrooms are the caviar of Japan. They grow around the roots of trees such as red pines and have fat stalks that can reach 20 centimetres in height. They have a strong smell and a spicy, some say cinnamon-tinged taste.

Gathered by hand from September to November, they are hard to come by – and so very expensive. Today, depending on the size of the harvest, they can cost as much as $800 a kilo. The researchers found that back in 1982, they were similarly pricey. To spend $50 on mushrooms was a considerable outlay. Spending $50 on big bags of rice was fine because that money came from a general grocery account, but money for matsutake came from the precious and smaller luxury account, so this was not a decision to take lightly.

We also assign our money to different timeframes in our minds. Money for today, money for tomorrow and money for a rainy day. Through the creation of mental accounts, we are able to make quick judgements about when to buy something and what it's reasonable to spend in different situations. They help us to exert self-control over our spending.[9]

Some people go as far as to set up separate bank accounts to reflect these mental accounts, even if that means paying interest on the debit in one while others are in credit. It's irrational in one way – overall you are losing money; but understandable in another – you've worked hard to build up that savings nest egg and it feels wrong to raid it to pay this month's credit card bill. Banks do offer mortgage deals where the interest you earn on savings is offset against the interest on your mortgage, but still 98 per cent of people in the UK in 2014 chose to separate their savings and their debts.[10] We don't like the idea of one big tally, especially when there's a mortgage involved, because then we'll always feel we're massively in debt.

Our use of mental accounts also helps to explain why we make judgements about the value of discounts within the context of the total price. It all depends on which mental account the money comes from.

When my husband and I bought our house and failed to shop around for a solicitor, it was partly because these fees seemed inconsequential in comparison with the price of the house. But it was also because we were chalking the fees up to a particular mental account, in this case a special one – the 'once in a lifetime buying a house' account. In reality of course the money we were shelling out to the solicitor was coming from my actual current account, which was rapidly looking very empty.

It is very important that we can assign money mentally in this way. If we didn't do it, we wouldn't take risks or make long-term investments, and we wouldn't have the economic activity and the prosperity to show for it. Mental accounts allow us to escape from the crippling financial caution that could otherwise grip us. In this sense, our evolving psychological attitudes to money allow modern economies to function.

But difficulty sometimes arises in trying to force our minds to put money into the appropriate psychological moneybag. Around 15 years ago, my husband and I decided to get rid of our car. Living in London, we found we were using it less and less, not least because parking spaces where we lived at the time were so precious that we were reluctant to surrender the one we had by using the car. It got to the point where, on the rare occasions we did decide to drive, we couldn't remember where the car was even parked. On one occasion, we wandered around for more than half an hour and then said to ourselves it was probably better that we take the tube after all, because if we drove we would only have had to spend ages later finding another elusive parking space.

It was getting ridiculous. Our Renault 5 was not so much a car as a white elephant. Selling it to someone who would use it regularly was clearly the sensible thing to do. Yet doing that would mean we would always have to take public transport. In London, this is generally reliable, but what about on late nights or if we wanted to travel out of the capital?

No matter, my husband said, just think of the thousands we'll be saving over the years. With no insurance, road tax, MOT, repairs or petrol to pay for, the money we saved could easily justify paying for a late night taxi home from a friend's house or a hire car for a weekend away.

His argument was logical and sensible – and we sold the car. But all these years later, I *still* find it hard to take the fare for a black cab from a mental account for everyday transport. Petrol and garage bills didn't feel like luxuries, but a taxi still does. So I rarely take one. Now that we have a garden and want to be able to fill a car boot with plants, we've started to wonder about buying a car again. In fact taking a taxi, and even having it wait for us, would still be cheaper, yet we can't quite bring ourselves to do it. It feels so extravagant to take taxis to garden centres. Yet a car, although far more expensive, seems reasonable. The explanation, I suspect, is that I've grown up in a culture where a car is considered essential for everyday life. A hundred years ago, things would have been different. A car would have been a luxury and paying cab fares relatively commonplace. In the future that might be true again. Maybe we'll be summoning driverless cars to come and get us instead of owning a car at all.

SETTLING OUR ACCOUNTS

So far, we've been considering mental accounts as if they are fixed things that we carry through life. In fact, with every transaction we open a new temporary mental account. Take buying an air ticket. These days flying is so common that a flight has almost passed out of the luxury item category. But it's still not an everyday purchase for most of us, and we are keen to assign the appropriate sum to the 'flight to wherever' account. As long as we don't go over that assigned sum, we'll be happy.

But the account isn't mentally closed until we've taken the flight, landed safely, collected our bags and got to our home or hotel. If an air traffic controllers' strike means we have to pay to travel by train instead, we are likely to add that unforeseen cost to the mental account for the trip and will now consider we made a 'loss' on the account. We don't generally chalk that extra train fare up to a 'rainy day account'. This was a particular trip for which we opened a particular mental account. So any unanticipated expense assigned to the account feels psychologically painful, almost irrespective of the actual amount.

To appreciate the point further, just consider the following example: instead of getting a cheap air ticket by booking long in advance, you pay top price because you only managed at the last minute to get the time off to attend your friend's wedding. You know you're paying perhaps a couple of hundred pounds more than you would have done otherwise but in this instance you are happy enough to pay it. After all, you're unexpectedly getting the chance to be there for your friend's big day. Yet change the circumstances back to having booked a cheap flight and then finding you have to take a train because of an air traffic controller's strike. The extra cost might be the same, but your response, I'd bet, will be very different.

The same mental processes, and mental anguish, happen when you decide a purchase is good value, only to discover that there are extras such as booking fees or seat selection charges. If the initial price had been a bit higher you might not have minded: you would have factored it into your mental account for the flight, but once you've established in your mind that the original price is what you're paying, any extra cost feels like a loss on the account or, worse still, a fine.

Because our minds work in this way, I'm surprised that certain budget airlines took so long to realise that their notorious practice of adding extra charges later in the booking process annoys people. If the executives of the company had taken the trouble to look at the welter of psychological research (which they're not alone in ignoring, I should add), they would have realised that what they thought was a clever business strategy was actually causing long-term brand damage. Our mental accounting makes us acutely alert to anything that feels like a rip off. In other words it helps us to exercise mind over money.

It's a finding I pick up in the next chapter. The strongest psychological reaction we experience in relation to money is the one that occurs when we know we are losing it.

4

TO HAVE AND TO HOLD

How we hate losing money more than we like making it, how Puerto Rican monkeys helped a researcher understand the financial crisis and why it's a mistake to choose the same lottery numbers every week.

HEIRESSES AND TRUSTAFARIANS aside, most of us don't 'come into' money. We acquire what money we have through a combination of the opportunities open to us and our own efforts. So it's not surprising that what we have, we want to hold. What is surprising perhaps is that we seem to value this money so much that many of us would rather hang onto it than use it to acquire more money.

Try this test set by Daniel Kahneman.[1] You've been given £1,000. Then you're offered a choice: double your money on the toss of a coin, or take an extra £500. What would you do?

Most people go for the certainty of taking home £1,500. I know I would. But what if the test is changed slightly?

This time you've been given £2,000, and your options are as follows:

1. Go for a coin toss that could result either in you getting to keep the bigger sum or losing half of it, in which case you'd be back down to £1,000.
2. Take a fixed loss of £500, which would mean you'd take home £1,500 – no more, no less.

This time the gamble probably feels more attractive to you. Yet of course the potential outcomes are identical. You either opt for a certain £1,500 or you take a gamble that results in you taking home £2,000 if you win or £1,000 if you lose. I know this test very well, and yet every time I read it, I still find myself tempted by the coin toss in the second version of the test. So why do we view the two sets of options so differently?

It's all to do with presentation. In the first test, the safe option is presented as a gain. You had £1,000 anyway but without taking any risk you can increase the sum to £1,500. While in the second test, the safe option is presented as a loss. You had £2,000, now you're being asked to surrender a quarter of it.

The fancy name for our different thinking in these two instances is loss aversion. Our general propensity to loss aversion is one of the most robust findings in behavioural economics, and it influences many of the decisions we make about money. We all like the chance to win, but we'll put more effort into not losing. The thought of even a small loss holds more power over us than the prospect of a larger gain. Indeed as Amos Tversky and Daniel Kahneman, who developed the theory in this area, have demonstrated, our aversion to a loss is actually measurable. It is just over twice as strong as our attraction to a gain of the same size.

Another example of this aversion can be seen in our reaction to late deliveries. When we place an order for a new sofa, for example, we generally accept that it will take some weeks to arrive. Let's say the seller in the furniture shop says a month. Fine, we say. But how do we react if the day before the delivery date the company tells us our sofa won't now arrive for another fortnight? If the seller had said at the start that it would be six weeks we probably wouldn't have objected. But now we do. Strongly. We demand compensation. And research has shown that we would expect that compensation to be higher than the price we would have been prepared to pay in the first place for a 'guaranteed' or 'speedy' delivery date of four weeks.[2] That unanticipated wait of a fortnight is now viewed as a definite loss – which we hate.

And we are not alone. It seems loss aversion is buried deep in our evolutionary biology, because it's not just us humans who feel this way.

MONKEY BUSINESS

Anyone visiting the island of Cayo Santiago in Puerto Rico needs to wear glasses and a hat at all times to protect them from showers of urine. The culprits are the rhesus monkeys who delight in sitting high in the trees and peeing on the heads of the humans on the ground. Look up at the wrong moment without protection and you could find yourself not only wincing in pain and disgust, but contracting a kind of herpes called simian B virus, which can be fatal.

For Professor Laurie Santos from Yale University, the risks are worth it. Despite their antisocial ways, the Cayo Santiago monkeys have become habituated to humans, which means Santos and her research colleagues can get close enough to study their behaviour in the wild. One of the striking things about rhesus monkeys, and other species such as the tufted capuchins, is their skill at problem-solving. And that got Santos thinking . . . about the financial crisis.

Yes, that's right. Santos was on a tropical island studying urinating monkeys, and this led her to ponder on the economic crash of 2008. Bear with me on this one. Santos had in mind those investors who were so resistant to accepting losses that they continued gambling on the stock market, hoping for an elusive win, even as their losses grew and grew. She thought too of people who refused to sell their houses for less than they had paid for them, even though these home-owners weren't in negative equity and with prices slumping could have upgraded to a larger house. Both were classic examples of human loss aversion. The fear of losing out must be buried pretty deep in us, Santos thought. So could it be that the monkeys, our evolutionary cousins, were loss averse too?

To find out she had to return to the Comparative Cognition Laboratory at Yale, where she and her team have a group of captive capuchins. These monkeys have been trained to exchange shiny round tokens for food.

A capuchin called Auric heads to what researchers call the monkey marketplace. There he's given a pouch filled with tokens. He sees two research assistants behind a glass window holding out their offerings, slices of grape in a dish or occasionally a marshmallow, and he knows that if he puts a token through a round hole in the glass window he'll get some food in exchange. But Auric's a smarter monkey than that. He's also learnt to spot the best deals, choosing to go to the 'traders' who offer the most fruit or the biggest treat for the lowest number of tokens.

Like humans, Auric and his fellow capuchins 'spend' and 'value' their 'money' differently. Some use all the tokens in one go, while others hoard them. Some steal tokens from other monkeys, and do so even when they could have stolen fruit instead.

The capuchins are now familiar both with the way the marketplace works and with each of the 'traders'. Some trust has been established. But then a bit of trickery is introduced. One trader starts to vary the number of grapes handed over in exchange for one token. Auric and his friends are expecting two grapes – the number the trader displayed. And half the time they get two. But the rest of the time they only get one.

To confuse matters even more a second trader settles into a pattern of appearing to be about to give just one grape for each token, only to add in a bonus grape at the last moment, but only half of the time.

Now I expect you can see what is happening here? Auric and the other capuchins are taking part in a similar test to the one Kahneman does on us humans. And as you'll have realised, whichever trader the monkeys go to they have a 50/50 chance of getting two grapes or one grape. Even so, our furry friends demonstrate a clear preference for one deal over the other.

They head to the second trader 71 per cent of the time.[3] And loss aversion would seem to explain why. For his last-minute offer of a second grape must seem like a gain, while the first trader's late withdrawal of a grape feels like a loss. Just like humans, Auric and friends seem to hate a loss.

For Laurie Santos, this is evidence that the irrational bias towards loss aversion goes back a long way in our evolutionary history, perhaps as long as 35 million years. It's deep-rooted in us and therefore hard to overcome.

But why does it exist and persist?

The neuroscientist Dean Buonomano suggests loss aversion stems from the time when the main obsession of humans was to find enough food; in other words, to a time when we were more like capuchin monkeys. Buonomano's hypothesis is very simple. In these pre-historic times, human beings, like monkeys now, prized the food they already had over the prospect of gaining some extra food, especially as they had no good way of storing it. In these circumstances, getting extra food was welcome, but losing food could be catastrophic. It could result in starvation.[4]

This theory might get at the evolutionary root of loss aversion but doesn't fully explain why we continue making the same decisions in the modern age. And a particular issue for us now is that loss aversion can lead us to make poor, sometimes disastrous, financial decisions. Just think back to investors refusing to cut their losses during a bear market. In such cases, loss aversion doesn't just lead us to irrationally choose one option over another even though both options have the same outcome. It leads us to choose the option with the *worst* outcome.

THE BEST WAY TO LOSE WHEN PLAYING THE LOTTERY

Imagine you're a student. You're offered a free lottery ticket with the chance to win a 15 euro book token. You're shown the ticket, and you notice the number on it. Then you're given the chance to swap that ticket for a different one. In return for swapping tickets, you'll get a free gift – a pen embossed with your university's name. Would you agree to exchange the tickets or not?

When students at Tilburg University in the Netherlands were given this choice only 56 per cent of them went for it, even though their chances of winning the book token were the same and so they might as well have had the free pen.[5]

Perhaps you're thinking it was the lousy gift that explained their reaction. Couldn't the researchers have tempted the students with a slightly more enticing freebie? Maybe, but that's not the issue. The important detail here is that the students were shown the number on the original lottery ticket. This meant that having swapped their original ticket for another, if the number on the original was drawn out of the hat, they would know they'd made the wrong decision. So they were prepared to pay what's known as a 'regret premium'; in other words missing out on the free pen (which was a guaranteed gain) in order to avoid the potential disappointment of missing out on a book token (which was a highly unlikely loss) later on.

Further proof of our tendency to behave this way comes from the fact that other students who were *not* shown the number of their original lottery ticket were much more likely to agree to the swap. For these players, the regret if their new ticket didn't win was diluted. All they'd know (and they knew this in advance) was that this winning ticket *could* have been the one they swapped. But the chances were remote: one in a few hundred or a few thousand – depending on how many tickets were issued.

Here then is a tip for anyone thinking of playing the National Lottery. Always pick different numbers and make no attempt to remember the numbers you picked in the past. If you pick the same ones every week and for whatever reason miss a week, you expose yourself to the potential agony – infinitesimally remote as it is – that 'your' numbers will come up. That can't happen if you adopt a random and amnesiac strategy. The exception is if everyone you work with belongs to a syndicate. If they have a big win, you're definitely going to know about it. So unless you think you can cope with all your colleagues becoming millionaires overnight while you don't, you might just have to join them to save the regret later. In which case it doesn't matter whether you have the same numbers or not.

That said, if you live in the Netherlands, some lottery organisers are one step ahead. In a fiendish example of the exploitation of regret aversion, they've designed a lottery in which everyone's unique postcode is automatically entered into the draw. Although you can only win if you've paid for a ticket, in any given week you can look up to see whether you'd have won, if only you had bothered to enter.

Here then is a second tip, this time specifically for Dutch people. Don't do it. Don't ever look to see whether yours was the winning postcode, unless you've bought a ticket. You'll not be surprised to hear that researchers found that people anticipate far more regret over failing to enter this alternative postcode lottery than the Netherlands' National State Lottery, where the numbers are random.[6]

Another example of this tendency happened in my own life – and again it relates to my recent house move. The timing of that move meant that the removal men we decided to hire (see Chapter 3) were going to pack all our belongings into their van on a Friday, then drive the van to their locked yard and park up, before moving everything into our new house on the Monday.

We found it somewhat unnerving that everything we owned would be spending the weekend unguarded on a deserted industrial estate somewhere on the outskirts of London. Wasn't there a chance that however high the fences, thieves could break into the yard and steal the van? If that happened, there wouldn't be any compensation, the company told me. But we could take out insurance if we wanted to.

That seemed sensible. Yet the cost was several hundred pounds. This sounded like a lot to insure our belongings for just one weekend against an event that was presumably extremely unlikely. Or did the high premium mean that theft was not uncommon? I was determined to make a rational decision about whether to buy the insurance or just risk it. So what do you think I decided to do?

In Chapter 10, we will see how poorer people sometimes don't take out insurance because their poverty forces them to think about the difficulty of paying the premiums in the short term rather than the disastrous financial consequences of a fire, flood or theft in the long term. I didn't have this problem. If I'd really wanted to, I could have afforded to pay for the policy.

Given we know costs like these can seem inconsequential

in the context of a huge transaction like a house purchase, perhaps you think I opted to take out the insurance?

Well I did, but not out of relative thinking. And not because I was acting prudently either. No, the impulse to take the insurance in this case, as in many cases, was fear of loss. I wasn't making a purely rational financial decision. Instead I was, as it were, insuring myself against anxiety in the present and potential regret in the future. Regret aversion was at play again.

As it happened, I struck lucky. The removal van wasn't stolen over the weekend, but, more than that, it turned out the removal company had forgotten to take out the insurance policy on my behalf, so there was nothing to pay. The perfect outcome. No outlay *and* no regret.

THE POWER OF OWNERSHIP

Here's a classic study conducted by Amos Tversky and Daniel Kahneman back in 1990: students were told they would be playing the parts of either buyers or sellers. The sellers were each given the gift of a coffee mug and told it was theirs to keep or theirs to sell if they chose to do so. The sellers then named the minimum price they would be prepared to sell the mug for.

Buyers were now shown the mugs and asked to name the maximum price they would offer for one. On average the buyers were happy to pay a top price of $2.25. But for the sellers this wasn't enough; they wanted twice as much.[7]

Now you might suppose that both sellers and buyers were simply driving a hard bargain; that in the end they would settle on a mutually agreed price. But the sellers held out, even though it was pretty clear that, at nearly $5, they were asking for more than these buyers were prepared to pay.

This is called the endowment effect. In simple terms, it means we tend to value things we already own more highly. We endow them with a greater value. It happens even when we have only owned the items for a very short time. In this instance, the students hadn't even seen these particular mugs until the morning of the experiment. They hadn't paid for the mugs or even chosen them. And yet their determination to keep them was such that they named an over-inflated price.

It may seem hard to believe. Yet the findings of Tversky and Kahneman on the endowment effect have been replicated again and again in many similar tests. It's one of the areas where the evidence is really strong.

Consider this scenario: I come into your living room and see a cushion on your sofa. You only bought it the other week, and so it can't really be said to have great sentimental value. Yet even if I offered you a bit more than the price you paid for the cushion, I suspect you'd refuse my offer. The nuisance factor would come into your thinking, no doubt. You bought the cushion because you wanted a cushion. Sell it to me, and you have buy to another one. But it's not just the bother. The cushion is yours now. In monetary terms, it doesn't make a great deal of sense. How difficult would it be to replace the cushion with an exact replica? And by accepting my deal, you'd make a small profit into the bargain. But we don't always think purely in mercenary terms. With loss aversion, we want to hold onto what we have. The same happens here.

Of course, this strength of attachment doesn't apply to things we've acquired for the purpose of selling them.

Successful traders want to make a profit, but they also want to shift their stock rather than hang onto it. And as sites like eBay demonstrate, there are things we own, sometimes for years, which we will happily sell on. That said, it's often the case that inexperienced sellers start off setting the level of the bid threshold too high, probably because even though they don't want that old sideboard any more, having chosen to buy it once upon a time and then owned it for a while, its value is higher in their eyes than in the eyes of others.

If you've ever witnessed the reluctance of children to swap with their sibling when they've opened the wrong Christmas present by mistake, then you have seen the endowment effect in action. In a study conducted in New Mexico five-, eight- and ten-year-olds were given either a 'super-ball' or a keyring shaped like a toy alien. When the children were asked before- hand what they thought of the two gifts, they rated the ball more highly. But even so, when the children who had received a keyring were given the chance to swap it for a ball, 40 per cent chose to hold on to it.

To check there wasn't something peculiar about these two gifts, the exercise was repeated with other objects. Whether they were given the chance to trade a mechanical pencil for a highlighter or a calculator for a box of six coloured pens, the same thing happened. Children in all the age groups are on average twice as likely to stick with whatever they were first given than to agree to swap.[8]

Imagine you are looking to trade in your car and buy a new one. Your old car is in pretty good condition without too many miles on the clock and according to the Blue Book, the bible of second-hand car prices in the US, it looks as though you should get $6,000 for it. The first dealer you visit offers you $6,500 for your car and has the new model you want for $8,500. But knowing it's always good to get a second opinion, you visit another dealer. This one says your old car is only worth $5,500, but they have the same new car you want for just $7,500. Which deal would make you happier?

The net result is of course exactly the same. Either way you pay $2,000 to swap your old car for the newer one, but in a finding which by now probably won't surprise you researchers report that most people preferred the first deal. Yes, people would rather overpay for a new car provided they felt they were well compensated for the car they already own.[9]

The endowment effect is also at work when companies offer free trials. The inertia of most customers means that once people have been lured into taking out a subscription for a magazine with that apparently generous offer of six free copies, they generally maintain the subscription for years. But the second reason why free trials work is that people get used to having something – in this case, a magazine in the post – and by cancelling the subscription they are imposing a loss on themselves.

Let's return one more time to the capuchin monkeys in that lab at Yale. It seems the endowment effect influences their behaviour too. When given the chance to trade a piece of fruit for an oatcake, a foodstuff they like equally well in other circumstances, the capuchins are reluctant. Perhaps offering them an extra oatcake would be an incentive? But no, the monkeys still preferred to hold on to what was already theirs. They would only trade the fruit they already had if they were given masses of oatcakes in return.[10]

So the instinct to hang on to what we've got is as strong in us as in apes. Money should help us overcome this instinct. Yet it appears that such is our attachment to money that sometimes, far from lubricating the wheels of commerce, it can act as a brake. Even when we're offered more money, we won't let go.

Of course there are many situations where the existence of money does facilitate exchange. That is the point after all. But key to making that happen is getting the price right. And it's to that subject that we turn next.

5

THE PRICE IS RIGHT

Why a high price is not always a sign of quality, why your brain is a wine snob, why sometimes we'd rather pay more than we need to, why you shouldn't be fooled by the 'mid-priced' option and why you should never open a café called the Zero Dollar Diner.

WE'VE JUST BEEN seeing how we tend to over-value our own possessions. Let's turn now to the judgements we make about what counts as a reasonable price when we are buying things.

We do it every day, with purchases big and small. You might imagine it's a simple enough mental process. In fact, it's rather tricky. We are easily tricked, and our own minds sometimes seem to join in the fun and games. When we add in the fact that prices are not stable, it is no wonder that exerting mind over money can sometimes be very difficult.

NEW WINE IN OLD BOTTLES

Every month Rudy Kurniawan would spend around a million dollars on wine and then make even more than that from selling it. In 2006, his sales totalled $36 million. Although he was young and had seemingly appeared on the wine scene from nowhere, he was soon regarded as one of the world's foremost wine traders. He impressed established experts with the speed with which he learned the different wines and by his unusual interest in the details of labels and corks. In blind tastings he was brilliant at identifying producers and vintages. He could even spot counterfeit bottles, saying he had trained himself to do it, having been caught out in the past.[1]

Kurniawan had an extravagant lifestyle, appearing in magazines wearing a white leather coat and carrying his white poodle, Chloe.[2] His generosity was legendary. An evening would start with the Californian treating his friends in the trade to wines worth thousands of dollars from his own cellar. Then the party would move on to a restaurant, where Kurniawan would also insist on buying only the very best.

One strange thing people noticed was that Kurniawan always asked the restaurant to have the empty bottles couriered to his house the following day. He would tell the sommelier he was building a bottle collection in the garage at his Los Angeles home.[3] He had even engaged an architect to create a museum for the collection.[4]

There were other things that got people talking. For example, Kurniawan owned bottles dated 1923 from a domaine in Burgundy that wasn't founded until 1924. Unusually for a collector of the world's best wines, he was also known to buy large amounts of cheap red. And when his wine was auctioned, it would include greater quantities of extremely rare bottles than you normally find in a single auction.

But friends and colleagues could always come up with explanations. Perhaps the family who owned the domaine in Burgundy all those decades ago included a few bottles from the previous owners' vintage under their own label. Perhaps he'd been sold the occasional fake bottle. With the quantity of wine he was dealing in, it wasn't impossible.

Still, suspicions started to grow. The wealthy industrialist William Koch, who won the prestigious sailing race the America's Cup in 1992, owns more than 43,000 rare bottles of wine.[5] He bought more than two million dollars worth from Kurniawan and after a while he felt something was seriously wrong. In his efforts to expose Kurniawan, Koch hired cork experts, glass experts, label experts and even glue experts.

Around the same time the owner of one of the world's most prestigious vineyards, wine producer Laurent Ponsot, also became suspicious, alerted by one of Kurniawan's more blatant frauds. Ponsot didn't begin making his most famous wine until the 1980s, yet Kurniawan was discovered trying to auction bottles of it from 1959 and 1945. In the end, the evidence against Kurniawan was overwhelming. And when the FBI's Arts Crime Team raided his home, they found he was producing fake fine wine on an industrial scale. A washing-up bowl was full of old corks, while drawers contained sealing wax, glue, stencils, instructions for making labels, a quantity of the red seals you find on the top of unopened bottles and vintage labels neatly created using a laser printer. In the sink there were bottles in soak, ready to have their labels removed. Next to them was a box of genuine old labels taken from vintage wines, and beside the box, not a corkscrew but a device for putting corks into bottles.[6]

It turned out that for eight years Kurniawan had been buying cheap burgundy and blending it with top quality wine to mimic the taste of rare and expensive vintages. He poured this blend into old bottles, attached fake labels, and resealed the bottles with old corks. So how did he get away with it for so long?

Some commentators have complained that the winemakers, auctioneers and guests at tastings must have gone along with the fraud. But Koch and Ponsot were instrumental in exposing Kurniawan, who is now serving a 10-year prison sentence, and if you read interviews with others in the wine trade they seem genuinely troubled that they were fooled. After all, they were supposed to possess refined and discriminating palates. Some of these experts even clung to the idea that the bottles at the tastings must have been real and that it was only the subsequent sales which involved fakes. Yet that was not the case. The wines at the tastings were Kurniawan's own blends too.

What Kurniawan relied on was one of the oldest tricks in the book. It's a ruse beloved of con artists, because the trick is played by victims on themselves. In this case, experts were told the wine was a rare vintage. The look of the bottle and label confirmed it. So when they opened the bottle they tasted what they expected to taste. The confirmation bias was at play. The experts looked for information to back up their expectations. They were at a fine wine auction, and at a fine wine auction you generally get fine wine.

Now, Kurniawan was particularly skilled at fooling the experts in many different ways, but this is a chapter about price, and price was a vital component of Kurniawan's fraud.

Perhaps you recall an advert not for wine but for beer that was on TV a few years ago. The lager, drinkers were told, was 'reassuringly expensive'. The same was true of Kurniawan's wine. One of the things that gave the traders confidence was that the wines they were tasting had very high prices.

Since Kurniawan's conviction around five hundred bottles of his fake wine have since been destroyed and composted, but another 5,000 bottles were put up for auction by the United States Marshals Service at the end of 2015, in the hope of recouping some money for the victims of the fraud. Really? you might be asking. How can they be sure it's genuine? The ninth and final question in the accompanying FAQs anticipates this: 'How certain are you that none of the wine being sold is fake?' In response, the US Marshals admitted they couldn't be 100 per cent certain these particular wines were genuine, but said that to the best of their knowledge they were. Kurniawan did after all buy plenty of genuine wine in order to make his unique blends. Still, you'd think buyers might be wary, yet three bottles of 1911 Romanée Conti attracted a top bid of $45,600. Perhaps the connection with Kurniawan added some notoriety value? Perhaps people can't resist a bargain, even if they are not 100 per cent sure it is real.

The experts no doubt felt stupid that they were duped by Kurniawan but they can take some comfort from the fact that many others have been similarly fooled, even when they were under scrutiny in psychology labs. There is ample evidence from psychological studies that price has a big effect on our perceptions of a product. In these situations, we fall prey to money over mind.

One of my favourite studies involves drinking wine while lying in a brain scanner. True, it's not the way most of us would choose to consume our wine, not least because the requirement to keep your head absolutely still when you are in a scanner necessitates delivery of the wine into your mouth via a tube. But in order to work out what is going on in the brain when we taste a wine that we believe either to be vintage or cheap plonk, there is no alternative.

Hilke Plassmann's experiment at the California Institute of Technology involved 20 volunteers with a fondness for, but no particular expertise in, red wine. One at a time, they lay supine in the scanner with a tube between their lips through which different varieties of wines were piped from the room next door.[7]

Spitting the wine out wasn't possible, so instead the tasters were instructed to savour each type of wine for a certain length of time before swallowing it, before rinsing out their mouths with water and moving on to the next wine. Their task was simple: to say which of the wines they preferred.

The tasters were told that there were five different varieties of wine, ranging in price from $5 to $90. So they were alerted to the fact that some of the wine was top quality and some supermarket standard. But they didn't know which was which. All they had to go on, apart from their taste buds, was the information on price and grape variety (often false, as it turned out) which the researchers gave them as the wine was piped through the plastic tube into their mouths.

You'll realise straightaway that the researchers were looking for the confirmation bias, where people look for evidence to back up what they already think is true. And they found it. The tasters consistently expressed a preference for the wines they were told were top end and expensive, even though half the time they were in reality drinking a low-price wine.

But there was more to it than that. The activity in the tasters' brains suggested that the volunteers weren't just *saying* they liked a particular wine having been told its price. They weren't just trying to look good by claiming falsely to appreciate what they thought was the finer wine. No, in these instances, the brain scanner picked up increased activity in the medial orbitofrontal cortex, a part of the brain that lights up when we experience something pleasant. That is to say, whether or not it was truly an expensive wine, and whether or not they would have liked that wine in different circumstances (see below), the tasters *experienced* greater pleasure *at that moment* as a result of *thinking* the wine was top quality. It seems the brain is a bit of a wine snob.

It's quite a finding. Real pleasure can result from the assumption that a thing is expensive, even if it isn't.

Of course the experiment also showed that most people cannot tell a good wine from a bad one. Though in truth who is to make such judgements? An analysis of the results of 6,000 blind wine tastings (with no confidence bias at play) found that it's only the experts who prefer expensive wines; the everyday wine drinker scores the posh stuff rather worse than the *vin ordinaire*.[8]

Which leads me to another of my tips: don't go on a wine course. A much cheaper way of enjoying fine wines is to get your friends to buy low-price wine and tell you it's a 2005 Château Pétrus. Your brain will do the rest – for free.

Oh, and here's another tip. If you do happen to buy a pricey bottle of wine (though why would you?) or get given one (in which case you're forgiven), make sure to tell anyone you share it with just how expensive it is so that you really get your money's worth.

ENERGY DRINKS, HEADACHE PILLS AND AN ALL-YOU-CAN-EAT BUFFET

Enough of the noble grape, let's turn now to energy drinks. In this experiment, two groups of students were told to buy energy drinks that were advertised to improve concentration. Both groups were sold the same drink containing the same ingredients. The only difference was that one group was charged $1.89 for a can, while the other was told that because the university had managed to obtain a bulk-buy discount they would only be charged $0.89.

The two groups were then given a list of anagrams to solve, and the group that paid the higher price for their drinks solved more.[9] Why? The researchers concluded that the more expensive the drink, the more the consumer is going to want to believe that its properties – in this case improving concentration – are real, and therefore the group who thought they'd bought nearly $2 worth of concentration worked more intensely on the anagrams than the second group.

Similar studies have used expensive, branded painkillers and much cheaper generic versions that nonetheless contain the same active ingredients. People tend to report that their headache is easing faster if they think they are getting the 'reassuringly expensive' brand.

One study of more than eight hundred women regularly taking aspirin – sometimes a brand, sometimes a generic version – estimated that approximately a third of the pain relief the women experienced could be attributed to their belief that they were taking the branded drug.[10] The team involved in the energy drink study also asked students to keep a diary of any colds they caught over the next term, to report any over-the-counter remedies they took and to note how effective those remedies were at reducing their symptoms. Once again, there was a marked difference in how the students rated the medication. This time it was a single brand, but some of the students bought it while on special offer. For them, it didn't work quite as well as for those who had paid the full price.[11]

Of course there are two ways of viewing this phenomenon. On the one hand, you could argue that customers who buy expensive branded medicine are being ripped off – or to be more precise, are ripping themselves off by choosing it. After all, the only real difference between these drugs and generic ones is the price. On the other hand, price seems to be working like a placebo effect, somehow convincing us that we are actually experiencing a greater reduction of pain with the more expensive brands. And if your headache's really bad, you're probably not going to mind *how* it works, or how much it costs, you just want, as the old advert put it, 'pain relief when only fast will do'.

It might be worth paying more for your lunch too. Researchers at Cornell University carried out a study in an Italian restaurant in Upstate New York that was offering an all-you-can-eat buffet. We all know the problem with these buffets is that you eat more than you intend to, and end up with all sorts of things on your plate that don't really go together. Still they do seem like a great bargain. So what effect does the price have on how you enjoy your piled-high plate?

On day one of the Cornell study, a group was offered the all-you-can-eat buffet for $4; next day a second group had to pay double that price. Which group enjoyed the meal more? Well, you'll now be expecting to hear that it was the group that paid $8. And you'd be right. Both groups ate about the same amount, but the people who paid more got more satisfaction from the meal. And what's really interesting is that the second group felt they'd had about enough, while the first group thought they'd overeaten.[12]

Yes, that's right, the people who had the $4 buffet ate the same amount as people who'd paid double, but they enjoyed it less *and* they felt stuffed afterwards. The price had changed their perception of their own bodily sensations. The lesson would appear to be that when it comes to food, cheap is not necessarily cheerful.

This perhaps explains why hugely expensive restaurants serving miniscule portions get away with it. They know how the mind works. When they serve you a sliver of fish, one potato, and a mere garnish of salad costing £25, you convince yourself it's absolutely the perfect amount and you simply couldn't eat another thing.

EMOTIONAL THINKING

When I backpacked around India more than twenty years ago there was one store in Delhi that seemed to have more Western customers than any other – the Cottage Industries Emporium. The reason it was so popular was simple. Every item was labelled clearly with a fixed price. Of course that meant that customers often ended up paying more for a silk scarf or an inlaid box than they might have paid in the street markets outside where they can bargain. But for most Westerners, including me, it was more comfortable to be faced with a fixed price and to use this single piece of information to make a decision about whether it was a fair price and whether or not you wanted to buy the item.

By contrast, bargaining for most Westerners is a difficult and emotionally draining experience. You start by asking the stall holder what the price is, and invariably get a response along the lines of 'You tell me price.' You make an offer that seems reasonable, but that's dismissed. And then, it's back and forth, back and forth.

Personally I've always found bargaining a 'no win' process. On the few occasions I have managed to get what I think constitutes a low price, I've ended up feel guilty, fearing I've deprived a poor man of a few rupees that he needs to feed his family. But if, after 10 minutes of haggling, I eventually settle for a higher price than I think is reasonable, then I feel *I've* been ripped off. It doesn't matter that the sum involved is probably only a few pounds at most.

The experience of bargaining abroad illustrates how fluid our attitude towards a 'good deal' can be. It's not just a question of getting the lowest price, or settling on an agreed price, custom and practice come into it, as do feelings and emotion.

One Saturday afternoon in a park in San Francisco, a couple of six-year-old girls were selling homemade lemonade from a stall. If people stopped, they were told they could pay any sum between $1 and $3 for the lemonade – whatever they thought was fair – and they could keep the cup it was served in.

The little entrepreneurs were in fact a front, acting for a group of psychologists who were studying the effect of signs with different wording on people's propensity to stop and spend.

Sometimes the sign on display read 'Spend a little time, and enjoy C & D's lemonade'. (C & D were the little girls.) Then after 10 minutes, it was switched for a sign saying 'Spend a little money, and enjoy C & D's lemonade'. And there was a third sign too, simply exhorting people to 'Enjoy C & D's lemonade'.[13]

Most people walked straight past the homemade lemonade stall and carried on with their Saturday afternoons. However, when the sign suggested spending a little time rather than a little money twice as many people stopped, they rated the lemonade more highly, and the amount they gave was on average $2.50. When the sign only mentioned money the donation dropped to $1.38, while in the control condition, where neither time nor money were mentioned, the results fell somewhere in the middle.

It seemed as if the mention of spending time made the experience of buying lemonade something more personal, a moment to savour, a treat rather than a bloodless financial transaction. However, this is one of those experiments where the control condition might have something quite important to tell us.

The girls made fairly good sales with the sign that said 'Enjoy C & D's lemonade' too. So maybe what's really interesting about this experiment is not so much that the mention of time encouraged people to spend, but that the explicit mention of money acted as a deterrent. Perhaps the second sign rather too pointedly suggested the girls were after people's cash and this was somehow deemed inappropriate? If adults had been staffing the stall and it had been obviously a commercial enterprise then things might have been different again.

Anyway, the point is that a little bit of emotional manipulation, reframing the sale of lemonade as a human interaction, altered people's perceptions of a fair price. No doubt the same would have been true if another sign had said 'Enjoy C & D's lemonade: all proceeds to help poor children'.

WHY YOU SHOULDN'T COMPROMISE (BUT OFTEN DO AND DON'T REGRET IT)

It should be becoming clear that our judgements about money are not always rational, that our thinking is influenced both by particular amounts of money and the forms money comes in. The tricks money plays on our mind are particularly exquisite when it comes to price.

Imagine you go to an electronic store in search of a new laptop. When you walk in, you're faced with counter after counter of computers. The choice appears huge, but when you look closely you realise that there are just three in the size that you want.

One is a white, gleaming design classic, but it costs way more than you were hoping to spend. There's one for half the price that will do, but when you look at the specifications the memory is smaller, the processor is not as fast, and – if you're honest – it looks a bit cheap. Or there's a third one, which is still a bit expensive, but it has cleaner lines than the cheapest one and more memory. Which do you go for?

The third one, of course; that reasonable option – the one that is neither top of the range nor bargain basement. But how freely did you come to this decision? The research suggests, not very freely at all. These days, stores are very canny about the way they display items. They know that relatively few customers are going to buy the really expensive laptop, but by displaying it alongside the other computers, the next most expensive one comes to seem 'mid-priced'.

The display is making use of what's known as the compromise effect.[14] It's an effect that has a powerful attraction for us. It always seems sensible to avoid the extremes and take the middle course. When I was house hunting, I often found that although I'd only booked to see two houses, one particular estate agent would arrange for me to see a third in the area, well above my price range, explaining 'You might as well view it while you're here.' He was hoping the compromise effect would alter my thinking. He knew what my price limit was and that it was unlikely I'd suddenly decide to bust the budget on a much more expensive house. But that was never his intention.

What he was trying to do by showing me the house I could never afford was to change my view of the other houses, to move me from thinking that although they were smaller than I wanted and the road wasn't that nice, compared with the pricey house, they were quite good value, something of a bargain even.

This psychology can work even with something as inconsequential as loo rolls. The supermarket adds some really fancy ones to the display, not in the hope of getting lots of people to trade up from the mid-priced brand to the 'luxury, quilted toilet tissue'. No, what they're really doing is trying to ensure people stick with, or go for, the mid-priced toilet paper and don't trade down by buying the really cheap ones. Dozens of psychological experiments have confirmed this effect.

To take one study as an example: participants were given

catalogue descriptions and pictures of SLR cameras and cassette recorders along with their prices, and asked which two models of each they would choose to buy. (As you might have guessed from the technologies in question, this study took place in the 1980s.) With just two options, the split was roughly 50/50, with half the people opting for the cheaper model and half selecting the expensive one. But the addition of a third, higher-priced option led to between half and two-thirds of the participants choosing what was now the mid-priced option, while the rest split between the cheapest and the most expensive.[15]

The compromise effect involves loss aversion. A luxury item has the best features, but has the big disadvantage of a high price. The cheap version wins on price, but has the big disadvantage of inferior quality. The mid-price option wins on neither quality nor price, but at the same time it has no big disadvantages. And remember that when we are weighing these things up, we give more weight to disadvantages than to advantages. We'd rather avoid a loss than make a gain. Our compromise choice plays to that sense.

The good news is that, the chances are, we probably won't regret it. Unless there is something seriously wrong with the item, we're usually happy with the one we've chosen. This is largely because once we've acquired a product, we don't have other similar ones to compare it with. Just think about it, you were very torn when you were choosing between all those flat screen TVs in the department store, but now the one you have in your living room – probably a compromise choice – fulfils your needs and you don't think about the TVs you might have bought instead. More than that – and this returns us to the endowment effect – you probably really like your flat screen TV more than other people do. It's yours and so you (over-)value it.

With their General Evaluability Theory, behavioural scientists Christopher Hsee and Jiao Zhang found that people generally rated objects more highly if these objects were viewed alone.[16] They give the example of a man looking for an engagement ring for his fiancée. In the jeweller's shop, the smaller, cheaper diamond rings the man planned to buy seem tiny in comparison to the larger, more expensive ones. His beloved is bound to prefer the bigger rocks, the man thinks. But if he sensibly buys the ring he can afford, the likelihood is that when he gives it to his fiancée she's delighted. All she sees is the diamond ring on her finger. She doesn't worry about the more sumptuous jewels in the shop. Or at least she doesn't until she happens to pass the jeweller's window . . .

I've experienced this syndrome, not when buying diamonds, I hasten to add, but when I needed a new suitcase. I knew the dimensions I wanted, but when I got to the shop that size of suitcase seemed rather small compared with the huge suitcases on display. Foolishly, I convinced myself to go up a size, and of course paid more than I intended, only to get home and find that my new suitcase only just fitted through the front door.

What I should have done was follow the advice I'm about to give you. Whenever you are about to buy something, imagine how that item will look on its own when you get it home. The one that suits your needs may be the smallest and cheapest of the lot, but so what? Try to ignore the similar products, particularly the bigger and shinier ones. You had no intention of buying something that large or expensive when you set out, and you shouldn't be swayed now you're in the shop.

Well, sometimes you might be. (You're allowed to treat yourself now and again!) But remember, when you get that impulse-buy home, it will be the only thing of its kind that you own. It won't sparkle in comparison with anything else. Of course you'll probably be pleased with your extravagant purchase and convince yourself that you couldn't have done without it, but then the same would also have been true of the less expensive version.

PAINFUL PRICING

Although, as we've seen, we can often be fooled by price, when we're sure something is over-priced we react strongly. Indeed it induces real pain. There's evidence that the part of the brain called the insula is activated when we think a product is too expensive, the same part of the brain that fires up when we anticipate physical pain.

Knowing this, it occurred to one group of neuroscientists that monitoring a person's brain activity would be a good way to predict whether or not that person might buy something. Of course a brain scanner was needed again. Volunteers were asked to lie in the scanner while pictures of boxes of chocolates and other products were flashed up on the screen in front of them. They were then given the prices of the various items they'd seen and asked whether they would like to buy any of the 40 products. After coming out of the scanner they were asked to rate how much they liked each product and what they thought of the price.

What happened was this. When the right insula (activity

isn't always the same in both parts of the insula) was activated during the revelation of the price, the volunteers in
the scanner tended not to buy the item. In effect the brain
saw the high price and went 'Ouch! Too much.' If it's not
activated, people think the price is okay.

In other cases, the price caused the nucleus accumbens
to be activated. This is part of the reward circuit of the brain,
where various types of neuron are fired if we have sex, take
drugs or eat food we like. It also becomes more active when
we anticipate a financial gain. This was sometimes followed
by activation of the medial prefrontal cortex, which is associated with combining information about gains and losses.
So in these instances the brain was saying: 'Pleasure ahead,
and it's also a bargain.' In these situations, the people in the
scanner were more likely to buy the item.[17]

By looking at the activation and deactivation of these three
areas, the neuroscientists were able to predict with 60 per
cent accuracy whether or not a person would buy a particular
product – better than chance, at 50 per cent, but maybe not
ground-breaking. They had just as much success by asking
people how much they liked the product and what they
thought of the price. So brain scanners are an expensive way
for companies to find out whether people like their products,
when they could just ask them.

The researchers suggest there could be a use for brain
scanners, however, in situations where what people say
doesn't tally with what they do. They don't specify which
situations those might be. For this technique to be worth the
trouble, you would need to find circumstances where people
don't feel able to express their views of price honestly. I
predict that it will be some time yet before many companies

start using these kinds of methods to choose price, rather than more tried-and-tested approaches.

HOW MY HUSBAND GOT HIMSELF A LEATHER JACKET FOR MY BIRTHDAY

Discounts add another layer of complication to decisions about whether a price is fair and whether or not we should spend our money on a product. The way a discount is framed can make a significant difference to our considerations.

Supermarkets are very keen on three-for-two deals or BOGOFs (buy one, get one free). They encourage people to buy more items than they would otherwise, of course. So, though the shop's profit margin on each item is reduced, the amount of actual money they take increases. But also, the very existence of the bargain draws our eye to that particular item. So while we might congratulate ourselves on resisting the marketing trap by buying only one item and not three, can we be sure that in the absence of the three-for-two-deal we would even have bought the single item?[18]

Another issue that clouds our judgement of discounts is our old friend, relative thinking. £10 off a £20 vase is obviously a better deal than £10 off a £50 vase. The first discount is 50 per cent, while the second is only 20 per cent. But of course the money saved is the same, and the bargain is only worth having if you like the first vase. If you don't, and if before you saw the discounts advertised you originally planned to buy the second vase, you'll have made the wrong decision, whatever the percentage reduction in price.

In our household there was a famous occasion some years ago when my husband went out to look for a birthday present for me, but happened to walk past a shop selling a man's leather jacket costing £500. It was a beautiful brown jacket designed by Nicole Farhi, but, even so, he didn't need a leather jacket, he hadn't come out to buy one, had never spent that kind of money on clothes, couldn't afford it, and if he was going to spend anything like that amount he should be spending it on a gift for his lovely wife. So he walked on . . .

Only to find himself inside the jacket shop, where the assistant told him that there was a special offer on that day and that if he went to buy a copy of a particular newspaper and brought it back in with him he could save £100 on the price of the jacket. £100 in exchange for a 30p newspaper! This kind of deal couldn't be missed.

So he bought the newspaper, he bought the jacket, and he didn't buy me a birthday present. After all, although he'd made a saving of £100, spending any more money that day would have been extravagant.

In the end, he did get me a present, but as I recall a rather modest one. As for the jacket, well . . . 'It's a bit of a classic, beautifully designed and cut, the sort of thing that is always stylish and never goes out of fashion.' These are my husband's words. Whenever this story gets told, he repeats them. And the story gets told quite frequently even now because my husband still wears the jacket 15 years later, so if value is the cost of an item of clothing divided by the number of times you wear it (plus the times people observe what a cool jacket it is, I hear my husband adding) then perhaps he really did get a bargain.

But still, he was royally 'had' that day. He was a victim of money over mind and could easily have been suckered into buying something that he wore only a few times before putting it to the back of the wardrobe and forgetting about it. It just goes to show how, in certain circumstances, 'great deals' can short circuit the good-sense wiring in our brains and lead us to have a blow-out.

REFERENT THINKING

We've already returned in this chapter to relative thinking, which leads us to see small cash reductions on lower priced items as discounts worth having, when the same sum taken off a more expensive item doesn't seem worth bothering with. Now in this short section I'm going to introduce a related, but fundamentally different, concept called referent thinking.[19]

This type of thinking often affects how we evaluate prices, because we tend to judge the fairness of a price based on how much we expect things to cost. We're experienced shoppers. We have a reference price in mind that signifies what we think would be a reasonable price for most items.

So how you assess a £5 saving on, say, a box of chocolates, depends in part on what you expected the chocolates to cost in the first place. If your reference price for chocolates is £10, you're not going to view a £20 box marked down £5 to the 'bargain price' of £15 as fair. That's because, to your mind, under the influence of referent thinking, you've actually 'lost' £5 on such a deal. And remember, there's nothing we hate more than a loss.

In one American study, people were told to imagine they were looking for a blanket for about $50, but in the shop it turns out that the best price is $75. Would they drive 5 minutes

to get the same blanket in another shop on special offer at
$60?[20] We've already discovered that affluent people tend not
to bother with such savings if it requires them to make an
extra trip. Getting in the car for the sake of saving $15 hardly
seems worth it.

But in this case, most people said they would make the
effort. And the reason they thought differently was the reference price. They were specifically told that the price they
should be looking to pay for a blanket was $50. Being quoted
a price that was 50 per cent higher therefore seemed too
steep. The actual extra cost was not the important point here.
It was the difference between what they expected to pay and
what they were being asked to pay that mattered.

So how come this only works sometimes? The explanation
from the experts is that it depends on how different the
actual price is from the price you expected. If there is no
difference, you will use relative thinking to make your decision about whether to drive further for the bargain. But if
it costs more than you expected, referent thinking takes over
again. Unless the difference is huge and the price is far, far
more than you expected, in which case relative thinking
emerges again.

ANCHORS AWEIGH

When you get your credit card bill, do you pay it all off
every month, pay the maximum you think you can afford,
pay the minimum required, or something in between?

One option you don't have – if you live in the US or
Britain anyway – is to pay nothing at all. There's a reason
for that. In these two countries, credit cards are used more

than anywhere else in the world, and authorities – who were concerned that too many people were racking up huge debt – enforced regulations requiring credit card companies to print a compulsory minimum payment on the monthly bill.

At first sight, it seems like a good idea. People are forced to confront their debt and to pay at least some of the balance off each month. Yet research by Professor Neil Stewart from the University of Warwick has found that the minimum payment could have an unintended effect.[21] What he and his team discovered was that when people are faced with the compulsory minimum payment, which is not particularly high of course, it leads them to pay off less of the debt than they might have done otherwise. And another team found that if an optional higher repayment was suggested, people tended to pay off more than they would otherwise.[22] This is due to a well-established psychological effect called 'anchoring'. It works like this. A price is suggested to you, and you think, 'Why not use that as a guide, a hint as to a fair price, but then adjust the figure according to your own assessment of the right value?' It sounds like a sensible place to start, particularly if you have little or no real idea of what something should cost. The problem is that first figure can be far more influential than we think. And of course it can be inflated – or set artificially low.

If you're buying a house, for example, the asking price gives an anchor and your assessment of what the house is really worth moves in relation to that. (Incidentally, this is why, when you get your home valued, you should never tell the estate agent what other valuations you've had. It'll lodge a price in their mind and they won't be able to give a truly independent assessment.)

Through the course of this book, I'll show that some of the mistakes we make about money are easy to avoid once we know how to recognise them. With anchoring, though, it might not be so easy. Anchoring has such a robust effect that, even when people are warned about it, they don't always change their behaviour.[23]

With house prices or credit card payments, the numbers initially confronting you are at least related to some financial logic such as the market rate. But anchoring can influence our notions of price in more extraordinary ways.

For a start, consider this, well, priceless example. A study showed that people were prepared to pay more for a meal from a restaurant called Studio 97 than one called Studio 19, the sole reason being that 97 was the anchoring number in the first case, and 19 in the second![24] The delightful lesson here for aspiring restaurant owners is that you should seriously consider calling your place The Trillion Pound Café. You'll make a fortune. But never, ever go for the Zero Dollar Diner.

Another example I like is that when people were asked to draw lines of certain lengths on a piece of paper, and then asked to estimate the average temperature in Honolulu in July, those asked to draw longer lines gave higher temperatures.[25]

Anchors have a crazy amount of power. Whichever way people are presented with an initial number, or even encouraged to generate their own – be it their phone number, the figure on an athlete's vest, a number on a roulette wheel – that number makes a difference to their estimates of everything from the weight of the Roman Emperor Julius Caesar, to the freezing point of vodka, to the year the telephone was invented.[26] The numbers don't even have to represent the same types of measure; a weight expressed in kilogrammes can influence the price you're prepared to pay in dollars. It seems people can't help but have their thinking skewed by anchor numbers.

Here is a pair of questions from one of the classic studies: Was Gandhi more or less than 140 when he died? How old was he when he died? And here's another pair: Was Gandhi more than nine years old when he died? How old was he when he died?

Obviously the first question is nonsense, since nobody has ever lived to the age of 140, but when people are asked that question first, the average answer they give to the second question is 67. If instead they are first asked whether Gandhi was older than nine when he died (another nonsense question for anyone who's even vaguely heard of the Mahatma), their average answer for his age at death is brought down to 50. (If you're wondering, Gandhi was in fact 78 when he was assassinated.)[27]

Now, picture this scene: a boardwalk on the West Coast of the United States. Among the stalls of aromatherapists, psychics, crystal sellers and head masseurs are two tables, side by side, one apparently selling CDs, the other sweatshirts. It's a laid-back, chilled out Californian scene. But what people out on the boardwalk didn't know was that some seriously heavy science was going down that day. Because these stalls were staffed by undercover researchers studying the impact of what's known as incidental pricing.

In keeping with the Californian vibe, passers-by who showed an interest in the CDs were given the chance to name their price. True, a device was used to ensure that people didn't just go for stupidly low figures, but rather worked out what they were really prepared to pay. Still, if the price was reasonable, the CD was theirs.

Meanwhile, next door, the sweatshirt stand was sometimes displaying a sign saying the sweatshirts cost $10, while at other times the advertised price increased to a whopping $80. Now, the cost of the sweatshirts should have been irrelevant to people considering the CDs. Yet even so, the average price people were prepared to pay for the CD when sweatshirts were advertised at $10 was $7.29, but that rose to $9 when the sweatshirt price was $80.[28] Afterwards, every single customer insisted that the price of the sweatshirt had not swayed them. But how else can the difference be explained?

Unlike some hypothetical studies, this research had the advantage of using real customers. But still, it was clearly a somewhat artificial situation. This led the same researchers to analyse five years' worth of real-life sales at the annual Classic Car auction in the States. Collectors come from around the world to this auction. They can inspect each car. They have precise ideas about what they're looking for, and there are plenty of guides in which they can look up typical prices. These are people who should be making informed bids.

Even so, the researchers found that if a cheaper model of car was sold immediately after a high-end model had been sold, the final sale price went up.[29] So, in the case of a Plymouth Barracuda, when it was sold after a classic Mercedes, the price rose by an astonishing 45 per cent compared with the average sale price.

An even more serious, indeed alarming, example of how

anchoring can impact on people's thinking happened in a German study. A group of junior lawyers who had begun to judge cases in court were given the details of a case in which a woman had been caught shoplifting. They were then asked to roll a pair of dice, which had been loaded to give a total of either three or nine every time. Next, they were asked whether they would recommend a prison sentence of more or less than the number of months shown on the dice. Finally, they had to state the exact prison sentence they would give.

Those lawyers who had seen a score of nine on the dice gave the woman an average sentence of eight months, but those whose dice had shown the number three gave her just five months.[30] It was of course a hypothetical situation again, and hopefully in real life judges aren't rolling dice immediately before making sentencing decisions. But the lawyers in the experiment were well aware that the numbers on the dice were totally irrelevant, and yet they were still swayed by them.

Anchoring has been well established in dozens of studies. When the anchor number is clearly financially relevant, such as the asking price in a house sale, then it's thought our psychological processes are close to the kind of conscious deliberations that Daniel Kahneman would call type 2 thinking, the kinds of decisions that we make slowly and carefully, as opposed to the more rapid, intuitive type 1 thinking.[31]

But when the number is irrelevant, something else seems to be going on. In these cases, our thinking is somehow influenced without us realising it. This is known as 'priming', a controversial topic to which I'll return in Chapter 11. So how can these studies teach us to resist the anchors that sway us in the wrong direction?

CONTROLLING THE ANCHOR

The most obvious way to retain control is to ensure that we are the ones to drop anchor, as it were – while always remembering that if you're the seller you want the anchor to lie on the high side, and if you're the buyer you want it to be a low figure.

Starting with selling: if you set a high anchor, you are – at the very least – likely to sell at what you consider a fair price. First, you and the potential buyer are now working around your initial figure, putting you at an advantage. Second, through the well-established cognitive phenomenon, the confirmation bias, the would-be buyer is likely to start looking for information to back up the high price you've established as the starting point, whereas if you'd set the price low, the buyer would have been looking for flaws in the item you're selling.

Now, there's one proviso to adopting this strategy. That is those situations where you have no idea what the thing you're selling is worth, or what someone might be prepared to pay for it. In this case, it's probably better to let the buyer bid first. After all, in these circumstances, if you set the anchor price ridiculously high, then you risk driving your potential buyer away; while if you go too low, the buyer will certainly accept the deal, but you'll have fleeced yourself.

But then what if the other person goes first and bids ridiculously low? Should you then counterbid with something similarly high?

The same situation might happen if you're looking to buy.

You think the price set by the seller is unjustifiably high, but do you respond with a price which you feel is actually way too low?

Research conducted by the psychologist Adam Galinsky suggests not.[32] His advice is to concentrate on the price that you had in your mind before the other bidder dropped their anchor. Any dealing around their price, even countering with a similarly silly lower offer, still means you're both fixed to that initial anchor. It is better to break off negotiations completely and to reframe around a new starting point.

Once again, our desire to avoid losses comes into our thinking. In one study, students were put in a role-play situation in which they were asked to imagine they were negotiating the best possible price when buying a condominium. The results showed that a lot depended on whether the students saw the seller's asking price as a potential gain or a loss. If that asking price was rather less than they expected to pay anyway, the student buyers were much happier to negotiate. In this situation, the students saw the transaction as one in which they could only gain. But if the anchor was higher than the price they had in mind, they were more likely to walk away from any deal. In this case, the students felt whatever they did they'd be facing a loss.[33]

The real-life lessons from the work on negotiating suggest that, if you are buying, you need to find a way to avoid the seller feeling they are making a loss, because by now we know that we hate a loss. So if you are putting in an offer for a house, your offer needs to feel better than they had hoped for, rather than worse. You could begin by suggesting that you feel the property is worth an even lower price than you propose to offer, but quickly add that you are prepared to pay over-the-odds for it and state your lower-than-asking-price offer. If you do this, compared with the price you suggested it was worth, your offer will feel a little more like a gain than a loss.

Of course many of the experiments into the effects of anchoring have the drawback that they were conducted in a laboratory. Finding out what someone might do in a hypothetical situation is very different from observing what they'd actually do in a real one. The advent of eBay has helped here. On eBay, negotiations are transparent for everyone to see. As such, the online market provides a great experimental playground for psychologists such as Adam Galinsky, Gillian Ku and Thomas Mussweiler.

One auction they studied involved a Hawaiian-themed shirt made by Tommy Bahama, the 'purveyor of the island lifestyle'. It was a bit too loud for my tastes, I must say, but plenty of people disagreed and put in bids. And the key to success for sellers – the researchers have found – is to set no starting price. This encourages potential buyers into the auction who then start bidding against each other. All the action then draws others in, but by now the initial bidders have invested time and energy in the auction and they don't tend to withdraw. The upshot is that the seller gets a higher price at the end. By contrast, sellers who set a starting price, particularly if it is on the high side, get less traffic and lower sales.[34]

Research has shown that the anchoring effect is stronger when people are unfamiliar with a situation, when the information comes from a trustworthy source and if people are feeling sad. This last finding is particularly intriguing, and it rests on the fact that when we feel sad we put more effort into cognitive processing, which in this case makes things

worse, as we are more likely to look for evidence that justi-
fies a high price.

Likewise, the findings of the few studies done into the
impact of personality on our tendency to let anchors sway
us show that the more conscientious and agreeable we are,
the more likely we are to think things through thoroughly
and to be more trusting. And this puts us at most risk of
being duped by over-inflated charges.[35]

All in all it seems you can pay a high price for low spirits
– and for being nice.

5½

LOOSE CHANGE

Tips for waiters, why a light touch is best and the problem of the shared bill.

HERE I DIGRESS briefly to explore one of the few situations where we are forced to discuss money openly, or semi-openly at least. When a group goes out for a meal, at some point someone has to deal with the bill. How should it be divided and what about the tip? In a group, the answer to these questions is never straightforward.

Let's start with the tip. Individuals have different ideas about an appropriate figure, which depend not just on the quality of the service or their generosity, but also on where they are from. I was once chased along the street in Manhattan after the waiter at a sushi restaurant decided my tip was insufficient. We had left 12 per cent, which would be fine in Britain, but the waiter was not happy and demanded more, saying we obviously had no understanding about how things work in the US. In Japan, it's the opposite and tipping at all can be viewed as insulting.[1]

Then there's the question of who to tip. My old street had two restaurants, two hairdressing salons, three dry cleaners and a shoe mender. Why, in the UK at least, do we tip the waiters and the hairdressers, but not the dry cleaners or the shoe mender, both of whom might also have done a lovely job?

But if you are someone who works for tips (and of course some employers pay unfairly low wages, assuming that tips will make up the difference), I have three pieces of advice for you, or maybe more, gleaned from the psychological literature.

The first is from a naturalistic study conducted in 1986 in a restaurant in West Lafayette, Indiana. For a week the amount people tipped and the method of payment used were recorded. When paying in cash, people on average (and this was in the US) tipped just under 15 per cent.[2] But with a credit card, chiming with what we saw in Chapter 2, that rose to almost 17 per cent. That said, if you are a waiter, then before you act on this research and encourage your customers to add the tip onto their card in the hope of getting more, you need to know of course whether your company passes on those tips to staff or pockets them.

When I was a waitress as a teenager, I didn't know that there were clever psychological methods for getting big tips. It was well over a decade too late for me when two French psychologists, Nicolas Guéguen and Céline Jacob, discovered that a light touch was the key. Not a light touch in conversation (although in another study they did find that handing the customer a card with a joke on it along with their bill led to higher tips), but an actual light touch on the upper arm.[3] Their research was inspired by studies from the 1980s that had found that if you ask someone to do something, they are more likely to say yes if you touch them on the arm at some point. Whether you are asking them to lend you 10 cents, sign a petition or sample some free pizza (that's assuming you need any encouragement for that last one), they say yes more readily.[4]

It's a technique that also works if you're ever trying to sell a second-hand car. Working with the psychologist Damien Ereceau, Guéguen found that when a man selling a car touched a potential male buyer on the arm, the buyer later rated the seller to be more impressive.[5] A light touch like this appears to foster a sense of warmth and intimacy. It demonstrates what a nice person you are and that you are fully focusing your attention on them.

So how much difference does a touch on the arm make when it comes to tipping? The unwitting participants in the experiment carried out by Guéguen and Jacob were customers sitting alone in a bar, in an attractive spot in the town of Vannes, on the coast of Brittany. In France, people don't always tip if they are just buying a drink. In fact, in this bar on the day of the study, only 10 per cent of people left something for service. But if the waitress briefly touched each customer's arm as she asked them what they would like to drink, that rose to almost 25 per cent.[6]

This pair of psychologists seems to take a particular interest in tipping. (Perhaps they used to be waiters.) For instance they have also found that if waitresses wear red rather than white or black t-shirts, it makes no difference to the tips female customers give, but that men give more[7] and that a bill presented on heart-shaped dishes garnered more tips than round or square dishes.[8]

Now it might be a mistake to try to put too many psycho-logical research findings into practice all at once. But if you're working waiting tables then the best evidence would suggest wearing a red top, touching customers lightly on the arm when you present them with their bill on a heart-shaped plate and cracking a joke. On the other hand if you're a customer and your waiter touches you on the arm, while wearing a red top, then presents you with your bill on a heart-shaped plate and cracks a joke, pause while you consider the actual service you received before you decide how much to leave.

A final piece of advice, which any experienced waiter already knows, is to avoid serving the tables occupied by groups. They are less likely to tip generously. Researchers have suggested that this might be down to the diffusion of responsibility among the group. No single individual feels that it's their job to pay generously. Having said that, it depends on the type of restaurant you're working in. In one study, at the International House of Pancakes in Columbus, Ohio, the groups didn't tip well – 11 per cent tips compared with 19 per cent at tables for one. But at the classier Smuggler's Inn not far away, groups were just as generous as the singles and couples.[9] Do the expensive restaurants have more staff, ensuring that there's still an opportunity to pay attention to the individuals in groups?

There is another possibility that seems to be overlooked. Maybe on the group tables, the serving staff simply fall victim to the shared bill effect. We've all been there. Fifteen of you go out for dinner. You all calculate what you think you owe, and the unlucky person with the job of adding it all up will inevitably find there's a shortfall. Who's most likely to pay the price? The waiter, with a reduced tip.

Why does the shared bill so often go wrong? There are two ways of splitting the bill of course. Adding the service and then using the calculator on someone's phone to divide the total equally – the method which leaves the non-drinkers and the less greedy subsidising everyone else. Alternatively everyone roughly calculates what they owe based on what they ordered, then adds a bit for shared drinks and service and passes a few notes up the table. When it's announced that the bill is short, reluctantly everyone will put in a bit more until there's enough, each slightly resentful that someone hasn't paid their share.

Occasionally someone might deliberately and dishonestly give too little. But usually that seems accidental, and the shortfall happens again and again. Over the years, and especially if people's earnings go up, allowing them to be more generous, experience leads people to overpay deliberately and the problem is reduced. Or at least it is publicly. They still feel they've overpaid. So what's going on here? The answer, it appears is that some individuals round down every estimated figure slightly to their advantage. By the time it's added up, a little under-estimate here and there suddenly turns into quite a shortfall.

The economist Uri Gneezy, who does some particularly imaginative studies on the psychology of money and who we will hear more about later, wanted to investigate what is known in game theory as the Unscrupulous Diner's Dilemma. This is a dilemma that happens not at the end of the meal, but before we've even ordered our food.

Some groups think it sensible to agree on how the bill will be split before anyone orders. That way everyone knows where they stand. This sounds like a good idea. But if the decision is made to share the bill equally, regardless of what anyone orders, then this is where the Unscrupulous Diner can really enjoy themselves. They can order the oysters, followed by the lobster, then the (inexplicably expensive) cheese plate and a brandy, of course, to finish. The tee-total vegetarian who just wants a main course can subsidise their meal. But would anyone actually be as mean as to change their order and go for the pricey stuff, just because they know the bill is shared?

According to Uri Gneezy's experiment, yes they would. He divided students into groups of six and gave them the opportunity to go out for dinner. Students were told beforehand how the bill would be calculated. When they were instructed that they would pay for whatever they, as an individual, ordered they tended to choose a reasonably priced meal from the menu. But if they knew that the bill would be shared, suddenly the more expensive items on the menu seemed appealing. For some it seems the Unscrupulous Diner's Dilemma wasn't such a dilemma after all.[10] Of course if everyone does it, it doesn't really matter. Everyone ends up paying more, but everyone gets a better meal. But as we'll see, that's not usually the case.

These students were strangers, whereas in real life a group meal is usually with friends, who you hope wouldn't seek to take advantage of each other. But if you think of the number of times there's a shortfall in the total, even though everyone seems to be honest, then it's likely that it is happening among friends.

Gneezy questions why we would ever agree to share the bill equally. To him it makes no sense. In his study, people were asked beforehand whether they would prefer to have an individual bill or to pay a share of the total, and 80 per cent of people wanted to pay only for what they themselves consumed. So why don't people always choose that approach in real life? Because there are other costs. There's the hassle of working it all out, the awkwardness when there isn't quite enough and, worst of all, the social cost of appearing stingy.

These days an increasing number of apps can keep track of bills for you and work out at the end what everyone needs to pay, and those can help. But for the moment even these helpful devices aren't going to answer that most socially awkward of questions: who drank all the wine?

6

MONEY THE MOTIVATOR?

How money makes you run to catch that train, why paying children to do better in exams has mixed results, why it's only worth introducing financial incentives if you can keep paying them long term, and why small payments can help people quit drugs and cigarettes.

IF YOU WANT staff to work harder, pay them more. If you want a salesperson to sell more cars, raise their commission. If you want a child to learn her times tables, promise her extra pocket money for each set she memorises. Call it bribery. Call it a sweetener. Call it an incentive. But it seems to work. Or that is what we tend to assume.

The British government uses payment-by-results to induce agencies to help the long-term unemployed find jobs. And multinational corporations tell us they have no alternative but to pay huge bonuses to their senior executives for fear they will otherwise go elsewhere. The clear implication is that money is the main motivator when it comes to managers working hard for their shareholders (though curiously today senior staff members seem to need this motivation more than cleaners, and didn't need such large incentives until about 30 years ago).[1]

In this chapter, I'll be looking at the situations where money *can* help to motivate us. We'll come to situations where money is clearly not the answer, where other factors serve to motivate us and alternative rewards are more appropriate later on.

DANGLING FROM BARS AND RUNNING FOR TRAINS

In the 1950s the neurologist Robert S. Schwab was working at Harvard Medical School. Investigating illnesses such as Parkinson's disease and the auto-immune condition myasthenia gravis, he was the first scientist to trial several medications that later became standard treatments. A man known for his good ideas, he was influential in developing the techniques used to establish that brain death has occurred in a patient. He was also a keen sailor. After dark, he would take his boat out along the wide waters of Boston's Charles River and then have a colleague at the hospital on the bank flash lights in a window at just the right moment to guide him back to safety. The same ingenuity was clear in his choice of experimental methods. For instance, his interest in the way that muscles fatigue led him to wonder whether tiredness could be overcome by the right kind of motivation.

In 1953 he tested the ability of individuals to hang from a bar by their hands. How long could a man bear the pain in the flexor muscles of the wrist before he gave up? Usually the men managed an average of 50 seconds.[2] Dr Schwab tried egging them on with words of encouragement and even hypnosis. This took the average hanging time up to 75 seconds. But then he offered the men money. He showed them a $5 bill (the equivalent of about $35 today) and told them it would be theirs if they could better their two previous attempts. Suddenly participants were able to find the strength to hang up there for almost two minutes.

In this case it seems pretty clear that a straightforward financial incentive was the motivation to try harder. And sometimes in the real world money has the same effect. Take fruit picking. Paying employees, often casual workers, not by the hour but for every punnet of raspberries they pick, makes sense. The workers are incentivised to focus on the mundane task in hand and are duly rewarded for harder work. Of course there is some innate pleasure in fruit picking – many of us enjoy blackberrying on autumn walks – but the mellow fruitfulness of this leisurely endeavour is a long way from the hard realities of modern agri-business. On the whole, both enterprising fruit growers and their industrious fruit pickers gain from piecework. Only the lazy worker loses out.

So for very specific and innately uninteresting tasks, money seems to work well enough as a motivator. But perhaps the strongest finding of all from the dozens of studies that have been done into the influence of monetary incentives is that payment by results – so beloved by certain politicians and businesses – doesn't work beyond a certain point.[3] The evidence couldn't be clearer: For most tasks beyond the simplest, if an individual is promised more money, the harder they work or the better they do, the less prepared they become to make any efforts for which they are *not* paid.

For his next experiment Dr Schwab headed to Boston's North Station to observe the behaviour of commuters. How would money affect their motivation? He wasn't interested in the punctual businessmen who stood briefcase-between-feet on the platform in their raincoats and trilbies, in good time for the train. Instead he focussed on the men who were running late, who had left the office with too little time to guarantee boarding the train they wanted to catch.

Although these men couldn't be bothered to be punctual, Schwab noticed that they would race along the platform in an attempt to board a leaving train, rather than just waiting for the next one. But how far were they were prepared to run? How strong was their motivation to catch that train?

Dr Schwab positioned himself on the platform ready to calculate the distance by counting the number of railroad posts each late-comer would pass. In the early evening the late running men would sprint just twenty yards before giving up. As the evening wore on – and the desire to get home rather than wait in the station grew – the sprinting commuters would run almost twice as far in the hope of making the train. But when it came to the last train, the men's determination to catch the train shot up measurably.

'Dignity was thrown to the winds', he wrote, 'and subjects would cry out and wave their arms, and sprint up to 70 yards down the station platform, hoping that someone would see them and stop the train.'[4] Remarkably, these energetic displays of desperation more often than not worked. The train driver would generally slow down to let them board. (I'm not sure that would happen in Boston today.) But what did this finding prove?

Schwab's initial conclusion seems reasonable enough. The

late runners wanted to catch that last train more desperately than the earlier ones, because missing it cost them money. If they missed earlier trains, all they suffered was a delay. If they missed the last train, however, it hit them directly in the pocket. The remaining options were to pay up to ten dollars for a taxi home or more than that for a room in Boston.

Yet even Schwab realised that money was not the only motivating factor in this example. As he put it, the men also faced the 'awkwardness of explaining this [a night spent in town] to the wife'. (We can speculate that they might also have preferred sleeping in their own bed or avoiding the queue for late night taxis.) Clearly that extra charge for getting home was one element pushing them to charge down the whole length of the platform, yet the way money influenced behaviour in this example was almost certainly more complex and interesting than a straightforward desire to avoid a financial penalty.

Presumably some of these commuters on occasion *chose* to have a late night in the city even though it would mean missing the last train home and having to pay for a cab or stay in a hotel. And in these planned instances the fact that they were incurring an extra cost wouldn't have bothered them at all. They would have factored the ten dollars or more into their thinking.

Yet when they weren't expecting to incur this cost they went to quite desperate lengths to avoid paying it. What was driving them up the platform therefore was not just the thought of the financial penalty but a sense of frustration and injustice: 'I've paid for my ticket, and I'm damn well going to get this train even if it nearly kills me!'

In both cases the monetary loss is the same, but the

psychological impact of the loss is much greater in the second case than the first. In a visceral sense, the $10 fare *feels* like a lot more money in this instance.

PAYMENT FOR RESULTS

So it wasn't *just* the money that had Dr Schwab's businessmen hurtling down the platform in pursuit of the last train. But money certainly came into their mental equation – and the idea of money serving as a prime motivator retains a strong hold over society and governments.

More recently in the United States money has been used to tackle poor performance in schools in a series of controversial experiments. This time the sum involved was large. Very large. The project, organised by the Harvard economist Roland Fryer, paid out a total of $9.4 million to 36,000 children. And it was the children who got the money, not their parents, which led some parents to lobby to change the scheme. Meanwhile opponents, and there were many, said offering financial rewards devalued learning for its own sake. Indeed such was the storm over the idea that when Fryer discussed it on CNN he received death threats.[5] All of which goes to show how money, particularly big money, stirs up passionate emotions.

But what of the results?

The first of the trials began in New York, Dallas and Chicago in the autumn of 2007, with others following in Washington and Houston. Each city had slightly different incentives. In the New York project, fourth graders (nine- to ten-year-olds) could earn $25 for doing well on tests, while seventh graders (twelve- to thirteen-year-olds) could earn $50 for each A grade they achieved. This allowed them to earn a maximum of $500 during the school year, half of which was put into an account, untouchable until they left high school, but the other half of which they could spend immediately. The Chicago scheme was similar. But in Washington the students received money not for high grades but for good behaviour, regular attendance and timely homework completion.

Conventional wisdom would suggest that whatever the ethics, such large incentives would yield results. And there was some success. Though not uniformly in all five cities. In fact the outcomes were decidedly patchy.[6]

In New York and Chicago, the payments had little impact on grades overall, although in Chicago school attendance improved. In Washington, results on reading tests rose for some students, but scores for other subjects didn't. In Houston, maths scores improved in the particular areas they had been paid to study and it only made a small difference to their maths grades overall.

In Dallas, however, things really did change, due to a crucial difference in the way the trial was run.

Here children were offered money, not for obtaining good grades but for completing particular tasks – in this case, reading books. They were much younger, at only seven and eight years old, and they were given $2 for each book they read. They could choose the books from a selection and could read them at their own pace. They took a comprehension test to prove they had read it and while there was no direct reward gained for higher reading comprehension scores, that's exactly what the children achieved. Which is not surprising when you think about it. After all, it's by reading that you get better at reading.

Now, there are a couple of things to note here. First, that as we'll be discovering in Chapter 7, bribing children to read books might rob them of what's known as intrinsic motivation. It could take away their love of reading, so that once the payments have stopped, they never pick up a book again. The researchers did look to see what happened next. In the year after the payments stopped students were still doing well on reading tests, but there was only half the improvement. Gradually the effect of the payments fades away.

However, it's the second aspect of the Dallas experiment that is most important to our understanding of how financial incentives of this sort work. In Dallas, the children were paid to complete a task which they *could all do* as long as they *put in the effort*. In the other cities by contrast, payment was not for effort but attainment, not for reading text books but for getting high grades. Of course, by concentrating hard in lessons, doing homework and revision, some children could increase their chances of doing well in the tests. But for others, however much effort they put in, they didn't know how to get the A grades that would earn them the payments. After each of the tests in the New York project, students were asked what they could do in order to get better grades next time, and couldn't really answer the question.

The students in New York, Washington and Chicago were certainly keen to earn the cash, but by contrast in Dallas and in Houston the task was specific, clear and within the control of the students.

Despite achieving some success, the learning from the Harvard experiment has not been widely applied in the US – or indeed in other advanced schooling systems. It seems there is still a certain moral queasiness about introducing monetary incentives into schools – a reaction which, as it happens, dates back almost two hundred years. As early as the 1820s, the Society for Progressive Education – again in New York – tried paying school children for high academic results, only for the scheme to be abandoned after a decade amid fears that this was the wrong sort of encouragement for a child and that they might end up developing a 'mercenary spirit'.[7]

One of the issues perhaps is that in richer countries the incentives offered are just not life-changing enough to make a difference. Perhaps in poorer countries they would have more impact. Such schemes have been tried widely in lower income countries including Colombia, Costa Rica, Jamaica, Kenya, Mexico and Pakistan.

In Mexico, the Progresa scheme paid families a large sum, as much as half their salary, to ensure their older children went to school every day. In terms of attendance, the scheme worked, particularly among the problem 14- to 17-year-old age group, where attendance rose from 64 per cent to 76 per cent.[8] There was even a knock-on effect on younger siblings, despite the payments not applying to them.[9] Yet higher attendance at school only resulted in a 4–10 per cent increase in attainment, depending on which years and age groups you compare.[10] An improvement worth having, but, just as we saw in Chicago in the Harvard experiment, getting children to go to school doesn't necessarily get them to learn.

But a scheme introduced in the Colombian capital, Bogotá, in 2005, was a spectacular success.[11] This time students who graduated from high school received a $300 bonus, enough to pay for college fees. Before the bonus was brought in, only 22 per cent of young people graduated from high school.

With the bonus that rose to an impressive 72 per cent. How can this be explained?

It could be that lots of talented students were failing to graduate from school because of financial pressures, but once the $300 graduation bonus was introduced the calculation changed. It was economically sensible for them to stay on at school and utilise the ability they already had to pass their final exams.

A key element though was the size of the incentive relative to earnings in the country. $300 in Bogota in 2005 was a lot of money. Getting the bonus could make a real difference to your life and enable you to study in a way that you couldn't before.

After comparing schemes from around the world, Professor Robert Slavin from York University concludes that financial incentives are only successful in richer countries, like Israel, if they target the very poorest people. Meanwhile in low-income countries, the schemes work best when conditions are well defined and concurrent efforts are made to improve teaching in the schools. What is also clear is that incentives are better than penalties, and payments are more successful in concrete subjects like maths than in other subjects.[12] Even then, they are an expensive way of enhancing results, so it is arguably better to invest the money in improving the education system overall.

BLOOD MONEY

There are some circumstances where even the suggestion of a financial incentive makes people feel uneasy. With advances in surgery, more blood transfusions are taking place, and the global demand for blood is higher than ever before. At the same time the criteria for donating blood have been tightened for safety reasons and so finding enough donors is becoming more difficult.[13] How then do health services get the blood they need? Paying donors to give more regularly seems an obvious answer, and in some countries that is what happens.

That said, there are some drawbacks. The World Health Organisation cautions against paying for blood donation. Their reasoning is two-fold. First, they point out that payment of a fee transforms the giving of blood from a philanthropic act to the selling of a service, and that in these circumstances the pool of people wanting to donate blood actually decreases. People's identity is shaped by how they earn money. If you are a teacher or an engineer, you might be happy to be paid for that, but not for donating blood. The payment turns something honourable into something shabby and mercenary.

Just think about it. If that smart, dark blue, folded card you get as a voluntary blood donor in Britain was to fall out of your wallet or purse in front of friends you would probably feel rather proud. Now imagine them seeing a receipt showing the Blood Transfusion Service had paid you £20.

Moreover poorer people might feel they have no choice but to give blood, when they don't really want to.[14]

The second reason the WHO gives, and it's a crucial one, is that payments can compromise the safety of blood supplies because it is people who are most desperate for money who are then drawn to donate. The issue here is that this group is statistically more likely to take part in risky, blood-contaminating behaviours such as sharing needles. Not all or even the majority of paid blood donors will be intravenous drug users of course – but the consequences of using infected blood for transfusion are so serious that health services have to be ultra-cautious.

These reasons seem persuasive, but where is the solid evidence that payments put off the right people and attract the wrong types? Well, in some surveys, potential donors – and in particular women – do claim they would be deterred by cash incentives. But then there's always the possibility with hypothetical situations that people will say what they think looks good.[15] Perhaps in real life, with no one looking on and making moral judgements, people act differently?

Because so many countries have banned cash payments, there's a lack of research into the effect of actual money on actual behaviour. The best we have is experiments using other incentives.

For example, a field trial conducted in Argentina found that the promise of a t-shirt and a supermarket voucher worth the equivalent of £1.35 made no difference to the numbers donating, but vouchers worth £4 and £6.70 did.[16] More people came forward and the blood they gave was safe. In the US and Switzerland, experiments also found that the more valuable the incentive, the more donation rates rose.[17] And these studies got round the potential safety danger by rewarding people simply for turning up at the clinic and filling in the form, rather than for actually giving blood, which removed any incentive for people in high-risk groups to lie about their behaviour so as to get the payment.

These limited trials would suggest therefore that the WHO's concerns about the negative effects of paying blood donors are misplaced. But to really know, it would be good to compare them with trials involving hard cash. A Swedish study often quoted as doing just that, in fact promised lottery tickets to students rather than cash.[18]

Overall, the research that's been done on this subject so far suggests that a system of financial rewards might help when there's an emergency shortage. Low- and middle-income countries store smaller quantities of blood and rely more on last-minute donations, but there's a gap in literature when it comes to the effectiveness of payments in these countries.

However, despite some circumstances where incentives can work, the whole idea of paying for blood donation seems to create a sense of unease. Of all the situations where we should act altruistically rather than with money in mind, this one seems to be among the most obvious. After all, we are being asked to help save the lives of fellow human beings. Who can put a price on that?

In the aftermath of the 9/11 terrorist attacks in New York in 2001, large numbers of people across the US came forward to donate blood. Many had never done so previously but wanted to feel they were doing something to help. It was a laudable act, but alas short-lived – the majority of those post-9/11 blood donors have never given blood again. And research shows this is the general pattern with emergencies. Blood donation shoots up at the time. But 60 per cent of donors don't return.

This is surely not surprising to anyone interested in psychology. People often get swept up in national or international tragedies and want to 'do their bit'. Once the news cycle moves on, however, there's not that same sense of being part of a collective endeavour. It's why fundraisers for charities put a premium on signing up people to give monthly donations through direct debits. One-off appeals are all very well but all too quickly the payments stop coming in. By contrast, 'regular giving' supplies charities with a steady income that allows them to pursue long-term projects sustainably.

In an attempt to turn 9/11 blood donors into regular donors, the blood centre in San Francisco tried two slightly different approaches. The people who had given blood for the first time after the New York attack were split into two groups at random, one of which was telephoned and given this message: 'Hello, I'm from the Blood Centers of the Pacific. I'm calling to thank you for your blood donation following the September 11 tragedy and to let you know that currently we have a patient having a liver transplant who needs twenty units and matches your blood type. Can we schedule an appointment for you to come in and help us out again?' The other group was told an identical story, but with just one difference; if they decided to give blood again they would get a free t-shirt.

Now the experimenters were surprised that the offer of a t-shirt made no difference: roughly 20 per cent agreed to give blood again in each group.[19] But I'm surprised at their surprise. Told the story of your match with a transplant patient, would the added incentive of a t-shirt really make a difference to you? In the circumstances it might even seem tawdry.

Of course, a very large sum of money would hardly be less so, morally speaking, but at least such a sum could be life-changing for some people. The t-shirt by contrast devalues the act of giving blood while amounting to nothing much at all in the way of an incentive. As we've seen from other studies, a much better idea if t-shirts are to be involved at all would have been to reward people with one *after* they'd given blood, by way of a 'thank you' gift.

In 2008, sixteen-year-old Jeremy Thomas from Coral Springs in Florida was found guilty in court of smoking in a shopping centre when he was under-age. The judge gave him three sentencing options: pay a fine of $53; complete seven-and-a-half hours of community service; or donate a pint of blood.[20] I've not been able to find information on which he opted for, but giving blood would have been the least onerous option in terms of time and expense. Yet in other situations where offenders have been offered this chance – drivers who've accidentally killed people in car accidents for instance – not everyone takes it up.[21] Some prefer to pay the fine. As far as I know, there's been no research into why people might act this way. But we can speculate that offenders may feel that to give blood in these circumstances is morally uncomfortable. Certainly with the dangerous drivers, such a penalty seems rather too close to the notion of an 'eye for an eye' or paying a blood sacrifice. And then there's this issue of feeling coerced. At least Jeremy Thomas and the others weren't told they had to give blood. But still, it was far from a free choice. In Jeremy's case, he could even cost his dona-tion precisely – it was equivalent to $53. And from the wider societal point of view, him donating blood as his punishment was not likely to have been helpful in encouraging voluntary donation. After all, people in Florida might think that the case set a going rate for a pint of blood or that giving blood is so unpleasant that it's considered a punishment.

It goes to show how important it is to think through the unintended and long-term consequences of such initiatives.

The Portuguese government failed to do this in a well-known recent example. In 2004, a scheme was introduced in which people who gave blood twice a year had their fees for using Portugal's National Health System waived. This had the effect of increasing donations while the initiative lasted. But when it ended – you've guessed it – donation rates went down. Donors – in particular the ones who'd started giving after the fee waiver was introduced – had got used to the incentive and gave blood less often when it was withdrawn.[22] It may be that it would have been better not to introduce the incentive scheme at all. But what was certain was that introducing it, then withdrawing it, was a mistake.

This is yet another example of loss aversion. And it has a powerful effect on us in such situations. While we might begrudge doing something for nothing (particularly if we think we should be paid for it), what we really hate is losing a financial benefit we've become accustomed to.

The lesson for blood transfusion services worldwide is clear. By all means run a small pilot to see if cash payments for blood donation do increase giving. (It's surprising no government seems to have done this.) But make sure you run it for a number of years – to see if the financial incentives lead to a sustained increase in donation rates over voluntary arrangements – and, crucially, don't introduce a payment scheme nationwide unless you are certain it is affordable long term. That is likely to be an expensive way of demonstrating something that should be obvious; that yes, money has motivational power, but only as long as the money keeps being paid.

CAN MONEY MAKE YOU QUIT?

Around the world, there have been many attempts to pay people to become healthier. One of the earliest initiatives was the Progresa project that I mentioned in relation to education, which began in Mexico in 1997, was renamed Oportunidades, and is now called Prospera. Poor parents were given money or vouchers if they took their children to school each day, but there was another condition too. The children had to have all their vaccinations. The incentive scheme seemed to work and this led – again with some success – to the use of financial inducements in other low-income countries.

Inevitably this excited interest in the high-income countries. Some initiatives have attempted to induce people to exercise or eat more healthily. But the most fascinating schemes psychologically are those that have tried to persuade people to give up dangerous habits – smoking and taking drugs.

In comparison with the poorer countries, the sums on offer are not life changing. But what does seem to happen is that the offer of money lures people into schemes they might otherwise reject, and then it acts as a positive focus and a tangible reward as people progress towards their personal goals. While apparently a small element of the schemes, money seems to be a key factor, demonstrating once again money's unique psychological power over us.

Giving up smoking is very difficult. Studies have shown that for every hundred people who attempt to quit, even with the help of proven methods such as counselling or nicotine patches, only six succeed.[23]

How was it then that mother-to-be Marie was able to

prove to me, in a small booth at the chemists, that she hadn't touched a cigarette for months? After all, this was her third pregnancy, but the first pregnancy throughout which she had not smoked 20 cigarettes a day – despite the well-known health risks smoking causes to babies. The reason she was trying, and succeeding, in giving up this time was that she was receiving money in exchange.

If she could get negative tests each time she blew into a disposable plastic tube attached to a carbon monoxide sensor in the booth in the chemist, she would get £150 in vouchers to use in a shop of her choice.[24] She told me she would spend it on baby clothes. Her determination was impressive, but there was something immediately curious about it. A financial incentive ten times bigger had been available to her during her previous pregnancies – the amount she would have saved by not buying a packet of cigarettes every day for nine months – approximately £2,500. So why did she view the relatively small incentive offered by the health promotion scheme so differently from the money she could have saved on her own?

Of course it wasn't all about money. The regular contact with encouraging staff definitely helped. Also, everyone knew she was taking part, and it's been demonstrated again and again that pledging to friends and family that you're going to do something makes you much more likely to do it. Her kids were particularly interested in their mum kicking the habit this time, because she had told them she would buy a present for each of them with the money she saved.

But still, there was more to it than that. And the key thing was the way Marie viewed that monetary voucher. It was more than a tool for obtaining baby clothes; it was a tangible reward for success, external validation of how hard she worked. This is why it was more important than the money she was saving through not buying cigarettes (which she accrued as well of course).

In other research, when women like Marie were asked whether the money they earned through such schemes was decisive in getting them to give up smoking during pregnancy, most insisted it wasn't, yet without the money they don't do it. So maybe it's fair to say that it wasn't the prospect of the increased spending power of that money which motivated them. Instead the money was a goal to aim for.[25]

And it seems money is peculiarly effective in this way.

When researchers at Newcastle University did a meta-analysis combining the results of the best studies they could find on the use of financial incentives, not just to encourage people to give up smoking, but also to attend vaccination sessions or cancer screenings, or to take up exercise, they found that as little as £3 could make people 50 per cent more likely to change their behaviour.[26]

When it comes to smoking during pregnancy, a Cochrane Review, which selects the very best studies from around the world and weighs up the evidence, found financial incentives to be the single most effective intervention. So much so, that 24 per cent of women were able to quit compared with 6 per cent using other methods.[27] Now, some of these studies only followed people up for seven days, and of course it's much easier to give up smoking for a week than for the full nine months, but other research did follow women throughout their pregnancies. Relatively small monetary payments were often successful in protecting the health of babies.

Beyond the term of the pregnancy, however, results are

less positive. A recent study followed up women who had been on a scheme like Marie's. The aim was to find out if six months after the women had given birth, they were still eschewing the cigarettes.

Disappointingly, of those who had given up during pregnancy more than 80 per cent had started smoking again once they'd had the baby and the financial incentives stopped. Still, nearly one in five (17 per cent) had succeeded in staying off the nicotine. By contrast, among a group who'd been enrolled in a quit smoking scheme during their pregnancies but not given financial incentives, fewer than 1 per cent were still off cigarettes by the time their baby was six months old.[28]

So it's perhaps a case of two-and-a-half cheers for the power of money to help mothers to give up smoking, but at least many babies were protected before they were born. What though of other examples of using money to help people quit?

KICKING THE COCAINE HABIT

Tom works in advertising in the sort of environment where cocaine gets snorted at parties. Tom tried the drug and loved it. So much in fact that he was soon spending a thousand pounds a week on his habit, and – despite his well-paid job – he was building up debts he knew he could never repay. Several times he went for professional help and briefly gave up, but in the end he always returned to the cocaine.

Then he was offered the chance to take part in a different kind of scheme to help him conquer his substance abuse. This time, in addition to the practical and psychological advice on breaking his addiction, he was required to go to the clinic three times a week for a urine test. And for each clear test demonstrating he was off the drugs, he was paid £2, which the clinic kept for him. He was told that after six months he could collect his earnings and spend the money however he wished, with the proviso that he must buy something which would help him move forward with his life.

Tom decided to save up for the textbooks he needed for the distance-learning course he wanted to take. Others on the scheme chose a bicycle to get themselves fit, a chest of drawers for their clothes, or in one case a new lock for their front door to prevent other drug users from getting into their flat.

Whether the bike, the chest of drawers or the lock did the trick we don't know, for Tom the end result was that after the six months he was still clean. This was far longer than he had ever managed before, and when I met him he told me it was the cash that was the key to his success.

On the face of it, such a claim stretches credulity. Remember the total amount of money he could earn was just £6 a week, or £24 a month. In total, the not-so-grand sum of £144. By comparison, his savings from not buying cocaine ran into tens of thousands of pounds. Rationally, those savings should have been a far bigger incentive for kicking the habit than the money he had gained for his textbooks.

To understand why these schemes can work we need to consider that each of us constructs our own idea about what money symbolises for us. For Tom, the main point of his £2 bonus for proving he was clean was not that he was now better off by £2, or that he had £2 to spend on something. No, as with Marie, the point was not the money itself, or

the spending power, it was that this particular sum represented a public success in his personal battle to get off drugs.
We also need to think back to those psychological moneybags.
For Marie, cigarettes were an everyday cost which would
come from her mental account for necessities, while the
vouchers from the scheme put money into a very different
mental account, the one for treats.

Having told me the money was key, Tom went on to say
other things that showed it was just one element of the
success of the scheme. For example, he said he waited with
great anticipation for the moment when the testing strip gave
a positive result, even though he knew full well he had not
taken drugs in the previous 48 hours. The result, like the
small cash bonus that went with it, was another external
validation that proved to be motivational. Likewise Tom said
he enjoyed hearing the congratulations from staff and
marking his progress up the ladder on the chart he'd been
given. The thought of failing just one drug test – which
would have meant him going back down to the bottom of
the ladder and losing his bonus pot – filled him with dread.[29]

Despite what Tom said, the money was just a small part
of a reward system. In no real-world sense was he being
incentivised to give up drugs in return for a financial boost.
And among all the other elements of the scheme – the
structure the regular testing brought to his week, the motivational impact of charting his progress, the support given
by the staff and the satisfaction Tom got from being told
he'd done well – the money was perhaps the least of it. But
still, small as it was, he'd earned it. And it was money posi-
tively gained rather than just saved along the way.

It is this type of money that we value the most. Money

that's hard won, that comes to us through real effort. It's for this reason, I think, that experts working on such schemes rightly bridle at the notion that clients are being bribed to change their behaviour, as some critics suggest. The word bribe implies something unethical. You bribe someone to throw a sports match or to leak secrets, to encourage dishonourable behaviour. In the cases of Marie and Tom it was different; the money they were getting reinforced positive behaviour patterns. The term the experts use is 'contingency management'. It's a fancy way of saying that people are helped to control their behaviour through a system of rewards and incentives.

Nonetheless the idea of rewarding drug users for kicking a habit that is after all illegal does make some people feel uneasy. Why, critics argue, should drug users make money from quitting – even small sums of money – when those who don't and never did take drugs get nothing? It's for this reason that staff at addiction centres are often initially reluctant to take part in schemes where monetary rewards are offered. The reason they are increasingly persuaded is that these schemes do seem to work.

Tom's case is just one story of success. A meta-analysis of 30 studies provides the real evidence of the effectiveness of this kind of scheme.[30] True, in about half of the studies the positive effect was small, but in the other half it was moderate or large, meaning far more people stayed off drugs after payment than using more usual methods. To quantify the difference, the average drug user on a voucher scheme is more successful than two-thirds of those not getting vouchers.

Some schemes worked better than others, of course. Immediate rewards seem to make a significant difference, with vouchers proving twice as effective if they are given without delay, rather than saved until the end of the programme. Other findings suggest monetary rewards are particularly effective in helping people to overcome tobacco, alcohol or cannabis addiction. They seem less successful with other drugs (perhaps because harder drugs are more power-fully addictive). Finally, and on the whole, the higher the payments, the more successful the scheme. (Though as we've seen in Tom's case, it is possible in some cases to help someone to quit a hard drug with small payments that are delayed to the end of scheme.)

All in all the evidence is pretty compelling – and, just to be clear, drug users weaned off one drug through such schemes don't tend to turn to another. And there is no evidence to suggest that cash incentives increase the chance the money will be used to buy drugs.[31]

GAMING

I was at a press conference in London in 2014 at which clinicians were discussing the results of trials to get heroin users to take a course of vaccinations against hepatitis B. They had experimented with using vouchers, and the results were impressive. When no vouchers were on offer, 9 per cent of the heroin users came for all three vaccinations; after the introduction of vouchers 45 per cent came.[32]

What I remember most from this press conference however was the reaction of other journalists, most of whom – unlike me – had no idea that these kinds of payments were on offer. These other hacks assumed that if there was money to be made from such schemes then people were bound to abuse them, to game the system in some way. For instance, wasn't it possible that people would pretend to be on drugs when they weren't?

This possibility is taken very seriously. Participants in voucher schemes are always tested at the outset of the programme to make sure they really are drug-users. Indeed, such is the strictness of these tests that one project had an unforeseen and undesirable outcome. The users who hadn't taken drugs for a few days found themselves disqualified from the voucher scheme, with the result that they went back onto drugs in order to get accepted. Not gaming exactly, but an example of how a scheme (albeit a generally successful one) can encourage exactly the behaviour it is trying to prevent.

What though of the general extent of actual gaming? A recent study sought to investigate whether stop-smoking schemes using financial incentives were prone to such cheating. At a hospital in Chesterfield, pregnant women attending their first antenatal appointment were offered the chance to take part in a voucher scheme to help them stop smoking. Was it possible that women might lie about their addiction in order to get on the scheme and earn the vouchers? The researchers weren't going to rely on the women simply to be honest.

First, as with any such scheme, the researchers tested the women's carbon monoxide levels to establish whether they'd smoked a cigarette within the past few hours. But of course this allowed for the possibility that someone who was generally not a smoker had taken a few puffs before coming to the appointment in a deliberate attempt to boost their carbon monoxide levels. So a further test was needed.

This one was a urine test to detect levels of a substance

called cotinine. It's found in tobacco, and so if these levels proved low it showed more definitively that any women claiming to be regular smokers were not telling the truth. Finally, to catch anyone who might have been using nicotine patches, which also boost cotinine levels in the urine, saliva was tested for a tobacco-related substance called anabasine. All in all, it was quite an elaborate set of tests and one way or another any cheat was very likely to be detected.

So were any uncovered? Not a single one. The tests confirmed all the women who claimed they were regular smokers really were. No one tried to pass themselves off as a smoker when they weren't.[33]

So much for the worry that financial incentives can encourage gaming. Another concern, which we'll go into in more depth in the next chapter, is that financial incentives reduce internal motivation, leading people to rely on outside rewards only to return to their old ways the moment the payments stop. Does this problem arise in this area?

It is a criticism sometimes levelled at such schemes, and indeed it has led some researchers working in this field to complain that they are expected to achieve higher results than other healthy lifestyle projects.[34] Would a programme designed to encourage people to lower their blood pressure through exercise and healthy eating need to demonstrate that participants' blood pressure was still lower five years later, these researchers ask? Surely not, they argue, and yet they're expected to show that the people on their schemes remain drug-free long after the incentives have been removed.

It may be that too much is expected of such initiatives. But even so, it's only right to look for long-term evidence that people can stay off drugs, and some studies have demonstrated that they do.[35] For example, when drug users in a south London project had completed the programme, some asked if they could carry on coming in for testing, without any rewards. This is just the result that health officials would want to see from such an initiative. Initially the promise of monetary reward attracts people to take part, but as the scheme proceeds, that reward is seen by participants for what it really is: a symbol of their personal success in quitting drugs. At which point that success is enough on its own and the proxy for it, the cash, can be withdrawn.

Even so, it remains the case that once smokers or drug users come off schemes that have helped them to quit, there is a reasonably high chance of a relapse. Not only has the financial reward been withdrawn, but so has the support and structure that such schemes offer. It's for this reason that ongoing services can be so important. The initiatives I've been talking about are just a start. Given financial constraints in even the richest countries in the world, it is highly unlikely that payments to get people to give up unhealthy lifestyles, or take up healthy ones, could be afforded *ad infinitum*. That said, I think in these circumstances money can play a positive role – and can achieve results that couldn't be achieved otherwise.

7

JUST REWARDS

Why if you pay someone they might be more likely to turn to Playboy *in their break, why praise is often a better motivator than money (but don't overdo it), why you should never pay friends for favours and why the England football team always loses in the penalty shoot-out.*

IN THE LAST chapter we saw that money, properly applied to certain situations, is a strong motivating factor. But of course there are instances where it very clearly isn't appropriate. And the difficulty we face in a money-oriented culture is knowing when these circumstances arise. As we'll see, if money is used in the wrong situations it can have a very damaging effect – incentivising us do the wrong thing or stopping us from doing the right thing.

THE CUBE ROOT OF A CONTINUING CONTROVERSY

Let's start in the late 1960s and look at a controversy that begins with a 3D puzzle made from rosewood and a copy of *Playboy*, and ends with academics accusing each other of 'deliberate misrepresentation and inept analysis' and 'turning silk purses into sows' ears'.

It is the autumn of 1969 and in Pennsylvania every Tuesday and Friday a new issue of *The Tartan*, Carnegie Mellon University's student newspaper, is published. A group of volunteers keeps it going, writing the stories in their spare time and then meeting in two editorial groups to agree on the headlines. They discuss them at length, averaging 22 minutes per headline. Like so many student journalists, they're super-enthusiastic – not like the cynical old hacks in the professional media.

What they don't know, however, is that these headline meetings are being used for a psychology experiment – and, as so often happens with this kind of research, one group has been fed a fake back story. The editor has told the Tuesday group that he has some money left in this term's budget and doesn't want to under-spend, so he is prepared to pay them 50 cents a headline (just over $6 today) for each good headline they write for a limited period. They're also told they mustn't tell anyone, especially the Friday group, because he can't afford to pay them too.

What was the experiment trying to show? This time it was not straightforwardly that a financial incentive leads to harder work. After all, there are only so many headlines in any edition of a paper, so the amount the students could earn was capped. What the psychologist Edward Deci who ran the study wanted to know was whether the incentive would make the Tuesday group keener. Would it increase their productivity, in other words? As a measure of keenness he decided to use the speed at which the students produced usable headlines.

What Deci's study found is at first sight surprising. At the start of the experiment both groups took an average of 22 minutes to finalise each headline. But the students in the Friday editorial group, who worked just for the love of it, became faster at thinking up good headlines as the weeks went by, taking just 12 minutes on average by the end, while the other group showed little improvement, only getting to 20 minutes.

Most strikingly, while the members of the unpaid group continued to show up every week, apparently enjoying the process of coming up with headlines for free, there was a considerable drop-out rate from the paid group once the payments stopped. Not only had the financial incentive failed to induce faster work from the Tuesday group, but once introduced it seemed to have stripped the pleasure from the task, such that – when the payments stopped – students were no longer prepared to carry on.

In another of Deci's experiments, three larger groups of students were given a 3D puzzle to solve.[1] Named after the drug Soma, which suppresses negative emotions and gives you a 'holiday from reality' in Aldous Huxley's dystopian novel *Brave New World*, the Soma puzzle consists of seven different clusters of tiny rosewood cubes that fit together in cunning ways to form either a big cube or a variety of other geometric shapes. Against the clock, the students were required to construct four particular configurations illustrated on a piece of paper.

The first time round, all three groups spent the same set period of time – 13 minutes – on the task and then the experiment leader made an excuse to leave the room, telling them they were now free to do as they wished. As well as still having the Soma puzzle, there were, on the tables in the room, copies of the latest issues of the *New Yorker* and *Time* magazine, alongside some items you would not find in many psychology experiments today, an ashtray and a copy of *Playboy*! Unbeknown to the students, the other experimenters watched through a one-way mirror to see what they would do during the break.

It turned out there was no real difference between the groups – all of them tended to carry on working on the Soma cube just because it intrigued them.

In the second round, things got a bit more interesting. One group was told they would be paid a dollar for each solution they came up with; while another (without being told about their paid colleagues) was offered no reward. As for the third, well, we'll come to them.

Now you might think that the object here was to measure whether the cash incentive motivated students to solve the puzzles more quickly during the formal sessions. But this was not what Deci was most interested in this time. Rather, he was keen to see what effect the money had on levels of intrinsic motivation – the extent to which the students remained interested in the task for its own sake.

So the key part of the study was how the students behaved once the experimenter had left the room, telling them to take a break and that they could read the magazines or whatever. This time, just as in the first round, the unpaid students tended to continue playing with the Soma cube, apparently enjoying the challenge of trying to find solutions even though the official session was over. By contrast, the paid group spent much more time looking at the magazines (the academic paper does not record whether they preferred *Playboy* over the *New Yorker* or *Time*) or simply staring around the room.

The conclusion seemed pretty clear: the students had lost their motivation to work on the puzzles once they knew they weren't being paid to do so. Whatever intrinsic motivation they may have possessed had gone.

Deci also noticed with this group that some of the students were embarrassed when the money was handed to them. They all took the cash, just as they had accepted the deal in the first place, but payment seemed to have made the puzzle-solving less enjoyable. It had become work and that can't be fun, right?

But did this show that only a task done for its own sake can bring pleasure? That whenever a person is rewarded for doing something, they lose the intrinsic joy in it? Well, not quite. Remember that third group? This time round they weren't offered payment for doing the puzzles, but they were rewarded afterwards with generous praise. Their work was very good, they were told, better than that of most of the previous students who had taken part.

So how did they behave when it came to the break, and the chance to have some free time? Yes, you've guessed it. These students, glowing with a sense of achievement, took the greatest interest and pleasure of all in continuing to play with the puzzles.

More than that, when the three groups were asked to repeat the task for a third time – like the first time, without the offer of any payment – the behaviour in the break was much the same. That's to say, the first group's motivation levels were similar to the two previous rounds, the second group's levels had dipped markedly (no cash at the end this time, remember), and the third group, still buoyed by the praise in the second round, were the most interested.

THE POWER OF PRAISE

Deci's experiments seemed to show that, if anything, a monetary incentive was demotivating, proving no better than no reward at all, and less effective than praise.

Admittedly, these early experiments by Deci had very small numbers of participants, and the observed differences between the two groups were less marked than we would demand from research today. But more than a hundred studies and four decades later, researchers still frequently uncover the same phenomenon. For instance, small children given money to draw pictures will put down their pencils and crayons the moment the bell rings for break time, while those who are not paid carry on drawing intently.

Other research has also backed up Deci's findings on the pure motivational impact of praise. A child praised for their drawing basks in the idea that they've done well, they don't say to themselves, 'If they have to praise me, this can't be any fun.' Instead they enjoy the task even more.

Of course the praise has to be sincere and appropriate. I remember getting an email from a boss at the BBC, which just said: 'Thanks for all your work on this. We're lucky to have you.' Not pages of gushing plaudits, just these two short sentences. The goodwill engendered by that email lasted for many months, if not years. If everything was going wrong, and I was struggling to make a programme, I recalled that single email and remembered that my efforts were appreciated.

It came from someone I respected and the sentiment was not just well-judged, it was well-meant.

Research shows that wording is crucial. If you are the parent of a small child lacking confidence, it can be tempting as you pin their latest artistic creation to the fridge to declare that it's the best picture you've ever seen. But the evidence suggests this is the wrong approach. Children quickly see through it if you say their work is 'perfect' or 'incredibly good' as opposed to just 'good'.[2]

Another study found that when children with low self-esteem were told they had done an 'incredibly beautiful drawing', they were less likely to choose a challenging task afterwards than those who were simply told it was a 'beautiful drawing'. Just one word made a difference.[3] The author of this paper, psychologist Eddie Brummelman, advises parents to step back and think about the message they give, so as not to set standards so high that the child might fear failing to meet them in the future.

There's also a body of evidence from two decades of research by Carole Dweck at Stanford University, showing that praising a child for effort or the way they approached a task, rather than for results, is more effective because if children are constantly told they are clever, even if it's true, it can lead them to play safe.[4] Dweck told me she's even gone up to families in airports to correct the way they praise their children. Her arguments are so compelling that the parents seems to put up with her uninvited advice.

To return to Deci. His explanation for the behaviour of the students in the Soma cube experiment was that people need to feel autonomous, and that a fee undermines that autonomy – actions are no longer worthwhile in their own right.

Another study seemed to back up this conclusion. In Israel, there are several 'donation days' every year where high school students go door-to-door collecting for charity. The amount of publicity devoted to the day makes collecting easy because householders already know all about it. The main factor affecting how much each student collects is effort. It's up to them whether they collect all day or give up after half an hour. The economist Uri Gneezy, who's done lots of fascinating work in this field, took a large number of sixteen-year-olds and divided them into three groups. One was told how important the charity was and that the amount each student collected would be published. A second group was promised a bonus of 1 per cent of the money they collected. A third group would get 10 per cent. Both these groups were reassured that the bonuses would come from other funds and would not affect the total that the charity received.

So, did the students offered payment pace the streets for hours to raise as much money as possible for the charity and for themselves? No. The unpaid students raised 35 per cent more than those paid the smaller bonus. The larger bonus seemed to motivate them a bit, but still not as much as when they were paid nothing. The lesson here is not to avoid paying charity collectors and to rely on their good will, but if you want to pay them, beware of paying very small amounts. As Gneezy puts it in the title of his paper 'Pay enough or don't pay at all'.[5]

BACK TO THE CONTROVERSY

Now I said at the beginning of this chapter that work in this area of psychology has led to some controversy in academic circles. Why is that? It's because the findings appear to fly in the face of treasured foundational work in the behaviourist tradition, which showed that when our behaviour is reinforced with rewards, we repeat that behaviour with increased enthusiasm. Eventually we don't even need the original reward to carry on doing the behaviour. Animal trainers start out using a clicker in combination with a food treat. But soon the animals will do what the trainer wants them to at the sound of the clicker alone.

The father of behaviourism, B.F. Skinner, was a psychologist who put his own theories into practice, even in his own study at home. Today his daughter, Julie Vargas, lives in the house and as she took me down the wooden stairs to the basement of the grey 1950s bungalow in Cambridge, Massachusetts, she told me how the study had been left just as it was when her father died in 1990. The room seems suspended in time. Skinner's reading glasses are lying on the desk, as though he's just popped out of the room.

The walls are wood veneer, and the ceiling is covered in polystyrene tiles. Mid-century modern fans would love it. There's even an early TV set with a V-shaped aerial coming out of the top like a rabbit's ears. It feels as though it would have been the perfect set on which to watch the moon landings.

A sleeping pod, the size of a very large fridge on its side yellow in colour and cuboid-shaped, takes up one corner. After reading about what Skinner called a 'baby tender', in which he used to place his daughter (essentially a temperature controlled playpen with a window across the front – not as dramatic as it sounds, and the stories online about the great damage it caused to Skinner's younger daughter are a myth), a Japanese company sent the pod to Skinner because they were hoping to market it. Inside there's a mattress, a pillow, a TV set and a stiff, concertina-ed curtain which you can pull across and even lock so that you are safe in your little cocoon. On the other side of the room there's an armchair where Skinner would sit and read with the help of a large magnifying glass suspended from a stand.

He would listen to tapes played on a reel-to-reel machine and, ever the amateur engineer, use a makeshift remote control of sorts involving string and a cardboard lever that would allow him to operate it while remaining in his chair.

As I said before, Skinner didn't only write about his theories in this unique room, he put them into practice. Skinner was convinced that just like rats in a laboratory, people can be conditioned with rewards to do certain things, and that with the right design the environment we live in can have a big influence over our behaviour. So as soon as he walked into his office, he made sure that the conditions he had grown to associate with hard work and concentration were present. First he would turn on the strip light above his desk, a light so bright that he wore a transparent green visor to shade his eyes. The light switch automatically started a timer, allowing him to measure how long he worked. But for fear of clock-watching, he designed a cardboard flap that would hinge over the clock face. The flap flicked down, and it was time to start.[6]

More pertinent to our subject, Skinner's theories also led to the idea of the token economy, where residents in an institution (usually children) are given tokens in exchange for tidying their room, sitting quietly at lunch or not leaving any food on their plate. If they save up enough tokens, they can get a reward, which in turn reinforces the good behaviour they showed to earn the tokens.

If Skinner's ideas are right, money – the universally recognised token of reward – should increase motivation and certainly shouldn't undermine it, as Deci suggests. In an attempt to resolve the apparent contradictions surrounding motivation, there have been four meta-analyses, where the data from each of the best studies from around the world is combined and re-analysed in the hope of getting closer to a definitive answer.

Three of these come to roughly the same conclusion as Deci: that payment does tend to undermine intrinsic motivation, but one, conducted by Judy Cameron and W. David Pierce, points in a different direction. Their analysis did show that when tangible rewards are promised in exchange for a task, intrinsic motivation is reduced, but they concluded that these findings have been overblown and complain that researchers are often too critical of any experiments which aren't conducted within the paradigm they favour.[7] The result, they say, is that teachers and businesses have been deterred from using rewards, even in circumstances where they might work well.

As often happens when psychologists set out to resolve a major dispute in the field, no agreement was reached and the rows continued. Between 1994 and 2001, argument raged in psychology journals, with rebuttals followed by rebuttals-of-rebuttals.

For example, critics of Judy Cameron and W. David Pierce argued that as well as including studies which looked at interesting tasks, the two also included studies where the task was boring. It was no wonder, these critics said, that in these cases intrinsic motivation was unaffected by the incentives offered, because there would have been no intrinsic motivation to do the task in the first place. These studies therefore skewed the meta-analysis, the critics concluded.

At the end of it all, there seems to be little doubt that, under certain circumstances, financial incentives do undermine motivation. But as we saw in the previous chapter, this isn't true all the time. For instance, a one-off surprise reward, after the event, doesn't undermine motivation, whereas the requirement to start or complete a task for money does. And of course it does depend on the task.

Consider these two activities: clearing the table after lunch and spending the afternoon painting a picture. The first is never going to be enjoyable for its own sake; so if parents offer a child a gold star or some pocket money, that will probably work. The reward encourages the child to do the chore and is not going to ruin his or her pleasure in table-clearing for life, for the simple reason that no such pleasure exists. When it comes to painting, however, the reward might work in the short term, but the message sent out is the wrong one. If they are bribed to paint, it could erode their intrinsic motivation and take away the joy of painting.

Similar problems can arise among adults too. Take the example of catering for a big party. Perhaps the group of people you've got coming round to your house is so large you don't think you can manage on your own, and so you ask a friend to help out. As you're asking them a big favour, it might seem only fair to offer them a small cash payment – as well as your eternal thanks, of course.

But think again.

Studies have shown that the introduction of money can

transform such an interaction and cause it be viewed in terms of market norms.[8] Your friend starts to see themselves as akin to paid caterers and will soon mentally compare the small sum you're paying them with the fee professionals would demand. Or they will work out how long they are spending in the kitchen helping you and start costing their time according to the pay they receive in their usual job. The upshot is that a task they would have happily done for nothing, as a genuine favour, they do less happily for a small payment.

It is much better in these circumstances to buy your friend some chocolates or a book, or take them for a thank you lunch. The cost might well be less – but the friend will appreciate it more.

In a similar way, the American behavioural economist Dan Ariely warns against asking for favours from friends that relate to their line of work.[9] For example, if you need your drains fixing it might seem sensible to ask your plumber friend to help. The problem is that they know exactly what they could have charged you if you hadn't asked them to do this task as a favour. It could feel as though they are losing money by being your friend.

In both these instances, the satisfaction of helping a friend is lost because a personal interaction has been turned into a financial transaction. In the work environment such a transaction is fine; you pay the money and you get the service – you and the professional involved may well never interact again.[10] But a friendship is different. We expect it to continue. Sometimes you help your friend out, sometimes it's the other way round, but you don't keep a tally of who's up or down when it comes to favours. You don't need to. Any decent friendship will balance out these favours over time. That's what a friendship is: a naturally reciprocal arrangement. The moment you try to monetise it, to introduce notions of credit and debt, it feels all wrong.

To end this section, let's return to the row between Cameron and Pierce and their critics. Academic spats are nothing new. This is how science works. One person publishes a study. Others are then free to examine the way the data is collected and analysed and to scrutinise the conclusions reached. Over time a consensus is – or is not – reached. What's interesting in this instance, however, is how strongly all the parties felt. It goes to show, I think, that money is right up there with love or religion as a topic that fires passionate emotions. Money plays such a central role in our lives that the way it shapes our behaviour is one of those subjects that *really* matters to people. When experts think they've cracked one aspect of its motivational power, they don't take kindly to being told they might be wrong.

BIG MONEY, BIG PRESSURE

We've seen that money doesn't always have the motivating effect we might think. Indeed sometimes it is actively de-motivating. But what if the sum of money on offer for a task is not just a few pounds or dollars but an amount that could change a person's life? Never mind losing intrinsic motivation or worrying about market rates and the precise nature of the interaction, surely when there is a massive financial incentive people will try much harder and do much better?

Of course, it's not an easy proposition for a psychologist in a typical university to investigate. Studies involving small cash rewards are affordable enough, but research grants don't stretch to prizes comparable with City-style bonuses or lottery wins. To overcome the problem, Dan Ariely set up a study in 2002 in a rural village in Tamil Nadu, in Southern India.[11]

The villagers were given games to play that tested a range of skills from memory and thinking to creativity and physical dexterity. One of the games was Simon – so called because you have to do what 'Simon says'. As it happens, it was a favourite of my own grandfather's, so I know it well. You may have played it yourself. The game console looks like a plastic flying saucer and is about the size of a car steering wheel, with the top divided into four plastic segments coloured red, yellow, blue and green. The lights glow in turn in a random sequence, each accompanied by a buzz of a different pitch. The task is to memorise the sequence of colours as it flashes up and then reproduce that sequence by pressing the relevant buttons. It sounds easy, and when the sequence is only four or five colours long, it is. But as the sequences get longer, memorising them gets much harder. Both memory and, to be honest, patience are tested.

Another game required the villagers to steer a ball-bearing around a maze without the base tipping up and sending the ball falling down one of the holes.

Villagers were offered various sums of prize money for reaching specified levels in the different games. For some the sums involved were pretty negligible, even by local standards, but others were offered a once-in-a-lifetime opportunity to win the equivalent of six months' spending by an average person in rural India.

Remember, in Western terms the people in the study were poor. Half had a TV, half had a bicycle, but not one owned a car. There's no doubt that the incentive to do well at the games was strong, but would that determination lead them to succeed? The results surprised the experimenters.

What happened was that the pressure proved too much – in particular for those playing for the big prize. While there was little difference between the scores of the low and middling reward groups for most games, those with a chance to win a life-changing sum scored poorly in all games. To use a sporting term, it seemed they choked.

Any England football fan will be familiar with the concept of choking. In training, England's multimillionaire and highly skilled footballers have no trouble slotting in penalties. Yet when it comes to the European or World Cup finals, with millions watching on TV and everything hanging on these spot kicks, they all too often balloon their shots over the bar, or hit them straight into the goalkeeper's arms, or even – as happened once with David Beckham – fall over as they are running up to take the kick. Technically these players know exactly what they need to do, but the pressure on the day stops them performing.

Professor Geir Jordet from the Norwegian School of Sports Sciences has studied this phenomenon in detail by examining film footage of almost four hundred spot kicks from penalty shoot-outs during major tournaments. The biggest determinant of success is the team's previous shoot-out history. If the team had won the previous shoot-out, they were 85 per cent likely to score this time, compared with only 65 per cent when they'd lost previously.[12] Team ability made little difference, suggesting it was the memory of the loss that was affecting them, rather than their skill.

In football, one of the problems identified by psychologists is that players often believe that scoring penalties is mainly down to two things – luck and the actions of the goalkeeper. They tend not to think it's under their own control. To conquer that perception psychologists advise using a particular technique during practice sessions. The penalty taker should tell the goalkeeper in advance where they are going to shoot – left, right, down the middle, high or low. To the surprise of some players, this exercise shows that even when the goalkeeper is tipped off in a way that might seem to give them a much better chance of making a save, the penalty taker can still often get it past them. They do have some control.

Remembering that fact should help a player in an actual tournament, when of course the goalie has no idea where the ball is going to be placed. And there are all sorts of other tips and tricks that sports psychologists suggest as well. Yet ultimately the pressure often tells, with the result that the ball sails over the cross bar, or – to return to rural Tamil Nadu – the Indian villager messes up the simple game.

There are various theories as to why choking happens. The most obvious is that in high-pressure or high-stakes situations we shift from autopilot to a conscious mode of thinking. In other words, we think about the task too much – and in so doing, turn something simple into something difficult, something we can do into something we can't.

This is what happens when you've been driving for years, but then try to demonstrate to a learner how the clutch and the gears work, only to find yourself stalling and bunny-hopping along the road. You think so hard that you can't do it any more.

A similar reaction was observed in a series of experiments in which people played a tricky hand-held game called

Roll-up, which involves guiding a ball along a track between two metal rods in such a way that the ball falls into a particular hole. When participants were promised money if they succeeded, their performance diminished.[13] The prospect of the financial reward led them to try too hard.

Another factor that increases pressure and lowers performance is the distraction that comes from the knowledge that other people are watching you. In the Roll-up experiment, choking increased markedly when participants knew their competitors were observing them.

This is surely a big factor in penalty shoot-outs, as it is in other sports. If, like me, you enjoy watching tennis, you'll have seen it happen at Wimbledon. On the practice courts, the top players produce serve after serve with robotic consistency. But put them on Centre Court, with a crowd of 15,000 looking on, and a match-saving ace can easily become a match-losing double fault. The thought of winning (or losing) the title; the thought of all that prize money; the expectancy of the crowd – it all piles on the pressure.

This is why psychologists work so hard with tennis players on between-points routines. However bad the line call in the previous game, however tamely you returned that last serve into the net, however much your opponent's bouncing of the ball is bugging you, it is essential to start the next point afresh, calmly and with a focused mind. Of course, from the spectator's perspective, it is the unpredictability of the performance of even the world's top sportspeople at crucial moments that makes sports so exciting. If we knew the players could always ace themselves out of trouble on match point, Wimbledon wouldn't be so much fun. As spectators, we are aware of just how much is a stake, and so, of course are the players – which brings us to the third psychological theory (after distraction and a shift to conscious thinking) to explain why the prospect of a big prize can throw us off our stride.

The basis of this theory was demonstrated in a recent experiment at Cambridge University. Participants played a computer game where they chased an artificial prey, in the form of a grey dot, around a maze. One group had the chance to win just 50p each time they caught up with the grey dot; the others could win £5. Once again, the people offered the chance to win the bigger prize performed worse, and those who most wanted the money (indicated by a questionnaire beforehand) achieved the lowest scores of all.[14] The difference with this experiment was that the participants played the game while lying in a brain scanner. And what the scanner showed was that the prospect of winning big money seemed to trigger increased activity in the ventral midbrain, an area of the brain associated with rewards.

At first glance, that may seem neither surprising nor to matter all that much. People are offered a reward, so the reward pathways of the brain are stimulated. Isn't that what's supposed to happen? Well yes, but the consequence is that this increased activity in one part of the brain overwhelms another part. And that part is our working memory, our ability to consciously hold information and procedures temporarily in mind, as though on a mental Post-it note. To go back to the Indian villagers, all they could focus on were great piles of rupees. And that meant they had no space in their minds to memorise the long colour sequences in the Simon game.

Yet, of course, not everyone offered a big money prize or

playing for the title does choke. As the English joke goes, football is a game played by two teams of 11 players in which Germany end up winning on penalties. The German players face the same pressure as the England players – and can expect the same big rewards if they overcome it – and yet they seem to cope better. Likewise, the Serbian tennis player Novak Djokovic seems much less prone to buckling in Grand Slam finals than the British player I'm cheering on, Andy Murray.

In 2014, at Berkeley, California, a study by Esther Aarts observed a similar variation in the performance of participants when big sums of money were offered for succeeding at a computer task. Some followed the pattern we've seen above and choked, while others kept their cool and claimed the prize. The difference in performance was all down to the neurotransmitter dopamine. [15]

Using a PET scan, Aarts and her colleagues obtained a measure of each participant's baseline level of dopamine. If it started out high, then the promise of a bonus would in effect cause an overdose in a part of the brain called the striatum. This made the participant less able to concentrate in the way that they needed to if they were to score highly on the game.

The task itself was relatively simple. The computer flashed up boxes saying either LEFT or RIGHT, and all the participants had to do was to press one of two buttons to indicate which it was, but as fast as possible. To make it harder, sometimes the box was accompanied by an arrow pointing in the opposite direction from the meaning of the word. A symbol would indicate whether or not the arrow was relevant, but answering at speed while sometimes ignoring the arrows and other times paying attention to them is not easy and requires serious concentration. And in those players with a dopamine system that was easy to flood, the level of concentration required couldn't be achieved. This shows us what is happening in the brains of those who can keep their cool versus those who choke.

So as we've seen, for various reasons, money can increase your motivation without necessarily increasing your chances of success. And as we'll see now, a financial incentive can even backfire completely.

CROWDING OUT

Switzerland is famous for the number of referenda it holds. In 2013 alone, there were 90 held in individual cantons, as well as nine national votes. Back in 1993, the people of central Switzerland were asked to vote on rules regarding the siting of nuclear waste dumps. A week before the referendum, researchers conducted surveys in people's homes. They wanted to see the effect financial incentives might have on people's opinions.

To begin with, people were simply asked whether they would accept a repository for short-term, low- to mid-level nuclear waste in their area. Half of those surveyed said yes, despite the fact that 34 per cent feared it would result in the death of some local residents (which shows admirable civic mindedness or a crazy disregard for the risks, depending on your point of view). Next, money was introduced into people's calculations. Would they be more willing to accept the waste facility in their area if the government were to offer them annual compensation of between $2,000 and $6,000 per person? The money certainly made a difference to people's views, but not in the way you might expect. This time only a quarter agreed to have a dump near them.[16] Yes, this significant sum of money (even for the well-heeled Swiss) had served as a significant disincentive.

Perhaps the level of compensation wasn't enough? We've already seen that if you do offer to pay, you need to make sure you pay a sufficient amount. But no, that wasn't it. A higher level of compensation only induced one more person to change their mind.

So what was going on here? Why had the financial inducement actually reduced the acceptability of the nuclear dump? Perhaps it alerted people to the possible risk? After all, the government would surely only offer compensation if the dump was dangerous? It must mean the authorities have something to hide. Yet when the researchers put this point to the people surveyed, they insisted it wasn't that. So what was it?

The conclusion the researchers reached was that the offer of money had 'crowded out' people's sense of civic duty.

In the absence of the money, the Swiss citizens were prepared to accept the nuclear facility because they knew that a secure energy supply was important to everyone. But once they were offered money, they became more selfish and instead of making a decision based on the wider community's interests, they considered only their own narrow self-interest. The personal trumped the collective.

The same crowding-out effect could explain why the Israeli students collected less for charity when they were paid to do it. The payments crowded out their altruistic feelings. Once they were collecting in order to gain for themselves rather than to do good, they put less effort into it.

Take fines. In a truly civic-minded society, these wouldn't be necessary. We would return our library books on time, observe the speed limit and put rubbish in the bins simply because we wanted to be considerate citizens. Fines exist, however, because we sometimes fall short of this ideal and need a bit of a nudge to do the right thing. They also stop 'free riding' – where a person accepts there would be chaos if everybody threw rubbish in the street or raced around at 50 miles an hour in built-up areas, but thinks it's fine if it's only them doing it. By and large our system of fines works well, which is why we keep it, but its existence can alter the behaviour of some calculating souls.

I know of a shopkeeper in Soho in London who happily pays parking fines. *Happily pays parking fines?* I can hear you cry incredulously. But here's his calculation. Quite often he sees the traffic warden coming and can move his car off the yellow lines in time. But even when he isn't so quick off the mark, it's still cheaper for him to pay the occasional fine than to stump up the expensive prices charged at the nearest underground car park, which isn't even very close to his shop. The fact is this shopkeeper has reframed the fines as a charge for a service, and it's a charge that he's happy to pay. When he comes out of his shop and sees a parking ticket on his windscreen he's not even irritated. As far as he's concerned, that piece of paper wrapped in yellow plastic is simply the bill, a bill which appears on some days and not on others.

Of course this behaviour is selfish. The shopkeeper is convinced his car is not causing any danger or nuisance. But he would surely think differently if everyone did the same as him. That, though, is the point. He *doesn't* think in this way. And sadly he's not alone.

Just think how often you hear people talking about parking penalties and speeding fines as if they are unjustified nuisances: weapons in the 'war on motorists' or part of the apparatus of 'Big Brother'/'Little Hitler' local authorities. These fines have become divorced from the notion of decent civic behaviour that they were designed to underpin. In these circumstances, it's not surprising – though it's certainly depressing – that for people like the Soho shopkeeper, a fixed penalty notice is no longer a fine for transgressing a social norm but rather a payment for a service.

Unfortunately for the staff at the children's nurseries in the Israeli city of Haifa, the same thing happened there, in an example that's become well known in the field of behavioural economics.

Haifa's nurseries tend to open from 7.30am until 4pm. In other words, they close before the end of the normal working day. This means that on some days, however hard they try, parents can't leave work early enough to pick up their toddlers on time.

So how did the nurseries cope with this problem? Not by turning the children onto the streets of course. No, they set up a rota so that each member of staff took turns to wait until the last of the parents arrived. No one really liked having to work beyond their hours, but they accepted it as part of the job.

But what if there was a way of encouraging the parents to pick their children up on time? Or rather, what if they were fined if they didn't? In 1998 two economists, our old friend Uri Gneezy and also Aldo Rustichini, tried this exact experiment. In six Haifa nurseries, they put a sign on the noticeboard warning parents that from the following week there would be a fine of 10 New Israeli Shekels (about $3) for any parent who was more than 10 minutes late collecting their child.

Now at the time, this was much cheaper than paying for an hour's babysitting, but still, it meant the parents were charged for something they had in effect enjoyed for free until then. The fines were levied for 12 weeks and added onto each parent's weekly fees. For the purposes of the study, the times at which the parents turned up at the six nurseries were logged. And to provide a point of comparison, arrival times were also monitored at another four nurseries where parents didn't face a fine for a late pick-up.

So what happened? Yes, you've guessed it, in the nurseries that had instituted the system of fines, the number of late arriving parents gradually started to rise. After a few weeks, the staff member left behind after hours found herself with twice as many kids to look after as before. In some nurseries there were more late pick-ups in one week than the total number of children, meaning either every parent was late at least once, or that some individuals were late almost every day.[17]

The influence of money in this case was clear. It had skewed the parents' attitudes towards the acceptability of arriving late – and in exactly the opposite way to that intended. Before the fines were introduced, the parents felt guilty when they made a staff member stay on beyond four o'clock. She was doing them a favour, and they didn't want to abuse her good will.

But with the introduction of fines the situation had been reframed: from taking advantage of a nursery teacher, to a paid-for service that you could choose to use if you needed it. It was now legitimate to be late, provided you paid your dues.

Not surprisingly, at the end of the 12 weeks, the system of fines was discontinued. But in another sign of how important it is to consider the long-term consequences of either financial incentives or penalties, the parents didn't revert to their old behaviour. Instead they continued to fail to collect their offspring in a timely manner. They had become accustomed to viewing the after-hours service as part of their contract with the nursery school even though the fines had been withdrawn. It goes to show how the introduction of money can warp a voluntary system if you're not careful.

8

MONEY TIPS FOR BANKERS

Why it's best not to empty your wallet in front of friends, why a free gift of thousands of pounds can be insulting and why large bonuses might be counterproductive.

NO DISCUSSION OF money as motivator is complete without considering bankers.

To the outsider, they appear to insist that only vast salaries, topped up with huge bonuses, can possibly keep them doing their jobs. Any curbs imposed on the City of London will have them all fleeing to Wall Street or Zurich. Yet how many Thames-side duplexes, bespoke suits, handmade shoes, bottles of champagne and luxury holidays can a man (and they are still mostly men) want? They have all these things and yet they must have more, they argue.

It's easy to condemn them but I want to understand them. We've already seen how big money can motivate poorer people, but how exactly is it motivating people who would seem to have more than enough? More to the point, is it motivating them in ways that have a value beyond their individual bank balances?

The ex-Canon of St Paul's Cathedral in London, Giles Fraser, tells a revealing anecdote about his erstwhile banker neighbours in the City of London. Fraser noticed that when young city types were in the pub together after work they sometimes played a game called 'Show All'. It's a simple game – if a vulgar one. One person shouts 'Show all', and everyone in the group has to reveal exactly how much cash they have in their wallet at that moment. The one with the most has to share it among the others.[1]

What does this game demonstrate about bankers' attitudes to money? A number of things spring to mind. First, that they all have so much that they're happy to play a game that could involve them surrendering a wad of cash just for a laugh. Most of the rest of us, earning far less, would shrink from emptying our wallets or purses to share with friends – which is why 'Show All' has not spread to the BBC, for example, or the health service. Second, there's presumably a large dollop of *braggadocio* about it. Or to put it more crudely, willy waggling. 'Look how much dosh we've all got!' But there's another element to the game that I think goes to the heart of the City's high-earning culture. Though the young bankers can afford to lose the money, they presumably don't want to, so their calculation must be that, however much cash they have, someone else in the group must be richer still. In all likelihood, it was this thinking that led one banker (in a possibly apocryphal but nonetheless entertaining story) to agree to take part in 'Show All' even though he was on his way to buy a second-hand car and so had £5,000 in his wallet – he still assumed one of the other players would have more.

Herein lies one of the key reasons why bankers, though rich already, still want more money: because they suspect the other guy has more. The amount you have demonstrates your relative status within this particular culture to the exclusion of almost everything else, and you only value yourself within that culture by reference to the size of your salary and your annual bonus. A friend of mine who once worked in the City told me that it doesn't matter if you're getting paid £300,000 a year; if someone you know doing much the same job is getting £400,000, then you feel undervalued. The whole system is so divisive that it causes real bitterness particularly as traders can't control stock prices meaning a lot of luck is involved. He compared it to paying nurses differing amounts depending on whether a patient had died or was only on the cusp of death.

I think we can already see how, within such a culture, the power of money to motivate is very likely to operate in odd and sometimes undesirable ways – a conclusion which of course has become commonplace since the financial crash of 2008.

Large salaries are one thing. But in this short chapter, I want to focus on the effect of the payment of bonuses that are a particular feature of what the financial services sector terms its 'compensation' packages for top employees. (And I'll be returning to the very revealing psychology of that term later.)

Now, the bonus system in the City is opaque (in many ways, one of which I'll also return to later). Unaware of the exact day on which their bonuses will be announced, during the bonus season staff wait nervously for their boss to call them into their office to tell them how much they're getting. By most people's standards the amount is substantial, but that doesn't mean that everyone is cracking open a jeroboam of Pol Roger vintage champagne later that evening.

Nearly twenty years ago, a few days before Christmas, a friend of mine went up to Canary Wharf to meet her boyfriend, who worked in a large investment bank. He had just had his bonus meeting with his boss. The moment he saw his girlfriend he burst into tears. She asked whether something terrible had happened. 'It has,' he said. His bonus that year was £18,000.

It was more than his girlfriend earned for working full-time for the whole year. Not surprisingly, she found it hard to be sympathetic. But of course, it was not the money itself that was the issue. The boyfriend knew it was a lot by any standards and that he lived far better than any of his non-banking friends. No, what so upset him was what an £18,000 bonus in his world at that time symbolised: failure.

He suspected that other colleagues had got bonuses of two, three, four times as much. And though he didn't need the extra money, he dearly wanted the recognition from his boss that it represented. Perhaps it was childish to start crying, but then he felt he'd been plunged back into child-hood. Teacher had given the other boy an A and him a D.

Whatever we think of the ethics of large bonuses, what of their efficacy? Perhaps my friend's boyfriend's colleagues deserved their A-star pay-outs, while he got his just desserts with his D for Dunce eighteen grand? In the world in which they operated, alien as it is to most of us, perhaps both had been appropriately rewarded for the money they'd earned the company and would be duly motivated to work harder next year?

At this point, you will be expecting me to introduce some

leading academic research that might throw light on these questions. But no. You would have thought given the billions the financial services sector shells out in bonuses that one of the big banks or other City institutions would have commissioned a rigorous independent study of the effectiveness of such incentives. But if they have, it's not been published. I at least could find no such study. It means we have to rely on related research to assess the effectiveness of bonuses. Let's look at studies from the previous two chapters, and apply them to the financial sector to see if we can come to some tentative conclusions.

First, most jobs in the City – especially at the top end, where the big bonuses get paid – bear no resemblance to dangling from a metal bar or picking fruit. To be fair to bankers, they're known to work long hours, but it is not clear that it is those long hours as such (or to put it another way, the pure effort they put in) that results in them bringing in high profits. Some do make their employers megabucks of course, but this is as likely to be a result of their skills or, as critics from Keynes onwards have pointed out, sheer luck. Psychologists such as Mark Griffiths, who research the psychology of gambling, used to study various types of gambling: staking money during a game (e.g. roulette), staking money on a future event, and lotteries. Now some study a fourth: speculation on the stock market.[2] That's right. Researchers have come to regard stock market gains and losses as so random as to be defined as gambling.

There is, of course, a whole range of jobs in the financial sector, and some resemble sales jobs, where payment by results or on commission is sensible enough because the level of personal input directly results in a measurable output. But there are as many other jobs where people work in teams and it is hard to distinguish – let alone quantify – an individual's role in success or failure, and a complex matrix of factors contributes to that success or failure. In these circumstances, the basic salary – which after all is usually generous in this sector – should be enough (as it is in most other sectors).

Okay, if the company does well in any one year then everybody could get a bonus, proportionate to their salary (and proportionate in the wider sense too). That, famously, is what the employee-owned company John Lewis does. Their scheme recognises that all employees, from the CEO to the check-out staff, contribute in their own way to the success of the business, and they all share in it in a way that is transparent and fair.

But, crucially, if John Lewis has a poor year then there is no shared bonus. One of the things that's most inexplicable and perverse (as well as damaging for the image of banking) is that top earners seem to get big bonuses even when the bank has lost billions. Researchers at Bristol University found that this applied in finance as well as in some other sectors. When stock returns were exceptionally high, bonuses and pay went up, but when stock returns were unusually low, they didn't drop accordingly.[3]

Understandably this makes the public angry, and – as we've seen from the evidence of how financial incentives work – it cannot be sensible. If nothing else survives from the heyday of Skinner and behaviourism, it is that rewards should be used to reinforce *good* behaviour, not bad.

One solution often suggested is to reward the chief executives of big banks, not with cash bonuses but with shares. The problem here is that there's plenty of research, which

I'll discuss in more detail in the chapter on saving, which shows that we don't value money in the future as highly as the money we own now. So receiving shares instead of cash could even be viewed as a loss.[4] But the advantage is that once the bosses own those shares, due to the endowment effect, they will do everything they can to make sure they don't go down in value.

In Chapter 6, we observed that financial rewards can be particularly effective when the task involved is innately tedious or repetitive, and that it would be hard to get people to do it without the inducement. Does this apply to financial services? Well, I must say I think I'd find working in the City pretty boring, but the sector attracts many of the world's brightest graduates. No doubt the big money is part of the attraction, but is it just that? Surely their fascination with devising ever more complex and leveraged products doesn't just stem from the money they can make from such wheezes? There is significant intellectual stimulation too. Some people love it.

Then there's the thrill of the deal, the trade. My one really wealthy friend works not in the financial sector but in publishing. I asked him once how interested he was in the magazine business, and he was honest enough to say it wasn't the quality of products as such which gave him the greatest buzz. It was 'sealing the deal'. He could never get enough of that, he said. Each new deal made him a lot of money as well, but he had got to the point in his career where it was the excitement of pursuing and winning the deal that really counted for him. I suspect something similar motivates many city traders and financial whizz kids. After all, it's not uncommon for people in the City to say they'll retire at 30, because by then they'll have made more than enough money. In fact, very few do leave at this age. Perhaps that's because they become addicted to money, but also they must enjoy the job too.

If I'm right, the addition of bonus payments into such high-end banking jobs should be the wrong thing to do. As we've seen from Deci and others' research in these situations the money stimulant is likely to rob the bankers of their intrinsic motivation or worse, attract people to the profession who have no interest in the job itself and are just interested in the money – in other words extrinsically motivated.[5] This has been raised as a particular concern in fields such as healthcare, but perhaps it matters in banking too. If money is everything, then when payments are taken away or reduced, it will be perceived as a loss and staff will be less willing to do the job than if bonuses had never been introduced in the first place.

It's just this argument (or a slight variant: remove the bonuses and the bankers will flee abroad) that defenders of the bonus culture deploy. But of course it's a pretty self-serving justification, and what the work of Deci and others really shows is that the financial sector should never have made bonuses such an integral part of remuneration packages in the first place.

This culture is so established that even big bonuses lose their power. It's a bit like the problem identified by Brummelman, Dweck and others where parents overpraise their children's drawings with ever diminishing or counter-productive results. If bankers keep getting – and expecting – that 'best-ever' bonus, it's not going to motivate them to higher achievements at all.

If bonuses are to be part of an individual's remuneration package, the research would suggest that they should be occasional and surprise one-offs, rewarding exceptional achievement. But even then the over-confidence bias can bring problems. Just as the majority of people consider themselves to be above-average drivers, which is of course statistically impossible, most of us also tend to overestimate our individual contribution to a project's success.[6] So bankers, like anyone else, are drawn to performance-based pay, believing they will do well out of it. This sets them up for disappointment when others make a less generous assessment of their contribution and the resulting bonus is lower than they expected. As with my friend's boyfriend, a huge monetary gift is transformed into a loss, and – as I've said before – there's nothing we hate more than a loss. And as researcher Ian Larkin from UCLA points out in his work on the topic, staff are going to compare their bonus with what colleagues receive (however hard managers try to keep the sums secret), which could even lead people to sabotage each other's work – hardly encouraging good team work.

Hardwiring bonuses into the permanent payment system robs them of their value. They should be a true 'well done'. Instead they are just part of the 'compensation' – that word again. Like the compensation for the Swiss nuclear dump, the message is a dire one, almost: *you're working in this lousy industry, we get it, so to* **compensate** *here's a tonne of money.*

This leads us to consider the big money question. Bankers' bonuses are definitely big money – by most people's standards. We saw earlier that big money sometimes does motivate whereas small payments don't, but then its efficacy is more of a factor where the sums involved can really make a difference in your life. My friend's £18,000 bonus, miserable as it was to him, would have transformed the life of a Tamil Nadu villager playing Simon for high stakes, but for him it was just more money he couldn't really spend. Or another holiday he didn't really need.

Because that is often the case, and because most of the time the work of bankers is not equivalent to a penalty in a World Cup final (though there are presumably big transactions that sometimes feel like them), I don't think choking is much of an issue. But given how catastrophically bad performance in the financial sector has been in recent years – trillions lost, institutions collapsing, the whole system tottering – you do wonder if big money has led some bankers to metaphorically overdose on dopamine. In other words, the lure of the big money prize has overloaded their brains and meant they haven't been able to focus on the mental tasks involved in the way they should.

Finally in this exercise of applying what we've learnt from the previous two chapters to bankers' bonuses, what about crowding out? Is the sector so money oriented that it's lost sight of why it is doing what it's doing? In a sense that is obviously true. Of course I'm not suggesting that providing financial services is just like giving blood. Or that our banking system should be provided by volunteers, like the RNLI or Mountain Rescue. If bankers were not paid, we almost certainly wouldn't have a banking sector. But it is frequently observed these days that the financial sector has become so obsessed with money begetting money that it's forgotten that its role is to oil the wheels of the real economy.

In a famous comment, made more powerful by coming from an insider, the then chairman of the Financial Services

Authority (FSA), Adair Turner, observed in 2009 that too much of the sector's activity was 'socially useless'.[7] If, as a result of the much-vaunted reforms that have taken place since then, it does become clearer that banks are providing a valuable and socially useful service to the wider economy, then the public reputation of bankers should rise. They will be better liked and respected. And perhaps it's naive, but will that kind of esteem be motivation enough? Bankers will do the job for the basic salary without needing the regular fix of a bonus, because they'll draw satisfaction from doing a good job. Too fantastic? But that's pretty much what we expect of nurses and teachers and social workers . . . I could go on.

I think it's clear that applying the best psychological research findings to the issue of bankers' bonuses would suggest that we need a radical reform of the system. Even the professional body for human resources, the Chartered Institute of Personnel and Development (CIPD), published an excellent report in 2015 surveying all the best research in the field and exhorting businesses to apply it.[8] But of course, for that to happen, the people locked in this ill-conceived bonus culture have to recognise that change is needed. For the good of us all, we can only hope enough of them do.

9

MONEY, MONEY, MONEY

*Why some people have lots, why most of us want
more, why enough is never enough and how having
more can make you happier (sometimes).*

FACING ONTO THE boules pitch in the Provençal village of
La Garde Freinet near St Tropez is a grand, high-walled,
peach-coloured house with sea-blue shutters and a wrought-
iron gate. In the war, the Nazis made the house their local
base. It is obvious why, as the house dominates the entrance
to the red-roofed village.

Broad steps wind up to double-height, triple-width glass
doors, which lead into the house. Either side of the doors,
there are Gertrude Jekyll-designed terracotta pots made at
Compton Pottery in Surrey at the end of the nineteenth
century, which – as garden enthusiasts will know – makes
them both much coveted and very expensive. This is clearly
the home of a person of taste – and some wealth.

Although Mike is in his seventies now, you wouldn't know
it to see him. He dresses like a rock star in skin-tight designer

jeans, with dozens of silver bangles and bracelets up one arm. At parties, he can often be seen doing his famous snake-hipped dancing.

He's a generous host, both at home and when buying champagne for his friends in the beach clubs of St Tropez. Money is there to be enjoyed, Mike feels, and he bemoans the minority of rich people he knows who he says are misers.

'Money is really important to me,' he tells me. 'People say it's all I ever talk about.' It's certainly been the driving factor in his life.

When Mike left school in Cheshire in 1950, his parents wanted him to take a safe position working for his uncle's insurance business. But Mike had other ideas. In the freezing winter of 1951, he got himself a job selling fire extinguishers. He was on commission and unable to afford proper boots, and he developed frostbite in his toes as he walked from farm to farm in the snow. But he learned how to persuade farmers to replace their fire extinguishers with his, and to buy a supply of refills that would last them far longer than their lifetimes. Within a year, his parents were complaining that it was inappropriate that he was earning more than the local doctor. He was on his way to becoming a successful businessman. But first there were a couple of detours.

Like so many boys, his dream was to play football for Manchester United. He got a trial at Old Trafford, but it wasn't on the field that he enjoyed good fortune. Instead, while he was in the city he spent some of his earnings from selling fire extinguishers on a night at the casino. In a game of blackjack he ended up winning another footballer's convertible Morris Minor.

This stroke of luck allowed him to leave home. The following day, at the age of 19, he piled his clothes into the car and drove off, never seeing his parents again.

Down in London he took another sales job, this time selling an early version of the telephone answering machine. Again he started doing well, but he still had dreams of fame, so he enrolled in drama school and afterwards he was offered a job in repertory theatre. But by then his interest in money had become established. 'I loved acting, but I didn't love it enough to go and work in rep and have no money.'

From then on there were to be no more diversions. He devoted his career to making money. And he was determined he would always have enough. More than enough.

His success now is obvious. But he hasn't stopped trying to make money and is still working on property schemes. He's over retirement age. He's got more than enough money to live very comfortably. But still he wants more. Why?

PENNY-PINCHERS AND CASH-SPLASHERS

We need money for life's necessities. We can all agree on that. But what constitutes a necessity? Here we're less likely to all agree. You might consider something essential, while I think it's a frippery. Faced with the need to economise, we're probably going to have very different ideas about the things we can't do without.

Things change over time, of course. Three decades ago, sophisticated computers that you can put in your pocket would have been barely conceivable. We would have thought having one was an extraordinary luxury, a play-thing for the super-rich. Now smart phones are viewed as essential in many parts of the world. Travel on a bus in some of the poorer boroughs of London and everyone seems to have at least one.

Likewise TVs: in the past, only the well-off had televisions. These days, even the most right-wing commentator is likely to concede that not having some way of watching TV constitutes living in poverty. Or eating out: when I was growing up, my parents hardly ever went to a restaurant. It was something you did on special occasions. Now if people can afford it, they eat out a lot. And it's no big deal.

But while attitudes across society change, we still have our own very different views on money, about what qualifies as rich or poor or how much is enough or more than enough. So, what shapes these different views? And in particular, why do some people seem so driven to make more and more money?

Over the decades various psychologists have developed typologies that attempt to group us according to our attitudes to money.[1] One was devised back in the 1970s by a pair of American psychologists, Herb Goldberg and Robert Lewis. They proposed twelve categories, based on their observations, it should be said, rather than through the rigorous analysis of data from hundreds of people that you would find in quantitative studies of personality. Nonetheless the money-types are intriguing, if rather unlikeable. Perhaps you can recognise yourself in here. Or as you get further down the list, maybe you will start to hope that you don't.[2]

1. The freedom buyer – you resent being required to do anything that might limit your autonomy and see money as a way of paying to not be told what

to do. You always buy the rounds in a pub because you don't want to feel indebted to anyone.

2. The freedom fighter – you dislike the way money constrains people and would like to see it shared out more equally. Maybe you feel guilty for coming from a well-off family. You might wish that money didn't exist at all and could be, in Goldberg and Lewis's words, a 'revolutionary activist', a 'concerned liberal', a 'misfit' or a 'nihilist'.

3. The compulsive saver – you save money for the sake of it. Every time you get paid you put a certain percentage of that money aside, almost as if you are paying a savings tax. You can't truly enjoy a holiday, particularly if you don't get paid holiday, because not only are you spending more than usual, but you are failing to earn anything.

4. The self-denier – you feel guilty if you spend any money on yourself, live in a cheaper area than you need to in order to save on rent and are first to hunt for any bargains in the supermarket. If you get any extra income, you spend it on anyone except for yourself. You are pessimistic about the future and don't dare spend any money that you don't need to.

5. The compulsive bargain-hunter – you don't like to spend unless there's a bargain to be had. You might spend hours looking for discount vouchers and finding the best prices. When a shopping trip is successful, it's not because you've bought a lot, but because you've saved a lot.

6. The fanatical collector – you collect not money, but anything else and can become obsessive. Once

you've collected these things you don't want to give them up. You might also be very competitive.

7. The love buyer – you are generous, but are using your money to buy admiration, attention or to get people to like you. Perhaps you donate large amounts to charity or give waiters large tips. You might spoil your children in an attempt to buy their love. Relatives might even resent you for being too ready to insist on always picking up the bill.

8. The love seller – you're kind to people and make others feel good about themselves, but really you are selling your love. You flatter your boss in order to stay employed. You only go out with partners who are richer than you and when friends fall on hard times you might be the first to abandon them.

9. The love stealer – are you a boss who pretends to care for your employees, but is actually only nice to them in the hope of keeping their wages low? Are you a performer who pretends to love the audience, but secretly has contempt for them? You might even steal items that have some special value for you.

10. The manipulator – you use money to get power, but also exploit people in order to get more money, sometimes even swindling them. You don't feel guilty about it.

11. The empire builder – you are determined to be a leader because you think followers are weak. You don't like others to question your decisions and independence is very important to you. You are driven and determined to find shortcuts to making money if you can.

12. The godfather – you bribe your children to be good. You are kind to others provided they do what you want them to. In restaurants, you specialise in complaining. You are happy to spend your money buying loyalty from others.

Mike told me that he is driven to keep making money because he wants security, which might put him in the Compulsive Saver category. But of course Mike also spends his money, so since it's not only about security I wonder if he is also a Freedom Buyer. As a young man, he became determined to make enough money so nobody could push him around.

Mike of course might disagree with my categorisation. And I wonder how he'd label me? Maybe a bargain boaster, since I do love it when people admire an item of clothing which cost me very little, or given the difference in our capacity to make money maybe a Money Dummy, one of the categories found in a much more recent typology of money attitudes.[3]

The problem with these typologies is that it's often hard to sum up people's behaviour around money using a single category. A better approach perhaps is to look at how our personalities relate to the way we behave around money. Such an exercise shows, for example, that people who score high on conscientiousness, one of the so-called Big Five traits in psychology that combine to make up our individual personalities (the other four are openness, neuroticism, agreeableness and extraversion), are more likely to have savings, or that entrepreneurs like Mike are likely to score high on stability and independence.[4] Within psychology there's also an idea called the locus of control, which describes our sense of being able to control the world around us. Entrepreneurs are more likely to have what's known as an internal locus of control, where they believe that they can change their own situation, while people in debt are more likely to have an external locus of control, where they believe that outside events are hard to control.

The relationship between different influencing factors can be difficult to tease apart. For instance, poverty also correlates with an external locus of control. In other words if people are poor they are less likely, probably with good reason, to believe that they can control what happens to them in life. Poorer people are also more likely to have debts. So, does having a personality with an external locus of control lead people into debt and thus poverty? Or does being in poverty form a tendency to get into debt which creates a sense of an external locus of control? (We will explore lack of money in more detail in the next chapter, incidentally.)

Other research has shown stable extraverts are more open, comfortable and care-free about their money. But while this personality type is extravagant with their money, at the same time they feel more in control of it. Research conducted in Sweden has found that people who score high on emotional intelligence tend to be less money oriented and not to value money as a sign of power or status. These are the people who are good at tasks like identifying emotional expressions when given a series of photographs of faces. They are also better at dealing with failure and challenges.[5]

By contrast, those who like money a lot were found in this research to be less attuned to the social environment. Was that why they turned to money for succour, because people made no sense to them? Or did their interest in money turn them away from people? Studies like these that take a snapshot in time can't tell us which came first. And of course they only tell us about averages. They can't predict how any particular individual, such as Mike, might behave. While Mike likes money a lot, he is certainly a 'people person'. He's also been good at dealing with failure and challenges. He doesn't value money as a sign of power or status, and yet he's money oriented. All these different attitudes are combined in one person. What these studies can do by looking at thousands of people is to indicate some broad patterns. For example, people who have had more education are on average less obsessed with money, which is not surprising perhaps because they might also feel they have a better ability to earn sufficient amounts of it. The research also reveals that younger people are on average less careful with their money, while older people are on average better at budgeting.[6] And yet, of course, you'll be able to tell me of exceptions, of students who are ardent savers and pensioners who spend, spend, spend.

No one in the field has managed to develop a theory that can account for everyone's views about money, explaining where they came from and why it is that we all seem to differ so much in our views towards something so everyday. But in my view, the most comprehensive and interesting work has been conducted by Adrian Furnham from University College London. He developed the Money Beliefs and Behaviour Scale, as well as a simple 16-item Money Attitudes Scale, which tells you which you value more – money as an instrument of power, security, love or freedom. Not the least of the reasons why Furnham's work is useful is that more than a hundred thousand people filled in the scale as part of a survey called the Big Money Test with the BBC.[7]

Among the things it revealed was that people were more likely to be overdrawn or refused credit when they were young, while bankruptcy affected more people who were older. Also, that people who considered that money gave them power were more at risk of having their car repossessed, while those who valued money for the security it gave them were less likely to get into financial difficulty. Men, it showed, were more likely to associate money with security and freedom, while women were more likely to admit to worrying while they spent money and to using shopping as therapy to manage their emotions. But the biggest difference of all from the test was that women were much more generous with their money.

Perhaps the most surprising finding from the Big Money Test was that, on the whole, people's attitudes towards money were not dictated by income. Whether people were rich or poor made no difference to whether they valued money for security, freedom, love or power. So perhaps we can conclude that at least some of our attitude to money is innate, as it were, that it comes *before* our financial situation rather than being dictated by it.

There is a temporal dimension too. Furnham has found that there is less variation in our attitudes towards money in the past, than when it comes to thinking ahead. For instance, older people, although they're better at budgeting, are more worried about money in the future, as are richer people. But although we might like the idea that for rich people having lots of money means having lots of money headaches that we could well do without, there is no doubt that it is still people with lower incomes who experience more finance-related anxiety.

If couples share similar attitudes to money, then they are lucky. When researchers at Kansas State University followed 4,500 couples in a longitudinal study spanning seven years they found that the biggest predictor of divorce wasn't arguments about the children or housework or sex, but arguments about money.[8]

The nature of these arguments differed from rows about other topics. For one thing, compared with arguments about housework, sex or in-laws, they were more likely to be heated, perhaps because money can represent so many different things within a relationship – power, disappointment and even mistrust. Interestingly however, the amount the couples were worth made only a marginal difference, so it wasn't that they were necessarily arguing because of a lack of money. At all levels of income or savings, couples argue about money.

Some researchers in this area of study believe that the reason that money can be so divisive within heterosexual relationships is that men and women have different attitudes towards the stuff. As we saw above with the Big Money Test, there would appear to be some evidence for this – women resorting to retail therapy more often, for instance. 'You spent *WHAT* on a pair of shoes!' Yet, as you'll recall, it was my husband not me who spent £500 on a leather jacket for himself while out shopping for a birthday present, and there is a study which shows that on average men are more extravagant than women.[9]

Another study of money styles found that men felt more competent in their handling of money and were prepared to take more risks with it. Meanwhile women were slightly more envious of their friends with money than men were, and felt that money was a sign of prestige and power, as well as a vehicle to it.[10]

And so it goes on. How much weight we can put on these studies, some from a decade or more ago, is hard to say. On the whole it doesn't seem to me that the differences between men and women's attitudes to money are more pronounced than the differences between different personality types.

I wonder whether the salience of money can explain why it is at the root of so many rows. We need to deal with it constantly, so it's hard to forget about it, and quite often two people will not agree, whether they are partners, mother and daughter, or brother and sister. Perhaps the only thing we know for certain about views on money is that we all have our own, and we all think we're right, so it's little wonder that it sparks arguments, or that those arguments can be so hard to resolve.

Those individual differences in our attitudes towards money don't exist in a vacuum, of course. A dramatic change in circumstances, such as winning the lottery, marrying a millionaire or losing your job, will inevitably change some of your views about it. Attitudes to money are less stable over time than something like intelligence, but more stable than, for example, job satisfaction.[11]

Now it's time to turn to one of the biggest questions of all about money. Does it make people happy?

WINNING THE LOTTERY

In 1995 Elaine was watching the TV with her two children when she saw all six of her National Lottery numbers come up. She had been quite lucky with the lottery before, winning small amounts, but this time the top prize was an eye-watering £2,704,666.

She was thrilled to win, of course, and elements of her life were transformed. Some of the money was used to start up a business with her husband – first a holiday village and then a restaurant. The couple knew that never again would they have to worry about financial security in their old age or where they would find the money for their daughters' university fees. But what about the big question. Did it make Elaine happier?

When asked, Elaine insists it's not money that matters. She recalls that when she was a child, her family was so hard up that she wore plastic bin-liners in her boots to keep the rain off her feet. And she remembers that every day from the age of eight she would let herself into the house after returning from school because her mother had not got back from work. So, yes, of course she is glad not to have any money worries now. But in the greater scheme of things money counts for little, she says.

Since her big win both her mother and her brother have died. In exchange for one more year with either of them, Elaine says, she would happily forgo all the lottery money. Indeed she would willingly return to the days when she had so little that her mother had to put bin-liners in her boots.[12]

Of course, Elaine's bad fortune losing her relatives was unconnected to her lottery win. But in other cases though, winning the lottery can cause its own misery.

William Bud Post III won $16 million in Pennsylvania in 1998, but five years later he was telling the *Washington Post* his win had been 'a nightmare'.[13] The list of things that went wrong in his life was long: a judge ruled that he must give a third of his winnings to his former landlady, he married seven times and divorced six of those wives, he went to prison for firing a shotgun at a debt collector, he was declared bankrupt and his brother hired a hit man to try to kill him. William insisted he was happier when he was poor and called his win the 'lottery of death'. Life was certainly simpler for him before his big payout.

For Abraham Shakespeare, who won $31 million in Florida in 2006, the end result really was that his number came up in the lottery of death. First a colleague tried to sue him for half the winnings, claiming that Shakespeare had stolen the ticket from his wallet. The judge found in Shakespeare's favour, but he soon tired of people asking him for money.[14] This was when he met Dorice 'Dee Dee' Moore. She said she wanted to write a book about how people were trying to take advantage of him. They became good friends and eventually he gave her full financial control of his assets. But it turned out that Moore was the one taking advantage of him financially. That was the least of it, though. In 2010 Shakespeare's body was found under a slab of concrete. He'd been shot twice. Moore was convicted of his murder and is now serving a life sentence in prison.

In other cases, winning the lottery can result in a public vilification because, guess what, not all those who win are good people. For example, there was outrage when one of the early winners of the UK's National Lottery was revealed to be serving a life sentence for attempted rape. He had bought the ticket while on day release from an open prison.[15]

These unhappy and undeserving winners are the exception rather than rule, though. Most people who defy the astronomical odds and win millions are nice, decent, ordinary people. Far fewer lottery winners than you might think squander the money in the infamous 'spend, spend, spend' fashion. Indeed, most save a good proportion of their winnings, and – when they do spend – they are proud to show that they do so responsibly. A study of Swedish lottery winners found people were careful with their money and keen to demonstrate that the money hadn't changed them.[16]

All of which is very interesting, I hear you cry. But what about the question of whether winning the lottery makes people happier?

The classic study of the impact on happiness of a lottery win dates from 1978. The researchers interviewed 22 lottery winners, 29 people who had become paralysed and 22 people who had been neither lucky nor unlucky. Although the lottery winners had more security and time for leisure, within a year of winning they were found on average to be no happier than people in the other groups. They seemed to enjoy everyday pleasures such as eating breakfast or watching TV rather less, possibly because these things paled in comparison with the huge thrill of their big win. They also became accustomed to their wealth and it stopped giving them extra happiness.

And the surprising, admittedly non-money-related, finding from the study was that the paralysed people had lower happiness levels than the control group but not by much. Their general happiness was still above the mid-point of the scale.[17]

It has to be remembered that this study was very small and didn't follow up people over time. Even so, later research has backed up the idea that happiness levels are relatively constant. Good and bad things happen to all of us, and levels of happiness fluctuate, but not by as much as we might expect. Through a process called hedonic adaptation, we get used to our new situation, good, bad or indifferent. That said, when life takes a turn for the worse, we adapt more slowly than when things improve. But even when people lose all their money, over time they tend to get used to it.[18]

So while few would pass up a massive win, we do know that such a change of financial fortune is not going to make a person much happier than they would otherwise have been in the longer term.

The finding that people who suddenly become rich can stop enjoying the small things in life is an interesting one, which seems to fit with a much more recent study from Belgium that I rather like.

Students were given a piece of chocolate, and a researcher timed how long they took to eat it. On average, the students spent 45 seconds savouring the chocolate. But if they were shown a photograph of money beforehand, this savouring time dropped to just 32 seconds.[19]

It's a strange finding, but the researchers concluded that once the students turned their minds to thoughts of money, they were less interested in the simple pleasure of a piece of chocolate.

The same psychologists also gave people a series of scenarios to imagine, such as visiting a beautiful waterfall. Then people were asked how they might react in that situation, choosing from a list of choices. People could tick as many or as few options as they liked, but the items that interested the researchers were those linked to the psychology of savouring. Previous research has demonstrated there are various ways in which we savour an event: we tell other people about it, we deliberately try to stay in the moment while we experience it, we show others that we're happy, and we anticipate and then reminiscence about the event.

What the researchers found was that the degree to which people savoured the idea of a simple enjoyable experience depended on how much money they had. Those with higher incomes and larger savings indicated they'd take less pleasure from the experience than people on lower incomes.

This phenomenon is known as the experience-stretching hypothesis. The idea is that once someone has been to a Michelin-starred restaurant and tasted the best meal in town, the simple joy of the tuna melt in their local café doesn't seem quite as appealing any more.

The Belgian team didn't stop there. They took their research a step further, again asking people how they would respond to seeing waterfalls and other attractions, but this time they showed them pictures of money first. Suddenly people on any income behaved in the same way as the rich people.

Here then is some evidence that having money – or even thinking about money – reduces pleasure. Or rather, it can reduce enjoyment of simple pleasures because having money – or dreaming of so doing – brings more extravagant experiences into your orbit.

Of course there are ways the rich can get around this tendency and still enjoy simple things. As a treat, I once ate at the famous London restaurant The Ivy. It's a well-known haunt of celebrities and the rich. Yet among the most popular dishes the restaurant serves are Welsh rarebit and cottage pie. Admittedly rather fancy and decidedly expensive Welsh rarebit and cottage pie, but therein lies the secret. The Ivy has developed a formula for providing rich people with comfort food in a way that satisfies their rarefied palates. I can make Welsh rarebit for myself any day, so I seem to recall I went for Dover sole.

In the unlikely event that you do ever find yourself suddenly catapulted into the realms of the super-rich there's an obvious lesson to take from the research in this area. And that is to behave like people who get steadily better off as their careers advance – a much greater number of people.

So, new millionaires, take it easy. Don't splurge. Obviously that's sensible financial advice anyway, but more to the point if you spend your suddenly acquired wealth on slightly nicer things rather than jumping straight to the best that money can buy, you'll spread out the joy you get from your cash over a longer period.[20] Bear in mind this finding too: on average, people get more pleasure from winning $25 in a lottery followed by $50 than winning $75 in one go.[21]

A HAPPY PARADOX

So far, it may sound as though money does not make people much happier. But of course we've been concentrating up to this point on people made suddenly rich. What about more common situations, where people become steadily better off and accumulate wealth over a period of years, even decades?

It is obvious that poverty can make people unhappy. Life satisfaction is undoubtedly improved by the alleviation of the suffering that it can bring. In experiments in Kenya, for instance, people with very little money were chosen at random and given approximately $400 or $1,500. With this new wealth, levels of happiness and life satisfaction did rise, while levels of stress and depression fell. But it was notable that if the money was to have an impact on a person's physiology, to change their physical and mental wellbeing, the larger of these two sums was needed. Levels of the stress hormone cortisol were measured at different times during the experiment, but they only fell significantly if people received $1,500.[22]

The Kenyan experiment would suggest that if you are very hard up, then the gift of a significant sum of money will make you happier. This chimes with common sense. Money removes some anxiety from life, allows people to buy enjoyable experiences, to live in greater comfort, and even to become healthier and live for longer.

For years a phenomenon known as the Easterlin paradox, named after the American economist Richard Easterlin, held sway in this field. It was based on evidence that although within a given country richer people are on average happier than poorer people, when you compare countries, the richer countries aren't necessarily happier overall than the poorer countries. The argument went that increased income certainly adds to the happiness of people, but only up to a point. Above a certain income level (anywhere between £10,000 and £20,000, depending on which study you look at), happiness stops rising. People reach a sort of happiness saturation level. They have all they need, and they can afford a few pleasures. Extra income might be nice, but doesn't make that much difference to wellbeing and life satisfaction.

If you're well off, you might be able to detect this pattern in your own life. You used to stay in backpacker hostels, then

B&Bs, now it's a hotel, and quite a nice one. You used to buy clothes in charity shops, then in high-street stores, and now you like designer clothes. When you first traded up, you experienced a surge of pleasure. But after a while you get used to these finer things and the pleasure in them dulls. At a certain point you plateau. You end up wanting Welsh rarebit not Dover sole when you dine at The Ivy. You start going to charity shops again or take up camping. (Or should that be vintage shops and glamping?) Anyway, you've reached the point where more money can't make you any happier.

A nice idea? But not necessarily true.

In 2013 Betsy Stevenson and Justin Wolfers from the University of Michigan published an analysis using samples that were far larger and tracked over a far longer time period than in previous studies. And what Stevenson and Wolfers found was that on average (and of course there will always be individuals who don't fit in with the general pattern) as people become richer they *do* get happier.[23]

More proof seemed to come from a Gallup World Poll in 2007, which showed that 100 per cent of the people in the poll earning more than $500,000 a year said they were very happy, compared with just 35 per cent of those earning less than $10,000 a year.[24]

So it's settled. Unfortunately for the rest of us, the richer you are the happier you are.

But wait, there was a problem. In the Gallup World Poll there were only eight people earning a salary as large as $500,000. And we still can't be certain that the impact of a bigger salary doesn't tail off at some point. Many experts still argue that the evidence suggests the law of diminishing returns applies, so the richer you get, the less difference a small additional sum will make to your happiness. This is a debate that will no doubt continue, with some experts now suggesting that any extra income above $75,000 a year doesn't make people any happier, while others persist in arguing that the richer you get, the happier you become.

GOOD AND BAD MATERIALISM

Regardless of the research, most people find it hard to believe that more money wouldn't make us happier. Just think of all the things you could do with it. The general public tends to predict a stronger relationship between happiness and income than even Betsy Stevenson and her colleagues would claim.

When psychologists at the University of British Columbia studied 400 Americans, asking them about their intuitions regarding the relationship between wealth and happiness, they found that people were fairly accurate at guessing the happiness levels of people earning above $90,000, but they underestimated the happiness of people with incomes below $55,000, even though a third of them were themselves earning less than this amount.[25] In other words, the participants were right that the richer people were on average a bit happier, but they exaggerated the difference between these people and poorer people.

When the researchers asked the participants to rate their own happiness levels, income only contributed a quarter of the difference between people. And when requested to imagine their own levels of happiness on ten different income scales, and those estimates were compared with the data collected from people actually living on such incomes, the participants overestimated how unhappy they would be if they earned a small salary.

This might be an example of loss aversion, of people fearing what would happen if they earned less than they did now and how difficult it would be to give up the things that they'd grown used to. That's reasonable enough of course. If an income drop meant relinquishing their homes and moving away from their friends and family, their happiness levels probably would drop. Still, these results tell us something important. If, as it seems, we have a tendency to overestimate the relationship between happiness and money, then it could lead us to strive for the wrong goals. Perhaps we should stop trying to earn more; it's not going to make us much happier, if at all. But it could divert us from pleasures we could enjoy now, with the income we have.

Yet this doesn't seem to be the general attitude. The desire to become rich seems to have increased in the last 30 or 40 years – at least, in the advanced economies. Between 1970 and 1998 the percentage of American students who believed that it was 'very important or essential' they become 'very well off financially' doubled to 74 per cent.[26]

As we've seen, this seems at odds with research into materialism, often defined as the desire for material goods and money to the neglect of other things, which appears to demonstrate that people who scored high on scales of materialism ended up less happy. More recent research, however, shows that the relationship between materialism and wellbeing is not as straightforward as that. For a long time, materialism was considered to be a personality trait that stuck with you throughout life – once materialistic, always materialistic.

For instance, on the Belk Materialism Scale people scored high on materialism if they displayed a combination of possessiveness, envy and meanness, none of which sound very attractive. But this fails to take into account the many reasons a person might want to own money and material goods. Going back to Mike Redd, for example, it was a desire for security and freedom, a determination never again to find himself desperate for money, which drove him to make it.

More recent theories of materialism take into account a person's circumstances. If Mike hadn't been so hard up in the first place, would he have placed such an emphasis on acquiring money?

The word materialism tends to occupy a morally negative space. Most of us wouldn't want to admit to being materialistic. We worry about our consumerist society and a sense that even though it keeps modern economies spinning, it leads us to buy things we don't need, and of course that's bad for the planet. But perhaps not all materialism is bad.

Here I introduce the psychologist Mihaly Csikszentmihalyi. He is famous for coming up with the concept of flow, where you become so completely absorbed in something you're doing such as painting or gardening that you feel such a sense of deep enjoyment that you don't even notice the time passing.[27] Anyway Csikszentmihalyi proposed two types of materialism.

There's the good kind, called 'instrumental materialism', which involves using material things to fulfil your personal values and goals. Then there's the bad kind, called 'terminal materialism', where you use your money and material possessions to improve your own social status and to generate envy in others.

Although research in the US and in Singapore has found that those with materialistic values are on average less happy, less satisfied with life and more anxious, it could all depend on a person's motives for wanting money. One study using entrepreneurs and business students, who we might guess are likely to want to make money, found that if they desired money in order to enhance their own status or to get power over other people, their materialism made them less happy. But if they wanted it for security or family support, then there was no impact on their wellbeing.[28]

Helga Dittmar, a psychologist from Sussex University, compared attitudes among a sample of people in Iceland with a similar group from Britain, examining six different motives for wanting to get rich. She found that people whose chief motivation was to overcome feelings of self-doubt had lower levels of wellbeing in both countries, regardless of whether they were rich or poor. Wanting money as a marker of success was associated with higher wellbeing. Wanting it in order to feel pride was associated with higher wellbeing in Iceland, but not in the UK.[29]

But the most interesting finding was one which Dittmar herself found rather unsettling. If poorer people said they wanted money in order to be happy, they were likely to have low wellbeing. Now this is not surprising perhaps, because this group didn't have the money they so desired. But the people in the high-income groups in both countries who said they were pursuing money in order to be happy, did have higher levels of wellbeing. So we could say they were on a fool's errand, because we know that more money only makes people a bit happier than before. Alternatively perhaps they knew what they were doing. They were happy now, so maybe their money had contributed to that, in which case, why not get more of it?

We should however be troubled by the relationship between materialism and loneliness. By following more than two-and-a-half thousand people for six years, Rik Pieters from Tilburg University in the Netherlands was able to demonstrate that not only did the more materialistic people become lonelier – perhaps because they were so busy pursuing money that they spent less time socialising, or because they trusted other people less – but it happened the other way round too. An increase in loneliness, after a divorce for example, often coincided with an increase in materialistic tendencies.[30] With divorce it's easy to see why, what with the sharing of the spoils of the marriage, and perhaps the likelihood of more straitened circumstances leading people to focus on money. Other people turned to material things after divorce in the hope of compensating for their loneliness.

But materialism wasn't all bad. It depended on the nature of the materialism. In this study, Pieters used questionnaires administered at various points over time. This allowed him to observe the sequence of events and to see which came first for different individuals, the loneliness or the materialism. Materialism was higher when people were younger or older, and intriguingly was at its lowest point at the age of 48. Sometimes materialism was good. If people took pleasure in their possessions and in their spending, just for the sheer joy of it, endorsing questionnaire items such as 'I like a lot of luxury in life' or 'I enjoy things that are not practical', this was often followed by a reduction in loneliness.

But others were caught in a vicious cycle of loneliness and materialism. People who were single were more likely to look to material possessions, almost as though they were a drug, which could make them happier. On the question-naire, they'd say yes to: 'I'd be happier if I could afford to buy more things.' But sadly, buying new things didn't help. The lesson from this study was that making new friends might work, but buying things in the hope of finding happi-ness wouldn't.

Which is not to say that money can't buy you happiness. As ever, it all depends. Mike Redd is no doubt happier now that he has the security and freedom he craved. He set himself the goal of making money, and he achieved it. But perhaps he'd have been just as happy if he'd made it as a Manchester United footballer (and at the time when he'd have been playing he wouldn't have become a multimillion-aire as a result). Perhaps a successful, but less lucrative, acting career would have also brought him satisfaction. He and we will never know. He seems to me to be a happy man now. But of course I know people – and you will too – with far, far less who are just as happy. Perhaps all we can say in the end is that having more money *can* make you happier, but happiness isn't guaranteed.

10

POVERTY OF THINKING

Why being poor can reduce your IQ and lead you to make bad financial decisions, and how you won't get a lot of sympathy from everyone else.

PERHAPS YOU FEEL envious of Mike Redd, living the high life in the south of France. Perhaps you also envy those people who became rich overnight as a result of winning the lottery. It won't surprise you to hear that psychological tests and brain scans have shown this response is commonplace. More disturbing though is that tests and scans also reveal that we feel disgusted by poor people. Yes, not understanding, or sympathetic, but *disgusted*. It's quite a finding and it shows, if such a thing needs showing, that the dice are loaded against the poor in many ways, some obvious and some very strange, but all very unfair.

DESPISING THE POOR

Why are we sometimes hostile to other people? Traditional research on prejudice suggests that the big factor is difference.

That's to say, we tend to dislike and distrust other people if they are different from us. What's more, when it comes to other groups, we are particularly likely to notice the differences between them and us, while in our own group, it's the similarities which stand out. Something called the stereotype content model takes this process a stage further. It argues that in order to decide on our emotional response to another person we make a two-step judgement. First, we ask ourselves whether they are friend or foe; in other words, do we consider them to be a warm character or not. Second, we judge whether or not we think of them as competent. It's by balancing these two judgements that we settle on our feelings. So, with older, frail people, for example, we might feel they're not very competent any more, but they're certainly no threat, so our strongest feeling towards them is pity.

When it comes to money, many of us consider rich people to be competent, but lacking in warmth, so our prevalent feeling is one of envy. And then there are the poor. If we consider that they're lacking in both warmth and competence, the resultant feeling is disgust. Indeed, so strong is this feeling that it can lead us to consider them as somehow less than fully human.

Now, hang on a minute, I can hear you cry. *I* don't feel like this towards poor people; quite the reverse in fact. Well, maybe. And neither do I. I'm just telling you what the research has shown, as shocking as it might be.

Among the more compelling evidence are brain scans taken at Princeton University in 2006 by the neuroscientists Lasana Harris and Susan Fiske.[1] They put volunteers in a scanner and showed them colour photographs of people belonging to different social groups. Some were clearly rich

– for example, businessmen in fancy suits; while the appearance of others was such that they were obviously not just poor, but destitute.

When the volunteers looked at the pictures of homeless people, two-thirds were prepared to admit that their immediate reaction was one of disgust – which was interesting, and disturbing, in itself. But what interested Harris and Fiske more was the activity in the brain.

The brain scans had shown that when the volunteers were looking at pictures of rich people, the medial prefrontal cortex was activated. This was in line with previous research, which had demonstrated that it is this area of the brain which is activated whenever we see another person rather than an inanimate object. To put it crudely, the grey matter flashes up a message saying 'same species here' and that tells us that we should relate to this other thing in front of us as a fellow human being, rather than a lawn mower or a pigeon or whatever.

But when the people in the scanner were shown the pictures of homeless people the medial prefrontal cortex failed to do its thing. Yes, that's right, the brains of the volunteers didn't register that the shambling guy with the matted hair, the shapeless coat and the broken-down boots was another human being. Instead the areas of the brain associated with disgust were activated. A vulnerable person was dehumanised.

When I saw this study I thought, as you might have done, of the vast and ghastly literature surrounding the Holocaust. How, you ask yourself, did so many German people (and others) come to treat Jewish people (and others) with such cruelty and inhumanity? How could they not see that, even in their most degraded condition, they were fellow human beings?

Perhaps this study is part of the answer. It's a shuddering and sobering thought. Disgust is such a strong emotion that it was even harnessed deliberately. When the writer Primo Levi described his long journey by train to the concentration camp during the Holocaust, he says the Nazi soldiers told him and his fellow Jews to bring money and valuables, but didn't suggest bringing something to use as a toilet on their long journey. So when the prisoners arrived at a busy Austrian railway station and were briefly released onto the platform, the first thing they did, not surprisingly, was to defecate in front of the waiting passengers. The Nazis had contrived to make them immediately appear disgusting and a little less human, making their appalling treatment seem a little less unacceptable.[2]

But let's get back to our attitudes towards the poor, which – while less chilling – still demonstrate a disturbing hard-heartedness.

Public attitudes research in the UK would suggest that, for a start, many of us think that if you're poor it's your fault. It also seems that, in some ways, attitudes are hardening. In a recent survey carried out by the eminent anti-poverty charity the Joseph Rowntree Foundation (which is named after one of Britain's great nineteenth-century social campaigners and philanthropists), 69 per cent of people agreed that, 'there is enough opportunity for virtually everyone to get on in life if they really want to. It comes down to the individual and how much you are motivated.'[3] This was despite the fact that many respondants believed that poverty was now something that could affect anyone because of the downturn in the economy. Meanwhile in another authoritative study of social attitudes, researchers noted that between 1994 and 2010 the percentage of respondents saying people were poor due to their laziness or lack of willpower had increased from 15 per cent to 23 per cent, while the proportion citing injustice in the system had declined from 29 to 21 per cent.[4] (Incidentally most people think poverty is just something that will always happen – with more than a third citing it as 'inevitable'.)

Sympathy for the poor appears to be in short supply, and one possible reason why surfaced when researchers from the Joseph Rowntree Foundation carried out group discussions among members of the public living in areas of high deprivation in two British cities. In every group, people would tell stories of families they knew who could not afford to buy enough food, but had brand new phones or the latest TVs.[5] As we'll see in the next chapter, we all hold strong views on what constitutes appropriate spending in certain financial circumstances, and when poor people buy things we regard as luxuries while saying they can't afford necessities we are particularly riled.

Overall, these studies suggest that a good number of people, and maybe even an increasing number, seem to think that the poor could just snap out of it if, to use a phrase beloved by some, they pulled their socks up a bit. And remember, this is not just the attitude of richer people, who might not understand what it's like to have money worries. These surveys and studies also involved less well-off people too, who we might expect to have more sympathy.

Perhaps we shouldn't be surprised that such attitudes persist, because other studies have shown that children as young as five have already acquired negative ideas about the poor that they carry through their childhood. This is particularly the case with middle-class children, while the attitudes of children who are poorer themselves tend to be more nuanced.[6]

In one study, researchers showed American children between the ages of five and 14 two photographs, one of a 'run-down' house badly in need of repainting and one of a 'nice' suburban house with a manicured lawn. The children were then asked to imagine who might live in the two different houses, what characteristics they might have and which of the children they'd prefer as friends.

Now, first of all, I'm pleased to be able to restore your faith in the goodness of human nature somewhat by reporting that the majority of the children participating in the study, whatever their own background, were generally quite nice about the imagined people in both houses.[7] But at the more detailed level, attitudes differed, largely along class lines.

For instance, while some of the poorer children spoke of how clean and well-organised life in the middle-class home would be, around one in five said they thought such people would be snobby, rude or bullying. 'They are richly happy, while poor people are lying in the snow,' one child said.

When it came to the people in the run-down house, some of the middle-class children said they thought a family living there were likely to be lazy, dirty or mean, and they could imagine them doing things like 'busting windows'. In contrast, children from low-income families themselves were more sympathetic. One said, 'If they're not rich or their clothes are messed up, some people laugh about them. I try to be their friend.' That said, some of the poorer children also demonstrated negative attitudes towards the imagined family in the run-down house, and they certainly seemed to be aware that wider society judged poor people harshly. For example, one of the reasons the poorer children said they would prefer to be friends with the poor children in the imagined scenario was because they felt they'd be less judged by them.

One of the most worrying aspects of the formation so early in life of negative attitudes about poor people is that it can lead to poverty becoming ever more entrenched. Other research has shown that children as young as six and seven think poor children are bound to do worse at school. The majority of better-off pupils will achieve their dreams, children told researchers, while less than a quarter of poor children will do so.[8] Where there's a lack of opportunity, these outcomes may be close to the truth of course, but if poorer children are led to take such a view there is risk that this will become a self-fulfilling prophecy. This is known in psychology as stereotype threat. A certain group underperforms as a result of constant reminders of the negative stereotypes that others hold about them. So for children from the low-income families, the concern is that they feel so fatalistic about their life chances that they don't even think it's worth trying.

And other studies suggest that more negative attitudes towards the poor than the middle classes persist into adulthood, with people rating those on low incomes as more likely to be lazy, dirty, unmotivated, unpleasant, angry and stupid.[9]

A troubling study from Oklahoma in the 1990s found that medical students, who are likely to have more poor than rich patients, became less positive about poorer people the longer they worked with them. By their fourth year of training, they said they were less willing to provide care for patients who couldn't pay for it and more likely to view them negatively.[10] This study was conducted a while ago, so let's hope for the sake of their patients that things have changed.

One reason why some people blame the poor for their

poverty is because they hold on to what's known as the 'belief in a just world'.[11] This is the idea that the world is on the whole a fair place, and that in general we get what we deserve in life. Holding such a world view can be reassuring, and it helps give people a sense of control. But the downside is obvious. It leads to the view that people are the authors of their own misfortune, so in the case of the poor, that they didn't study enough at school, or don't put in as much effort at work, or are feckless and spendthrift with what money they do have.[12] Indeed a study of attitudes towards homelessness conducted back in 1992 found that opinion ranged from sympathy right through to anger and disgust. Those who were more hostile were more likely to believe in a just world.[13]

But what of our attitudes towards the rich? If a person dislikes the poor, does that mean that they like the rich? Not necessarily. New research from Suzanne Horwitz at Yale University has demonstrated that these attitudes are independent, so it doesn't follow that if you dislike the poor, you automatically like the rich or vice versa.[14] Psychological studies using surveys tend to find that people say they don't like the rich, but the results of Horwitz's study using a version of the Implicit Association Test would suggest otherwise. This is a technique which aims to tap into people's real views, rather than those they would like the experimenter to think they hold. They have often been used to test racist feelings.

People sit at a computer while words flash up on the screen. Their task is to categorise the words as good or bad and to press a certain key for each. So 'excellent', for example, counts as a word meaning good. But they also have to categorise words as fitting into the category rich or poor. Here, 'high income' would fit into the rich category.

But here is the clever bit. People are told to answer as fast as they can. The computer is measuring how long they take. So if people are faster at answering when good words and rich words are associated with the same key on the keyboard, then it suggests they see a link in the meaning between those two words. These tests are hard to fake, and therefore provide a good picture of people's real views about a topic.

So, the psychologists in this study found that, despite what middle-class people said up front about rich people, subconsciously they tended to be pro-rich, but they weren't necessary anti-middle class (the study didn't include attitudes towards low-income groups). Further proof of this came when participants were given a story about two drivers crashing, one driving a pricey Jaguar, the other an old Toyota. Those who had shown up as pro-rich on the previous test were more lenient on the driver of the expensive car.

In other words, without realising it, we might admire the rich and this could result in us treating them more kindly than people with less money, in other words unwittingly discriminating against the poor. And if that's not bad enough for the people in poverty, because the world is not just, once they are there it can be hard to escape. Among the reasons is that poverty can lead people to make exactly the bad decisions which lead others to label them irresponsible.

HOW MONEY WORRIES CAN REDUCE YOUR INTELLIGENCE

Before the annual harvest, sugar cane farmers in the Indian state of Tamil Nadu have very little money left. At this time of year, they often have no choice but to take out loans or pawn their belongings in order to pay the bills. It was during one of these lean periods, back in 2004, that a group of psychologists asked 500 sugar cane farmers to perform a series of cognitive tests. Then a few months later, once the harvest was in and payment received, the psychologists got the farmers to repeat the tests.

The diet and general lifestyle of the farmers was essentially the same throughout the four-month study. The main difference between the pre-harvest and post-harvest periods was those money worries. The study found that this stress had a staggering impact on the farmers' cognitive abilities.[15] Their IQ scores were nine to ten points lower before the harvest when they had no money than they were after they received payment for their crops. This was enough to move them into a different IQ classification – from superior intelligence to normal or from normal to the rather unfortunately named 'dull'.

This study showed something that may seem obvious, but is obviously important: that when money is scarce it becomes more of a preoccupation. The Harvard University psychologist Sendhil Mullainathan, who's a leading researcher on the cognitive impact of poverty and was one of the authors of the sugar cane farmers study, puts it this way: people with money worries have less 'bandwidth' in their brain to focus on other things.[16] His work has shown that this diminished bandwidth can lead to a decline in measurable intelligence. Everyone knows that if they are forced to stay awake all night, the next day they find it hard to think straight. The impact of scarcity on thinking in Mullainathan's studies is equivalent to 80 per cent of the effect of an all-nighter.

A different study, in very different circumstances, also

showed how severely money worries can impact on mental abilities. This time the tests took place at a shopping centre in New Jersey in the United States.

People taking part were asked to imagine a hypothetical situation in which they'd just been told repairs on their car would cost either $1,500 or a tenth of that, $150.

With these bills planted in their minds, the participants were given two tests. The first is a type of intelligence test often used in psychology experiments. It's called Raven's Progressive Matrices, and it measures your skills in logical thinking and problem-solving. You are presented with a sequence of shapes drawn in black on white backgrounds, but there's a gap in the sequence. Your task is to choose which shape from a selection will logically fit into the gap. In the second test, instructions flash up on the computer screen at speed, telling you to press a button on a keyboard as fast as possible. It's impossible to predict what's coming next and so the test measures a person's ability to think and act fast.

What then did the experimenters find? First of all, and obviously, that performances in the two tests varied. Of interest to us though was the difference in performance between richer people and poorer people, bearing in mind that one of two prices for car repairs had been planted in their minds. While the better-off participants scored equally well (or badly) in the tests whether they were facing a car repair bill of $1,500 or $150, the less well-off participants scored much worse if they were facing the higher bill.[17] And remember, this wasn't even a real bill. It was hypothetical. No actual costs were involved and yet the money worry impacted significantly on people's cognitive abilities.

We've all experienced the problem of over-preoccupation, if not with money then with other things. Think of the lonely person scrolling down Facebook who notices that everyone else seems to be out having a good time with their friends. Or the man trying to give up smoking, who can't turn on the television without catching an old film in which the lead actor lights up. Or the woman who's just had a miscarriage, who seems constantly to hear that friends are pregnant. In all of these cases, it's not really that everyone else is out with their friends every night, or always smoking or having babies. It's that people with these characteristics have become more salient. They are noticed while other people are not.

The same happens with money. If you don't have it, you obsess about it. You can't get it out of your mind. Which is bad enough, but what the work of Sendhil Mullainathan and his Princeton University collaborator Eldar Shafir has shown is that the more you worry about money, the more likely it is that you'll be unable to take the right decisions to escape from poverty.

PAYDAY LOANS AND TUNNEL VISION

Each year 12 million Americans take out payday loans, and 54 per cent of these people find it difficult to pay the money back.[18] Indeed the US Consumer Financial Protection Bureau has found that half of payday loans are rolled over ten times, compounding the interest and the misery. The companies have come in for a lot of criticism and, increasingly, more regulation. But those who become indebted in this way also get blamed.

Others will say how can these people be so stupid? Don't

they know that instantly available, unsecured loans are bound to involve high interest rates that will make paying back the money more difficult? How do they think the payday loan companies make a profit and hedge against risk?

Yet the fact is, the companies who offer these loans are not relying on rank stupidity. Indeed it would seem they understand the psychology of debt very well, and in particular that when your income is low and uncertain, taking out a short-term loan can seem more responsible than being in debt long-term at lower rates of interest. Rational economics predicts that we want to consume now and pay as late as possible. But in fact, there's good evidence that most people don't like debt at all. They're debt averse. People want to pay off debts early, even if the debt is interest-free and so early repayments doesn't save them any money in the long run.[19] Yet in the case of payday loans the sense that the debt will be short-lived is often an illusion. Unforeseen life events or simply forgetting to pay instalments on time can mean the debt rapidly mounts up. So why do people fall for them?

Pew's Payday Lending Report found that it was both a fear of and a familiarity with debt that led poorer people in the US to take out quick payday loans. They needed cash for one reason or another, but didn't want a long-term debt hanging over them. Given their financial insecurity they thought it was reckless to make an arrangement that would involve steady repayments which they might not be able to meet. They just wanted money to tide them over for a short period until payday, when they would be shot of the debt. Or so they reasoned. In many cases, they never intended to have the loans for long enough for the high interest rates to matter.

These findings fit with other evidence that when people

are poorer they become more risk averse when it comes to spending money.

That's understandable and apparently sensible. The problem is that what makes sense in one way doesn't make sense in another. Not taking out insurance when you can't afford the consequences if the worst does happen, for example.

For many years I've listened to the radio soap opera *The Archers*, which features a family called the Grundys. They're often portrayed as rather feckless, but their decision not to insure the contents of their rented cottage was taken because they wanted to avoid paying premiums they couldn't afford. A sensible decision? Not when, as happened recently in the fictional village of Ambridge, the river Am burst its banks and many homes, including the Grundy's, were flooded.

Back in the real world, we all know that being online can be very useful, if not essential, these days. Yet if you're unemployed, you might think twice about buying a computer and signing up for broadband. Again, such a decision would seem at first sight financially prudent. After all, to pay for such a purchase you might need to take out a loan or put the cost on credit card. But the downside is that you are missing out on all the job advertisements on websites and you won't be able to fill in online application forms. So not buying that computer and getting online might mean you remain unemployed longer than otherwise. If you have very little money, it's necessary to calculate correctly the risk/ reward ratio of various spending (or non-spending) decisions, and that's not easy. The failure to get it right can compound people's relative poverty.

Here's a quick quiz. How fast could you come up with a

list of every state in the US? Perhaps a couple of reminders would help to get you started? I'll give you Ohio and Alaska.

Did that little headstart help you? Chances are it didn't. Studies have shown that people find it harder to name the rest of the states when they've been told two of them than if they'd been left to come up with all 50 on their own.[20] This psychological process is called retrieval inhibition.

It works like this. What you need to do in such a situation is to discount immediately those two states and move on to thinking of others. But instead your mind becomes obsessed with Ohio and Alaska, and you find it harder to focus on coming up with Connecticut and New Hampshire and South Dakota and so on.

When it comes to money worries in the real world, something similar happens. Let's get back to payday loans. People who resort to them seem to be displaying a condition that psychologists call tunnelling, where the mind's focus narrows. All that matters is getting hold of money as soon as possible to meet the immediate need, whether it's paying to stop the electricity being cut off or mending the car so that you can get to work. Where retrieval inhibition comes in here is that the narrow focus on the now drives out a wider focus on the longer term: in this case, not factoring in whether you can repay the loan come payday.[21]

If tunnelling is a significant issue for people with money worries, then it would suggest they are not responsible for the situations in which they sometimes find themselves. The poor are largely passive victims of the way the brain works. Others, of course, argue it's not poverty that leads to poor decision-making but the exact opposite. To put it bluntly, as the less charitable often do, the poor are more likely to make stupid decisions because they're not as intelligent as richer people.

So who is right? This is quite an important question with all sorts of moral and policy implications. For instance, should governments prioritise lifting people out of immediate poverty or spend more money on education? Does welfare help people to help themselves or create dependency? Should low interest loans be provided, or should the poor be forced to manage with what they've got?

THE MENTAL POVERTY TRAP

The psychologist Anuj Shah set out to address this issue. The participants in his research programme were neither poor nor stupid. They were students at one of the most expensive and prestigious universities in the world: Princeton. But for his experiment, Shah created an artificial situation in which scarcity impinged on the thinking of participants.

What he did was to get the students to play an American TV quiz show called *Family Feud*. In this game contestants are given a category – let's say, Beatles' hits – and then are asked to guess the most common answers given by a hundred members of the public.

British readers of a certain age will recognise that the game resembles an old TV favourite called *Family Fortunes*. The catchphrase of the host, a comedian called Bob Monkhouse, went along these lines: 'You said Yellow Submarine, our survey said . . . ' and the viewers would wait to see if that particular hit had been chosen by the public or not, with a wrong choice being signalled for some reason by the distinctive sound of the blowing of a wet electronic raspberry.

In Shah's version of the game, one group of students was, so to speak, 'time-rich': they were given longer to come up with as many answers as possible. The other group were time-poor, with a stricter limit on how long they had. Initially, both groups performed much the same, taking into account the amount of time allocated to them. At this point it seemed the time-poor group, conscious of time pressure, were focusing that bit harder.

But then the 'time-poor' group were told they could 'borrow' extra seconds if they felt they needed them. There was a price though. And the 'high interest' on the 'loan' was this: for every second they 'borrowed' in a particular round, they lost 2 seconds from their overall time.

So how did the time-poor group react? Remember their performance in earlier rounds suggested they didn't need extra time; they were performing as well as the time-rich group. Even so, they started borrowing seconds. It seemed their consciousness that time was scarce overrode other considerations. The short term trumped the long term. And gaining a few seconds now seemed more important to them than losing double that amount of time later. Their short-term performance didn't even improve. They made the wrong decision in all regards.[22]

What then does this study tell us? Well, seemingly, that in a situation of scarcity the pressure imposed on our thinking leads to poor decision-making. Specifically that it leads to irrational, short-termist thinking. And remember that Shah's study involved a group of people whose level of intelligence could in no way be said to be low. It was the circumstances they were put in that made them behave against their own broader interests.

Now I don't want to over-extrapolate, but this finding

does seem to suggest that it is the lack of money that leads to poor decision-making among poorer people rather than vice versa. In which case, blaming the poor for their poverty is quite wrong. In terms of attitude to money, research has shown that people on low incomes are not any more feckless than anyone else, but sometimes their decisions can get them deeper into debt.[23] In a very real sense there is such a thing as 'poverty of thinking' and to escape from that, what the poor need is financial help. Allowing people to borrow small amounts of money quickly and cheaply from mutual credit unions would be one example of such help. Such a service would provide poorer people with the money they need to meet immediate needs and give them the mental space to escape from what the scientist Johannes Haushofer calls 'the neurobiological poverty trap'.

Haushofer hypothesises that the difficulty of trying to survive without enough money raises levels of the stress hormone cortisol and that this impacts the thinking of poorer people. Haushofer's idea has been backed up by studies which have found that in families with low incomes, levels of cortisol are higher.

There could be other reasons for this rise in hormone levels. Illness, for example, which can lead to the unemployment that can result in family poverty. To come to firm conclusions, we need to know which came first, the high cortisol levels or the poverty. But it's striking that even toddlers in low-income families often have raised cortisol levels, and – even if they were ill – illness in a toddler would be less likely to lead to poverty.[24] This kind of research is in its early stages, and a few studies do contradict Haushofer's hypothesis, but the majority concur.

POVERTY AND THE BRAIN

Evidence from neuroscience would appear to add weight to this conclusion. Behind the forehead lies the prefrontal cortex, the part of the brain which plays a large part in inhibiting reckless spontaneity, encouraging us to wait patiently for greater rewards in the future, rather than always opting for instant gratification.

Say you are offered £10 today or £11 in a week's time. Your mental considerations in this case will go something like this. Given the small difference in the sums, it may well be rational to take the £10 that is available now. After all, something could happen during the coming week and the slightly bigger reward of £11 could be lost. But what if the two different sums offered were, say, £10 and £20? Well, in this case, it becomes highly sensible to wait. And that's what your brain should tell you if the prefrontal cortex is functioning properly.

You're probably thinking that this sounds like the mental processes I discussed in Chapter 3 when we saw how we'd generally be delighted to save £15 on hiring a bike but would consider such a saving inconsequential if we were buying a car. The mental process in that case is called relative thinking. In the context of the overall amount spent, is the saving worth the bother?

The mental process here is slightly different and is known as temporal discounting. How much is it worth to wait? As with relative thinking, economists have done hundreds of experiments on it. And guess what? Individuals vary in the deals they will accept. But a key factor in the different decision-making of richer people and poor people can often be this: can you afford to wait? In the richer person's case, the answer is often, yes. They don't need the £10 now because they've got plenty of money, which means they might as well hang out for the £11, and certainly for the £20. By contrast, a poorer person might need that £10 so badly that they decide to forgo a bigger sum later.

Yet if you think back to Chapter 3 again, this time to those Indian villagers prepared to take a 45-minute trip to save $50 on a household appliance, you'll see that in a different context poorer people react differently. So what's going on here? How can psychology be showing that poorer people tend to act more rationally in weighing up actual savings in the context of overall price but less rationally when faced with a choice between less money now or more money later?

A clue to this mystery lies in a technique called transcranial magnetic stimulation. This involves a large coil being held beside the head. The coil emits magnetic pulses that affect the electrical currents flowing in precise areas of the brain. It sounds rather Frankenstein-esque, but it's been demonstrated to be safe, and the effects on the brain are significant.

Most relevant to us is that when the stimulation is used to dampen down the activity in the prefrontal cortex, people become less likely to wait for greater rewards in the future and more likely only to consider the here and now. And what exists outside the laboratory that does the same? Chronic stress.[25]

Now it's not only the poor who suffer from such stress of course, but they are certainly highly prone to it. Struggling to make ends meet from day-to-day takes its toll. So could this explain why poor people sometimes resort to such destructive remedies as short-term loans at crippling interest rates? They are not acting out of foolishness or fecklessness, but because stress levels affecting the prefrontal cortex make them less able to take the future into account?

As I said above, more research is needed in this area, and it's always going to be hard to disentangle causality. But some of the evidence we already have is persuasive – and disturbing. For example, research has shown that financial poverty could damage the development of children's brains. In St Louis in the USA, children's brains were scanned once a year for between three and six years and the poorer children were found to have a smaller volume of both grey and white matter, and a smaller hippocampus and amygdala. The good news was that for those with good parents, the effects were ameliorated.[26] But what of those children growing up in families where parenting skills were not so good?

If more research finds that financial poverty reinforces poverty of thinking, there is surely a strong argument for social programmes to raise incomes. And that would represent a shift in the current drift of political thinking, which – as the French economist Thomas Piketty has shown – is allowing economic inequality to grow.[27]

11

BAD MONEY

Why rich people would be the first to jump in the lifeboats on the Titanic, *why envy is bad sometimes but not always, why we'll tell lies for money (as long as it's a substantial sum) and why some people can't resist throwing money away.*

ALWAYS BE SUSPICIOUS of clumsy people. This might sound a bit harsh. I'm a clumsy person myself, as it happens. But the reason I say it is because dropped wallets, pencils and paper abound in certain types of psychology experiments. When I lived in Brighton, you could tell when the Open University Summer School in psychology had started, because wherever you went in the town people were dropping things in front of you.

As a psychology student myself I knew what was going on. I noticed that close by other people were loitering casually with clipboards. They were there to observe the circumstances under which people would offer to help pick up the dropped things.

So what type of person tends to be most helpful in these situations? Well, those of you who subscribe to the idea that money is at the root of all evil will feel a bit vindicated perhaps. For some studies have found that the more money oriented a person is, the less likely they are to come to the aid of the clumsy experimenter.

SELFISHNESS OR SELF-SUFFICIENCY?

In 2006, a group of students took part in a study at the University of Minnesota in Minneapolis organised by the eminent psychologist Kathleen Vohs. As with so many groups involved in psychology experiments the students were, officially, weird. Or rather, WEIRD. That's to say they were all from **W**estern, **E**ducated, **I**ndustrialised, **R**ich, and **D**emocratic countries.

First, the students were given scrambled up strings of five words from which they were asked to select four to make a phrase. Some of the students were given a list of neutral words. So the rather Yoda-esque 'cold it desk outside is' would become 'it is cold outside'. Others were given money-related words. So 'high a salary desk paying' would become 'a high paying salary'.

The idea of course was to get some of the students thinking, albeit sub-consciously, about money.

What happened next was that one of the students, set up by the researchers, asked for help, pretending to be confused about how to do the puzzle. Which of the other students would come to their aid? Surely the nature of the puzzles they'd just completed would make no difference? Wouldn't their degree of helpfulness depend on something deeper than that? It seems not. For it turned out that the students who'd worked with the money-related words only spent half as much time helping their confused colleague. Whatever their other characteristics, the fact that they'd just been thinking about high-paying salaries and similar phrases seemed to make them more selfish.[1]

In another part of the study, the students played the well-known board game Monopoly. The game was arranged in such a way that some of the students had a big pile of money left over at the end, which they could use for a later game, while others were left with very little. Then one of those staged acts of clumsiness took place. Someone dropped a pile of pencils on the floor. And yes, again it was found that the students who were rich with Monopoly money – money that wasn't even real, of course – proved less helpful.

This study is an example of what is known within psychology as 'priming', the idea that when we are exposed to an image or some words that make us unconsciously focus on a topic, that image or those words can have a significant influence on us. The best-known experiment on priming is probably one which found that people who were given the task of unscrambling anagrams of words related to old age walked more slowly to the lift after the experiment. In other words, the idea of old age was so on their minds that they began to walk as if they were elderly themselves.[2]

These kinds of studies are always intriguing, and I've discussed them on my radio programmes many times because they're so popular. It seems we relish the idea that we are subject to unconscious influences, and perhaps especially if it makes us a bit more wicked than we'd otherwise be. It seems many of us experience a certain frisson at the thought that we are not totally in control of our behaviour. It perhaps explains why stage hypnotists who can make volunteers bark like a dog or quack like a duck are so popular.

Yet the whole idea of priming has caused something of a rift within psychology. This is because attempts to replicate some of the most renowned studies have not always worked out. For example, when other psychologists tried to replicate Vohs' money study, using exactly the same method, they didn't get the same result.[3] The same thing happened when researchers attempted to repeat a study in which some participants were shown pictures of $100 notes on a screen while being asked questions about their views on free market systems. In the original study, those shown the big value note were more likely to express capitalist beliefs than other participants, but again this has proved difficult to replicate. But to be fair, Vohs has responded to her critics in a new paper, raising the question of whether the samples used are truly comparable.[4] The replication attempt used students from the University of Chicago, which is famous for its strength in economics, so Vohs wonders whether more students might have a pro-free market stance to begin with, with the result that priming with money made little difference. The debate about priming is set to run for many years.

I hasten to add, that although there have been some isolated cases of fraudulent results within psychology in recent years, cheating is not the issue here. No one is suggesting that the psychologists who carried out the original experiments did anything underhand or unethical. Just that the results they obtained on a particular day with a particular group of participants couldn't be replicated in other circumstances, which perhaps weakens the original findings.

But this note of caution doesn't mean there's nothing in the idea that the mere mention or sight of money might influence our attitudes or indeed behaviour. For while some studies have contradicted the original findings, others have supported them. Vohs' money priming methods have been used in research all over the world. More than 165 studies have been conducted in 18 countries. To take one example, participants who had been primed with the thought of money by unscrambling money-related phrases were then asked various hypothetical questions. For instance, imagine you are working as an office assistant and are using the photocopier when you remember you have run out of paper for your printer at home. How likely would you be to slip a ream of paper into your bag?

In this study, those primed with money-related sentences were more likely to say they would stoop to this little bit of thievery from the office and to carrying out other unethical actions than people who'd not been so primed.[5] But remember, at this stage, people were only being asked how they would react in a hypothetical situation. Would they actually cheat in real life? The experimenters devised a way to find out.

Participants were invited to play a computer game in which they could win real money, and where – with a bit of practice – it became clear that there was an easy way of cheating to win more. Once again those primed with money were more likely to succumb to the temptation. The hypothesis of the researchers here was that money priming put people into a business-related frame of mind in which they made decisions based on what might be good for business rather than what was morally right. Which certainly could be the explanation, though doubtless many business people would resent the implication that cheating at a computer game is akin to being business-minded.

Not that priming with money always leads people to behave badly. In her original study, Kathleen Vohs found that even though money priming appeared to make people more selfish, it also made them more self-sufficient (a more worthy attribute), and that this too could explain why they were less helpful. For instance, when participants were given difficult but solvable puzzles, those primed with money didn't give up or ask for help as quickly as others who'd been primed differently. They worked on alone for an average of 16 minutes instead of 11. Likewise, in Vohs' experiment, which began with students shown either a screensaver of a fish swimming or money floating around underwater, those shown the money were three times as likely to choose to work alone rather than with a partner on the subsequent task.

All of which leaves us where exactly? Perhaps we are able to say that being money-minded does make a person quite single-minded. After all, when earning the stuff we tend to have to think about Number One. Which doesn't mean once we've acquired money we can't show generosity (as I'll demonstrate in Chapter 12). That said, there's also some evidence that the more money you have, the meaner you become.

WEALTHY AND CHILDREN FIRST (OR WHY BEING RICH COULD SAVE YOU IF YOU WERE ON THE *TITANIC*)

All of us can probably think of a situation in our own lives in which a better-off friend has been slow to reach for their well-stuffed wallet when it comes to buying a round of drinks at the bar. A relative of mine relishes a story in which a wealthy couple she knows invited her and other friends to a fortieth birthday party at their large, riverside home and then charged them (quite high prices) for the food and drink. 'Of course, it's by being so penny-pinching that they got so rich in the first place,' you hear people say to explain such behaviour.

On the other hand, for every notorious instance of a billionaire miser there are examples of rich people who are exceptionally generous philanthropists. Yet the idea that having money tends to make people mean and selfish persists. So what is the evidence for it?

Here's a statement: 'People like me deserve an extra break now and then.' Perhaps you'd agree, thinking that a bit of luck is always a good thing, and why shouldn't you have some. Perhaps you'd agree more fulsomely if you thought you'd not been very lucky in life so far. But what if you were quite happy, healthy and wealthy?

Well, in this book I'm focusing purely on financial wealth, not other aspects of good fortune, and when this question is used as part of a scale to measure entitlement, it's not the people with the least money – those who might be considered to be down on their luck – who most often endorse this statement, it's the richest people.[6]

Here's another statement. (I really like this one.) 'If I were on the *Titanic* I would deserve to be on the *first* lifeboat.' Of course we never know how we'd behave in a disaster situation. In our panic we might well push past others to survive. But surely no one asked this question in this way would answer that they are somehow entitled to escape from the sinking ship first. Yet a study showed that more rich people than poor people thought exactly this way. Isn't that staggering?

The *Titanic* test formed part of one of more than fifty studies that the American psychologist Paul Piff has conducted and in most, it must be said, the rich don't come out well. To answer perhaps the central question – are richer people more mean? – Piff assembled a group which included some earning as much as $200,000 a year, as well as others earning less, sometimes much less. All the participants were given $10. They could keep all of it, give all of it away, or keep some and give some away. Piff found the poorer people were more generous. On average those earning less than $25,000 a year gave away 44 per cent more than those earning between $150,000 and $200,000 a year.

In another study, Piff asked people to choose between circles of different sizes to represent either themselves or 'other' people. The result: the wealthier a person was the more likely they were to choose a bigger circle. Richer people were also more likely to agree that they were good at everything and never wrong, and to check their appearance in a mirror before having their photo taken.[7]

Mean, selfish, big-headed and vain. It's going well for the rich so far.

But remember, these people were rich before they took part in Piff's tests. Maybe it was not their wealth that dictated their behaviour, but their behaviour which helped them to become wealthy. That's to say, big money wasn't to blame for making them so loathsome, they were loathsome in the first place and that's how they got so stinking rich.

If this is the case, then money's out of the frame and the root of all evil is, well, evil. One possible way of proving this is to give money to people who don't usually have it and see if they take on the characteristics of the rich. To see if this might happen, Paul Piff resorted to a game of Monopoly again.

Crucially, participants were not from different wealth brackets in real life, but as a result of a coin toss one of the players in each game saw themselves as wealthy and one poor. How? Well, for a start the winner got to be the racing car while the loser had to make do with the old boot. But more than that, the winner started the game with twice as much money, got to throw two dice instead of one, and as if that wasn't enough, received $400 rather than $200 every time they went past Go. We're talking all the luck.

Not surprisingly, the advantaged players tended to start winning the actual game. But it wasn't that which interested Piff, who was watching proceedings through a secret one-way mirror. What he wanted to see was how these 'rich' people behaved. The answer was, in a word, obnoxiously. For example, they tended to be noisier, whooping triumphantly as they bounced their racing car along the board in pursuit of ever greater riches. And they even took more than their fair share of the pretzels from a bowl left out for both players.

After the game, these participants were asked why they thought they'd won. And guess what, they talked of the effort they'd put in and the wise decisions they'd made, but not one mentioned that they'd had an advantage from the start.[8] This reminds me of the findings of the classic 1978 study I mentioned on lottery winners in Chapter 9. Despite the use of the word 'lottery' in the title of the competition, which you'd think might be a clue to its random nature, almost two-thirds felt that they in some way deserved to have won.[9]

Again, it's an astonishing finding, and Piff concluded from

it that while, yes, competitive people, who often have selfish instincts, are good at making money, it can also be shown that having money, even temporarily, even when it's all just a game, shapes a person's behaviour, making them more self-centred and arrogant. It works both ways, in other words.

A NOTE OF DUTCH CAUTION

Had you been in the San Francisco Bay Area one sunny day, you might have seen people lurking behind the bushes next to a pedestrian crossing. Of course, as a reader of this book, you would have immediately realised that these people were not up to something nefarious, but were researchers conducting a psychology experiment. This time they weren't dropping things to see who helped out but were observing the behaviour of motorists at the crossing. The man behind the experiment was once again Paul Piff.

In California, as in many places, cars are supposed to stop if a pedestrian seems about to step onto the crossing. It's one of those protocols of road use, partly a matter of safety, partly of law, but perhaps above all of courtesy. And by now I hardly need to tell you what Piff's researchers observed. Yes, of course, all the people driving cheap cars stopped to allow pedestrians to cross, while only half the drivers of expensive models did the same.[10]

Let me hastily add, as Piff himself did, that the total number of cars observed in this study was pretty small. And to the extent that there's proof to show that being rich makes you mean and selfish, it comes not from single studies, but from an accumulation of evidence. Even then, there is also some evidence that points to the fact that being rich can make you generous and selfless. More to the point perhaps, none of these studies show or purport to show that *all* rich people are mean, just that on average the richer are a bit meaner than the poorer.

Of course it helps if a study involves a big sample of people and doesn't use proxies if they can be avoided. After all, taking the experiment above as an example, it could have been the case that one of the people driving an expensive car that didn't stop at the pedestrian crossing was not some wealthy businessman but a desperate car thief – or as Stefan Trautmann of Heidelberg University observed of Piff's study (using the language of the academic journal) 'low status individuals may over-consume highly visible goods', which translates as poor people sometimes have cars they can't afford.[11]

With the aim of avoiding such problems in his own work Trautmann used an authoritative survey carried out in the Netherlands. In it, a representative sample of 9,000 people are quizzed four times a year, and their socio-economic status is assessed using detailed questions about wealth, income, job type and job security.

Trautmann discovered that people of higher socio-economic status seemed to be more independent and less engaged with other people. He also found that the better-off people were more likely to be tolerant of tax evasion, though at the same time the less well-off were more forgiving of benefit fraud, which perhaps suggests that having more money doesn't make you more immoral, but rather that your notions of morality are dictated at least to some degree by your financial circumstances. All that said, however, the data from the survey only allowed Trautmann to draw conclusions about attitudes, not behaviour.

So what he did next was get a representative sample of the people in the survey to play various financial trust games. And when observing the actual behaviour of this smaller group, Trautmann found that richer players were no more likely to betray their opponents than poorer ones. Which doesn't of course mean that he now had definitive proof that the wealthy are just as likely as the rest of us to be generous and helpful (or mean or selfish) but rather that in this *particular* study no measurable differences could be detected. As ever, the watchword is caution. In psychology, as in all aspects of life, nothing is simple. If you do studies one way, you get one set of results; if you do them another way, you find something very different.

DICTATORS AND ULTIMATUMS

Take 633 millionaires and offer them the chance to be dictators and to issue ultimatums. Would this help us in our search for the answer to the question of whether the rich are any meaner than the rest of us?

Well, no, and – at the same time – yes. Sorry, but I can't really be any clearer than that, for the findings of this study – again, we are in the Netherlands for this one – were somewhat contradictory. Researchers managed to persuade a large private Dutch bank to allow them to invite their wealthy clients to take part in a series of games. As I say, a remarkable 633 millionaires agreed.

As part of the game, they were given real money to play with or indeed to keep. Not a lot by their standards – 100 euros to be precise – but even so, a tidy sum. One group played the dictator game, so named because the lead player is in sole charge and no one else has a say. Another group played the ultimatum game, where the lead player gets to make a 'take it or leave it' offer, but the other player has a choice about whether to accept. In this study, these other players were, the millionaires were told, earning less than 12,500 euros a year, so there was a huge income gap, but perhaps being so rich the millionaires didn't care about that, perhaps they'd be mean and selfish? Well, no, in fact – or not in the first game. On average the millionaires proved to be rather benign dictators, choosing to give away 71 euros on average, with just under half giving away the full sum. They were three times more generous than people usually are in this game.[12]

But what about those millionaires playing the ultimatum game? Now remember there's a crucial difference with this game, because the potential recipient has some choice in the matter. They can decide to refuse the one-off offer. And while you might think this is always irrational, decades of research have shown that if the recipient thinks the offer is too small then they will spurn it. Indeed, half of the people will say no if they're offered anything less than 20 per cent of the total sum. Suspecting this – for after all, givers as well as recipients generally have some notion of fairness in these circumstances – most lead players of the ultimatum game tend towards making a relatively generous offer. Remember, they get nothing themselves if the other person refuses their offer. But the Dutch millionaires didn't seem to be bothered about that. Perhaps in a sign of the financial ruthlessness that helped them make (or keep) their money, once they started thinking in terms of making a deal, rather than a straight donation, they became *less* generous. Indeed this time the average amount they offered was 64 euros, and fewer than one in three of them this time offered the full 100 euros to the much poorer person.

Incidentally, while we'll come on to charitable giving in more detail in the next chapter, it's worth noting here that this Dutch study provides a lesson for charity fundraisers and it's this: when looking to raise money from rich people it's better to ask for a straight donation rather than to imply that there's something in it for them, that it's some kind of investment. If you do the latter, then there's a risk your rich donor will put their hard-headed rather than soft-hearted hat on – with the result your charity will get less.

But to round off this section, what can we make of all these fascinating, often entertaining but somewhat infuriating and contradictory studies? Even the millionaires were more generous in the Ultimatum Game than people usually are. What we can say is that having money makes people feel more independent. (We saw how important that was for Mike Redd.) Given that, some richer people will decide to be generous with their money. After all they can afford to be and they, like the rest of us, get a warm feeling from giving money away. But, as we've seen above, and with all the caveats about the reliability of some of the studies, there are instances in which richer people appear to be less generous than the rest of us, not more.

FLYING FIRST CLASS

I fly abroad for work a few times a year, but always in economy. On budget flights, I've never even paid for speedy boarding or an assigned seat. I never dreamed that one day I would walk onto a plane and turn left.

But recently it happened. A technology firm in California asked me to give a talk to their employees and offered to fly me first class from London to San Francisco.

When I walked up to the first class check-in desk (no queue of course) the attendant seemed rather suspicious. Perhaps my sense that I didn't really belong there was obvious or my suitcase looks cheap. Still, my boarding pass was in order, and from that point on she – and indeed all the airline staff – could not have been more friendly and helpful. It was as if I'd passed through a portal into another, magical, world.

First stop was the Concorde Lounge, with its super-comfortable seats in muted greys and burgundies. It was eight o'clock in the morning but the lounge had the vibe of a late-night bar in a top-class hotel. As I waited for my eggs Benedict to arrive, I flicked through the glossy magazines and started people-watching. Presumably there were one or two inter-lopers like me – people who were not rich, whose flights had been paid for or who had saved air miles in order to upgrade and for whom this experience was a one-off – but for some, this was how they always travelled, this was just normal.

On the plane itself, I couldn't help but obsess about the other people in the first class cabin. Were they born into money or were they self-made? Were any of them very important or famous in some way? Was it possible some got their money illegally or at least unethically? I felt the urge to write a quick survey and hand it round.

Studies have shown that we have strong feelings about who does and doesn't deserve money and whether it is obtained in the right way. In fact, anyone rich can gain our disapproval. In one study researchers measured the movement in people's facial muscles when they were shown a series of photographs. When it was an old lady in the photo, and they were told she had got soaked by a taxi driving through a puddle, their facial expression was sad. When it was a rich-looking businessman in a suit who got soaked, people didn't admit to getting any pleasure from this, but the movements of their facial muscles suggested otherwise. They couldn't help but smile.[13] The possession of any riches can invoke this kind of *schadenfreude* (in addition to the admiration I mentioned previously), and if money is inherited or unearned people view it more negatively.

In his work on the sacred and profane meanings of money, the marketing scholar Russell Belk notes that all around the world there are fairy tales warning of the terrible fate that might befall anyone who stumbles across lost treasure.[14] It seems that deep within human culture is this notion that no good will come to people who have ill-deserved good fortune. As we saw in Chapter 9, this feeling even extends to 'people like us', ordinary people who win the lottery. Good luck to them if they're nice and spend their money wisely, we think. But woe betide them if they're scoundrels and just spend, spend, spend . . .

Back on the plane, the person behind me looked like a supermodel. Her legs were very, very long, and she managed to look elegant in the black pyjamas which the cabin crew had handed out to us at the start of the day-time flight and which (rather bizarrely) everyone wore. (It made us look as if we were wearing a rather classy prison uniform.) As we approached San Francisco, this woman went to the loo (which you may be pleased to know was just as cramped and grim as in economy, but with a fake flower in a little vase) and came out fully made-up, looking stunning, ready to face the paparazzi or whoever else was waiting for her.

Those of us who aren't rich often console ourselves with the thought that those who are must find it difficult to sleep at night. But my first-class flight gave me a glimpse into why most of the rich rarely feel this way. As I left the plane (the attendant thanked me profusely for travelling with them), and picked up my suitcase (they come first on the carousel – no hanging around), it struck me how being treated this way must make you believe you're important even if you aren't. Your sense of entitlement must increase, eroding any guilt you might feel about having so much, when others have so little. Yes, I am special and I do deserve to live like this, you must think.

All of which of course infuriates us and induces the most common reaction we have towards the rich: envy. This is why we smile when the man in a fancy suit gets drenched, and it's a feeling that can sometimes be so strong that it will lead us to do extraordinary things.

BURNING ENVY (SOMETIMES BAD/SOMETIMES GOOD)

Perhaps one of the most famous studies into envy was carried out by Daniel Zizzo and Andrew Oswald at Warwick University.[15] Volunteers in the study were all given the same chance to win a small amount of money. Afterwards it was revealed to everyone taking part that they'd all been given a bonus payment. But while for some this meant they ended up with £11, for others their final total was only £6.

This caused understandable resentment among those who'd lost out. The bonus handouts were entirely arbitrary;

those who got the higher amount hadn't deserved it in any way. It simply wasn't fair.

In life, of course, that's just tough. But in this experiment the losers had a chance to fight back. They were offered a deal. If they chose to, they could spend some of their money on taking cash away from those who'd lucked out.

In the language of economics this is called 'burning' money. But this didn't mean there was a KLF-style bonfire at the Warwick campus. In fact, no actual fire was lit, no cash was destroyed. All that happened was that money in the small economic system created for the experiment was removed from circulation. No one could have it. It was lost to all the participants.

For the purposes of comparison, the winners were also offered the chance to 'burn' some of the money of their rivals. They did so indiscriminately, while the losers chose to pick on the winners. They were the ones with something to 'gain' from the deal. That is to say, even though they'd lose out financially to an even greater extent, they would at least have the satisfaction of seeing the winners suffer.

Given this opportunity, two-thirds of the people took it. And on average, by the time each person went home they had seen almost half their winnings destroyed.

I think we can agree that while acting in this way might give us some wicked sense of satisfaction, it's not terribly admirable. If all we can do when we see someone with more money than us is to seek to destroy that money, we're not going to live in a productive society. It's a classic case of money over mind.

But envy doesn't always work this way. When I go round to my wealthy friends' house, I'll admit it, I do rather envy them. They have a small cinema in the basement, for good-ness' sake – who wouldn't want one of those? But of course this doesn't make me want to burn their house down. In fact, I admire the enterprise that led to them becoming so well-off. And in a small way maybe it makes me work harder in the hope of getting a bit of what they've got.

It's this element of admiration of the rich that can turn envy into a more positive emotion, and which has led Rik Pieters, whose work on materialism and loneliness in the Netherlands we considered in Chapter 9, to dub it 'benign envy'. Such envy is not bad, it's good. It helps to fuel aspi-ration and drives people to strive for success so that they too can have the money others enjoy.[16]

Pieters distinguishes this sort of envy from another type, which he calls 'malicious envy'. Now this term would seem to describe well the destructive envy shown by the people in the Warwick experiment. But in fact Pieters uses the phrase to describe envy in the way it is commonly understood, in other words as 'a feeling of resentful or discontented longing aroused by another person's better fortune, situation, etc.' – to use the Shorter Oxford English Dictionary definition. And as we'll see, this sort of envy doesn't generally result in a person wanting to destroy what the other person has. Not literally at least. Rather, it leads to a feeling of contempt, feigned or otherwise.

In his study of envy, Pieters asked students to look at a colour photograph of an iPhone and to read a description of some of its features. Next he asked them to imagine that they were working alongside someone who had such a phone. Half the students were then asked to imagine feeling jealousy combined with some admiration for their colleague with the fancy phone, while the other half were asked to imagine feeling jealous and begrudging.[17]

Next, the two groups of students had to rate how much they liked the iPhone, the effort they would be prepared to put into obtaining one and how much they would agree to pay for it. The key result was as follows: people in the benign envy group (those who imagined admiring the student with the phone) were prepared to pay what Pieters calls 'an envy premium'. And a substantial one. Indeed they said they'd pay nearly 50 per cent more for the phone than the malicious envy group (those who begrudged the student the phone). The experiment seemed to show that – even in an imagined scenario – if someone we admire has something we don't have, then we are more likely to want it and indeed to work to get it. (The price the students were prepared to pay for the phone in this experiment served as a proxy for the degree of effort we might put in to acquire what a person we envy already has.) So, in such a case what the Shorter Oxford English Dictionary describes as 'discontented longing aroused by another person's better fortune' serves as a spur to action.

But there is a caveat. This sort of positive envy seems only to work in situations in which the thing someone else has, and for which we long, is somehow achievable. Pieters uses the example of a neighbour having a better lawnmower. We see it, envy our neighbour for it, want it, and because it's only a lawnmower (and presumably our neighbour can't be *that* much better off than us) we determine to get one too. It's a bit like what used to be called 'keeping up with the Joneses'. The Joneses had the nicer house and nicer car, but they were still just the Joneses. Keeping up with the Kardashians on the other hand, well that's just silly.

Our strategy in the case of super-rich people like the Kardashians, or even more so with someone like Donald Trump, is to turn our envy into contempt, to despise them for having so much money while having absolutely *zero* taste. This is surely why magazines like *Hello* and *OK!* do so well. We enjoy being 'invited into the lovely home' of such-and-such a minor royal or Premier League footballer, because we're confident that it will be full of ghastly gold taps or white leather sofas. It gives us the chance to – metaphorically – trash the place, while making us more satisfied with our own, more modest lot.

A follow-up experiment by Pieters demonstrated this type of reaction. This time, his participants were able to bid either for an iPhone or for a Blackberry. Those imagining malicious envy were once again not prepared to pay as much as the benign enviers for the iPhone. They preferred to go (and pay more) for the Blackberry. It seems they wanted to differentiate themselves from their colleague with the iPhone (who they envied but whose success they begrudged rather than admired) by choosing another kind of phone entirely and convincing themselves that theirs was better.

Envy turns out to be quite a complicated emotion, and – judging by this research – a complex emotion to study. But for our purposes, the important thing to conclude from all this is that while envy often is negative, in some circumstances it can have a positive effect on us, at least to the extent of spurring us on.

WASHING YOUR HANDS OF MISERABLY SMALL LIES

Like envy, we don't generally approve of lying. There are some exceptions of course. What on *earth* is that monstrosity, you think, on first seeing the hat your friend is wearing at her daughter's wedding. *How* lovely, you say, when she comes over and tells you it cost £100. You're lying, of course, but it's a white lie to protect your friend's feelings. And then there are lies told for the greater good, such as insisting to the baddies that the man they're chasing ran *that* way.

There's another circumstance in which we are tolerant of lying, which is rather more surprising. It turns out we think lying is okay if money is involved (and the more, the better). It's one of those findings that might have you raising your eyebrows. But bear with me as we embark on one of the weirder trips into the way money messes with the mind.

Several psychological studies have found that when people have come into contact with something or someone they consider immoral, they spend a longer time than normal washing their hands. We might dub it the Lady Macbeth syndrome, for it's almost as if people are trying to cleanse themselves of an association with sin.

Strange as it sounds, this finding is so consistent that some psychologists now consider it to be a better measure of the strength of a person's moral disapproval of something than simply asking them what they think. And of course it avoids the issue of people telling researchers what they want to hear instead of the truth – a perennial problem for psychologists trying to investigate our attitudes.

One such group of psychologists is working in China, and

we'll get to them shortly. But in order to explain what they did, we need first to detour into a classic psychological experiment carried out by a man called Leon Festinger in the 1950s. In this experiment, participants were asked to complete a boring task but then to tell the next set of participants that actually it was quite interesting. In other words, they were asked to lie, for which they were paid either $1 or $20.

What this study demonstrated was that people in such situations experience what's known as cognitive dissonance, that is to say they feel uncomfortable because they are trying to hold two incompatible views at the same time, in this case knowing that the task was boring while also knowing that they had told subsequent participants the opposite.

So acute was the discomfort felt by people in this situation, so keen were they to resolve the dissonance, that when they were later asked to evaluate Festinger's study they convinced themselves it wasn't that dull after all. Or rather, those paid the lower sum reacted in this way.[18]

Those paid the larger amount reacted differently. In their case, the payment of that bigger sum moved them to feel that they were only doing it for the money anyway, which meant they didn't experience discomfort about finding the task dull and telling others it was interesting, and so when it came to evaluating the study they continued to insist the task was dull.

Now I hope you're following all this. There's more to come as we turn to the Chinese researchers.

In the Chinese adaptation of Festinger's experiment, it wasn't the participants who were offered the money to lie, it was a stooge. Again the amount paid to him for lying was sometimes small, sometimes quite a lot bigger. And crucially, the participants were witnesses to the lie, some seeing him paid the small amount, some the larger one.

At this point the participants thought the first part of the experiment was over, and as they left the lab the stooge shook hands with them. Only then did hand washing finally feature in the study, with all the participants asked to wash their hands carefully because, they were told, the next phase of the experiment involved handling precision equipment.

It sounds rather unnecessarily complicated perhaps. But there was method in it. And of course what the experimenters wanted to know, because they thought it would be a good gauge of the moral disapproval people felt about the lying, was how long the various participants spent washing their hands.

The results are noteworthy.

Those people who'd seen the stooge given a small sum of money to lie – just one yen (which is equivalent to about 12 British pence) – washed their hands for the longest period after shaking hands with him. The Chinese researchers concluded that this was a sign that these people didn't like the fact that someone had told a lie for such a pathetic sum of money. By contrast, those participants who'd seen the larger amount of money handed over to the stooge for lying washed their hands for a shorter period of time (7 seconds compared with 9 seconds). They seemed to disapprove of his behaviour less (and therefore feel less dirtied by his handshake) because the sum paid to him was a big one.[19]

After all this, I'd forgive you for thinking that all such experiments really prove is that psychologists think up some bizarre things. Nonetheless, these psychologists argued that the findings from this study show that we tend to excuse bad behaviour if it's done for money, but only if it's done for enough money. Perhaps a second experiment – also done by the Chinese group – will convince you?

This time people were shown a series of photographs of one man making sure he's the first to grab some money that's lying on the ground, by pushing another man over in the street. Sometimes the sum of money on the pavement was small. Sometimes it was large. And yes, once again, people considered it more acceptable to push the man over for a larger amount of money than for a smaller amount. Indeed the tipping point, as it were, at which pushing over became acceptable, was some three-hundred yen or about thirty pounds.

And how did the researchers find this out? Well, this time they just asked the participants.

Still unconvinced? It does seem to be one of those research findings that conflicts with our ideas of commonly held attitudes. But just consider this real-life example. We often hear stories on the news of people who act as drug mules, taking huge risks to smuggle heroin or cocaine through airport security. The real winners if the mules get through are, of course, the big-time dealers and the drug cartels. And yet the person carrying all the risk is the poor mule. So let me ask you this: which of these two mules do you have more respect for – Mule A, who's been paid $50, or Mule B, who's been paid $5,000? I'd bet you say the latter. Not because you admire B, but because if someone is going to take that massive risk, at least they should make it worthwhile. To do it for $50 just seems stupid. Likewise, we often have a sneaking admiration for a multimillion-pound bank heist and nothing but contempt for a stick-up in which the robbers escape with a few hundred quid.

CHEATING FOR CHARITY (AND WHY PSYCHOLOGISTS ARE APPARENTLY NICER THAN ECONOMISTS)

Perhaps the findings from the last section have left you feeling rather morally queasy. If so, the next study I want to share with you will probably make you better. Okay, it suggests that we're fine with cheating, but only if the money gained goes to someone else and is not pocketed by the cheats themselves.

This study was conducted at Bath University.[20] Students were asked to roll a dice under an upturned disposable coffee cup. They were then asked to peer through a little hole that had been punched in the base of the cup and to tell a researcher what number they could see. If the number was a one, the charity Cancer Research UK received a 10 pence donation, if it was a two, the charity got 20 pence, and so on.

Given how I've teed up this experiment, the results won't surprise you. Almost a quarter of people claimed to have rolled a six, which is a good deal more than you would expect by chance, and which means nearly one in ten of the students almost certainly lied in order to maximise the money the charity received.

Of course you might be thinking, why so few? In the circumstances, wouldn't everyone claim to have rolled a six and therefore maximised the money going to the cancer charity? Well, the probable reason that didn't happen is that the students had more than one go. In these circumstances, you can doubtless see why they didn't call 'six' every time.

That would have been a bit too shameless even for a good cause. They wanted their cheating to be somewhat believable, and so they called 'six' more often than was true, but threw in a few fours and threes for the sake of credibility.

What I didn't mention in relation to the experiment above was that it involved two groups of students. One group was studying economics and the other psychology. And the reason I didn't mention it was because the two groups didn't diverge significantly in their behaviour when it came to cheating for charity. But in a second experiment, where the cheating was for personal gain, things were different, and without wanting to be smug I must report that the psychologists came out of this rather better than the economists.

In this second experiment, the students were given three numbers and told to imagine these were the numbers from three dice they'd just thrown. They were then told that they should read out the sequence to a researcher, and that the first number they read out would be converted into a sum of money which they'd get to keep.

Of course the actual numbers a student was given could have been 1, 2 and 3, in which case that student would have got £1 if they'd honestly reported back. But then there was nothing to stop people lying. Perhaps not to the extent of suggesting they'd got 6, 6, 6: that would be pushing it. But if, for instance, you actually got 3, 2, 5, why not at least say the sequence went 5, 2, 3 so that you get £5 instead of £3?

A small deceit perhaps, but a deceit all the same. So what happened? Well, I've rather given the game away, but after the experiment the students were asked to fess up, at which point it was discovered that the economists were more likely to lie in order to keep more money than the psychologists.

Interestingly, this experiment is in tune with others that show economists are rather more ruthless about money-making than others. For instance, it's been shown that economics students give less to charity, with one study showing that the number who admitted to giving nothing at all was double that of students in disciplines such as architecture and, yes, psychology. Even when income and gender were taken into account, economics students were found to be less likely to co-operate in tests like the Prisoner's Dilemma. This is a classic test of co-operation that was developed in the 1950s. The premise is this. You and a friend are arrested on suspicion of robbing a bank. You're in separate cells and you can choose between confessing, turning your friend in, or protesting your innocence. If you both deny it, you'll both get a year in prison; if you both confess, you'll get eight years; and if one of you accuses the other, they'll get 20 years and you'll go free.

From an individual's point of view the rational response might be to confess, thereby avoiding the worst outcome, the 20-year sentence. However, if you can be sure that your friend will co-operate, you could both stay silent and each get a year, a far better result for you as a pair. It all comes down to whether you can trust your friend. Today, it's usually played on a computer screen and the prison bit might not even be mentioned. Instead it is framed in terms of co-operating or defecting in order to gain points or money. Economics students were not keen on co-operation, and in a 1981 study into how much fairness mattered, a third of economics students refused to answer the question or gave answers so oblique as to be uncodeable.[21]

Perhaps this is not all that surprising: after all, economics students are taught to see the world as one in which rational economic actors seek to maximise their economic gain, and by so doing create greater prosperity for all. But does their training in the use of economic models emphasising the virtue of acting in your own self-interest explain some selfishness in money matters among economists? Or is it rather the case that people with an interest in holding onto their money are attracted into the study of economics in the first place?

One study that sought to discover the answer compared students at the start and at the end of their degree courses, and found that those studying other subjects became slightly more generous as they approached graduation while economics students remained at the same less-generous level throughout.[22]

So, are all economists self-serving and money grabbing? The answer, of course, is no. Moreover, much of the most interesting work in economics these days is influenced by psychology and argues that the notion of ruthless, rational economic actors behaving in their own best interest bears little relation to reality. Indeed it recognises that as well as sometimes behaving co-operatively and generously, people can actually be quite poor at making the right financial decisions. And of course I do realise that some of my favourite studies in this book were conducted by economists.

In their 1978 book on personality and money, the psychologists Herb Goldberg and Robert Lewis list a whole page of signs that they say show that a person has an irrational view of money.[23] These include feeling uncomfortable if you have money left over at the end of the month which you haven't spent; knowing you're being taken advantage of every time you make a major purchase; and firmly believing that money will solve all your problems. What struck me reading the list was how many of the signs might apply to me. It's a comfort to know that more recent work in the field of behavioural economics suggests we all have what might be termed an irrational view of money at times.

But there's one group who make some particularly curious decisions, and it is to those people that we head now.

GAMBLING

Gambling is not about money. That is what most gamblers say, and certainly what former pathological gambler Paul Buck told me. Between 2003 and 2011 he lost £1.3 million through gambling via 93 different accounts. To pay the debts, he found a way of taking money from work. But he told me he would have gambled in cream cakes if he could have found a lorry-load of them or six inch nails if he'd known where to get buckets full of them. But what he could get was money, and it soon took over his life.

So for a few people like Paul, money is more than something to worry about it. Whether they gamble, hoard or spend it, money has become far more than a symbol or a means to an end. It has become a disorder. Not surprisingly compulsive spenders have been found to have low self-esteem, to feel conflict over spending and to view money as something imbued with status and power. Research with people attending groups for compulsive shoppers in the US cities of Phoenix, Tucson, Denver, Colorado and Detroit found that they scored lower on their desire for money as security than other people did, but higher on wanting money for the status and power it can bring. They were also more likely to view money as a solution to problems and as a way of comparing themselves with other people. As you might expect, they were more likely than other people to feel that they didn't have enough money.[24] There are very few money-related disorders for which there are formal diagnostic criteria, but gambling is the one that has received the bulk of the attention from researchers.

Paul had no interest in betting until he was 18. He was at Leeds University when he placed his first bet at the bookies. He had a large early win when he put £5 each way on a horse that won at 33:1. He can still remember the buzz of that victory 20 years later. But it wasn't about the money, he insists.

So what was it about? Was it the thrill of the gamble? Back in the seventeenth century the philosopher Blaise Pascal insisted that the possibility of a reward formed the main attraction in gambling: 'Make him play for nothing,' he wrote. 'He will not become excited over it, and will feel bored.'[25] Almost 350 years later, several psychologists have tried this in the lab. And it seems Pascal was on to something. If you wire people up to measure their heart rates, those gambling for real stakes will show faster-beating hearts than those playing for nothing.[26]

But what if you gave people the choice between a gamble and a sure thing, which would the gamblers choose? Researchers in Virginia in the United States had people play a game in which they had to choose between a guaranteed win of $2 or a 50 per cent chance of winning $2. The answer sounds obvious. If you want the money you take the first option. Or if suspense is your thing, you can pay to take the second. In advance people say they will go for the sure thing, but when you get them to actually play the game and to play 40 or so trials in a row, everything changes. Quite often the non-gamblers choose the more exciting option, possibly to liven up the psychology experiment. But when it comes to the gamblers, do they go for the thrill of the gamble? Surely that's what they really like. No, they opt for the sure thing.[27] This experiment would suggest that financial rewards do motivate gamblers after all. Or is it just that they soon learn that the house always wins out in the end, and – as their debts begin to build up – they have no alternative but to be very interested in any money presented as a sure thing?

As a gambling disorder develops, the thrill of winning money diminishes. It is no longer fun, but it can feel curiously safe. While Paul was at university, he didn't have the time or the money to spend much time gambling, but once he got a job in retail after he'd finished his degree, he began doing it every day.

He says his gambling was never about affording a luxury car or an island. But that he liked feeling safe when he gambled, as if he was in his own little bubble. Whenever he felt he was out of his comfort zone in his job, gambling took him to a place where he felt calm.

Then in 2001 he became a financial adviser, his salary tripled, and he climbed quickly from a problem gambler to a compulsive one and then rapidly to a pathological gambler. In his job, he was dealing with stocks and shares every day, gambling, some would say, on what might do well. He thinks this fuelled the gambling he was doing outside work. At first, there was the adrenaline rush of beating the bookies, but soon he was spending between £300 and £900 every day after work.

Once his wife and three kids had gone to bed, he would continue betting online. As he put it, 'Gambling became the centre of my world. It enveloped my brain completely. It's always in your mind where the next bet is.'

In the UK almost 1 per cent of the population is affected by pathological gambling. Researchers have tried to work out whether there are certain personality types who are more prone to developing such problems. There is evidence that pathological gamblers are more impulsive and also more obsessed with money, but perhaps once they've lost hundreds of thousands of pounds they can't be anything but obsessed with money, with the constant need to look for the chance to recoup their losses.[28] This is the ultimate example of money as both a drug and a tool. The next bet is always on a pathological gambler's mind. Even walking past a betting shop causes a response in their brains, just as the ephemera of drug-taking – scales, or syringes or mirrored surfaces – do for people addicted to drugs. Yet the money is also a tool. They *need* to be obsessed with money to find enough of it to continue.

What we need to know is which comes first – the gambling or the impulsivity. Most research just take a snapshot in time, but there is the occasional longitudinal study that follows people over time, such as one conducted in New Zealand. Just over a thousand babies born between 1972 and 1973 in Dunedin on the South Island have been followed up ever since, regularly flown from wherever they live in the world back to Dunedin to take part in interviews, physical examinations, blood tests and surveys.[29] Some people drop out, of course, but when the gambling study took place, 91 per cent of those original babies, now very much adults, were still taking part. This is an exceptionally high participation rate, which gives us an unusually representative sample. And having met the researchers on eight different lengthy occasions by the time this study on gambling took place, these young adults are likely to be happier to tell the truth than in other studies.

At the age of 18, each young person took part in a personality assessment. Three years later, in 1993, they were interviewed for the first time about whether they gambled. The first casino didn't open in New Zealand until the following year, but with more than eight thousand slot machines and plenty of horse and dog races, there were in fact more opportunities to gamble there than there were in the US at the time.

Those who gambled a lot at the age of 21 were found to have scored higher on risk-taking and impulsivity at the age of 18 than those who didn't gamble so much three years on. They worried more, experienced more anger and aggression, and felt victimised more often. This points to the personality factors preceding the gambling problem. Of course, when it comes to personality and behaviour, the direction of causality is always hard to establish, but considering how many other studies find that impulsivity is a risk factor, it seems likely that this aspect of personality played a part in leading them to gamble.

Other researchers have looked at impulsivity in the laboratory. Will people choose to have £15 now or £35 in 13 days' time? The gamblers tend to take the money now.[30] They also found that when people are in a particularly bad or particularly good mood, they are even more likely to behave impulsively.

When you place a bet, your cortisol levels rise, and your

heart rate increases while you wait for the result.[31] If you are new to gambling, the excitement of each bet reinforces your behaviour. You do it again. And maybe again.

But if you become a problem gambler, everything changes.

For Paul, the more he gambled, the more the thrill disappeared. 'From 2009 to 2011 there was no enjoyment at all. There were times I would wake up at two in the morning, go downstairs and put ten, or twenty or thirty thousand pounds on Brazilian football or Australian horse racing. I didn't know anything about either of them. Then I'd get up at 5am to see if I'd won, not that I really cared.'

Winning didn't help. He never considered using his winnings to pay off his bills. Instead he would hide the cash inside the spare tyre in his car. It didn't make him feel good. All he could think about was when to gamble it away again.

'I remember winning at horse racing on a Saturday morning. I turned £3,000 into £15,000, but all day it played on my mind this money was sitting in my account. As soon as my wife had gone to bed, I logged on to my computer and played online roulette. An hour and five minutes later, I had turned that win into a loss of £39,000.' It was then that he felt better. 'There was a sense of release when I was left with nothing to gamble.'

Some gambling programmes teach financial strategies as part of the treatment, but an Australian study found that gamblers' financial knowledge is no worse or better than anyone else's. In fact, like any gambler, Paul knew full well that in the end the house always wins. But there is a key difference in the way gamblers think. They may have financial nous in some ways, but they often make illogical decisions. Paul admits that he did so himself.

This is backed up by some of the most intriguing research on the topic. If I were to show you a slot machine showing two oranges and a strawberry, the chances are you would deem that a loss. You need three of the same to win and you only have two, so you lose. But problem gamblers see it as a near miss. Two oranges is almost three, so they nearly win. Likewise if their horse comes in second or third, they will interpret that as a sign that they're getting closer to winning, not that they lost their stake.

Even rats do something similar when faced with what the researchers call rodent slot machines. When they are given a drug called quinpirole, which makes them more obsessed with rewards, they behave as though losses are near misses.[32]

One particular distortion in the way we consider the odds of winning even has its own name in the world of statistics – the gambler's fallacy. And you don't have to be a gambler to fall for this one.

If people are playing roulette, for example, and the previous win was a black, 75 per cent of people will bet on red next, believing there's a better chance of red coming up. The next spin of the wheel is in no way affected by the previous one, so it's just as likely to come up black again. But we find that hard to believe. Gamblers even more so. And anything involving a choice makes them *more* confident. So if gamblers choose the number of their own lottery ticket, they are more convinced it will be the winning ticket than if the number has been chosen at random.[33]

Some of the most fascinating research of all deals with gamblers' brains. There's a neurological test called the Iowa Gambling Task, where people are given four decks of cards and asked to pick cards from any of the decks. Some cards win you money. Some lose it. Decks A and B are set up so that the wins are big, but the losses are even larger, so over time you lose. Decks C and D have smaller wins, but even smaller losses, so over time you can win more. Gradually people learn which deck they like and after a hundred trials most people favour decks C and D. But patients with damage to a part of the brain called the ventromedial prefrontal cortex (known as the vmPFC for short) continue to favour decks A and B, despite the large losses.[34]

Gamblers do the same. Psychologists have told me how extraordinary it is to watch such people do it, losing more and more money when it seems obvious that they should choose the other decks. But brain scans show that they have something in common with the people with damage to the vmPFC – they have less activity in this area than you see in other people's brains. We already know that people with a low functioning vmPFC find it harder to foresee consequences or to defer gratification. However – before we read too much into these studies – we have to bear in mind that some are very small, with as few as seven people taking part. But is it possible that the reward system in problem gamblers is underactive? Could they be trying to compensate for that? In other words, do they need to take bigger risks to get even small thrills.

The more impulsive people are, the more susceptible they are to errors in reasoning, which could explain the link between impulsivity and problems gambling. Research at the only NHS clinic in England specifically for people with gambling problems has found that gamblers are more likely than everyone else to have superstitious rituals, such as carrying lucky charms, or to explain losses away as bad luck.[35]

For Paul, what he loved about gambling was the escapism. He knew it was bringing him down, but couldn't stop.

In 2011, Paul was reading an article about the way pathological gamblers think and behave, when he recognised himself in the description. He spent the next six days online searching for tools which assess problem gamblers. On every test, he was near the top of the scale. His problem was very serious. So serious, that he decided he only had one option, which was to end his life. He attempted suicide and was unconscious for more than four hours. This was the prompt for him to go to the National Problem Gambling Clinic in a side street in London's Soho.

The clinic treats more than a thousand people a year and consultant psychiatrist Henrietta Bowden-Jones says sometimes they have gambled away their family home, usually with their spouse knowing nothing about their problem until it's too late. For many, gambling runs in their families. Some were sent to the bookies as children to place bets for their dads. Others were left in the street as kids for hours at a time while their parent was in the bookies. But not everyone has early life experiences related to gambling. Some suffered abuse or bullying, or grew up with a sibling who was very ill. For these people, gambling might feel like some sort of escape.

During eight weekly group sessions of cognitive behavioural therapy, clients consider the causes in their own individual case, assess the consequences, and learn practical strategies for giving up gambling and replacing it with something less harmful. Each gambler writes a list on a piece of paper of the things they think are good about not gambling. They keep it in their pocket and when they feel the urge to gamble, they take it out to remind themselves of why they shouldn't do it.

Paul was taught to avoid everything to do with gambling. He couldn't carry any money, had to avoid all computers and could never watch big sporting events. It wasn't easy. He put on weight, developed a rash on his face and frequently found himself shaking.

People's behaviour can shift surprisingly fast. Dr Bowden-Jones says the key is the combination of the removal of every temptation to gamble and the discovery of the right replacement activities. For a long time all their money has been spent on gambling, so going out for a nice meal or buying treats can act as a real incentive.

Four months after beginning treatment, Paul started to feel as though he had some sort of control over his life. And in the three years since, he hasn't gambled a single penny. He told me that now even the desire to gamble has gone. Today he runs a consultancy specialising in intervening in the workplace to prevent problem gambling. He says that people sometimes ask him whether he could place a bet occasionally without gambling becoming an issue again. So could he? 'I'll never know,' he tells me, 'because I'll never try.'

12

GOOD MONEY

Why giving money away (and even paying tax)
increases our happiness, why we don't always like
generous millionaires and why charity campaigns
might do better with less pretty children.

WE'VE JUST SEEN how money can have a bad effect on us,
or lead us to do the wrong thing. But I hope I've made it
clear that I don't think money is generally bad. Far from it.
It exists because it's useful, and – if we're in control of it, if
we exert mind over money – it helps us to do good things
and to lead, in the broadest sense, a good life.

Most obviously, money is a positive force when we donate
it to worthy causes. This is a classic win/win situation. We
achieve something worthwhile in the world but we also *feel*
warm about ourselves.

One morning, people walking down a street in the
Canadian city of Vancouver were asked to take part in an
experiment. Those who agreed were given an envelope
containing either a $5 or $20 note. The envelope also

contained written instructions. Half the people were told they should spend the money on themselves. The other half were instructed to use the money to buy a present for someone else or to donate the money to charity. In both cases, they had until 5pm that day to spend the money.

That evening, the researchers spoke to all the participants. The first group said they'd bought a variety of things for themselves – sushi, earrings and coffee were all mentioned. People from the second group bought toys for younger relatives, food treats for friends or gave the money to homeless people in the street. Then the researchers asked each participant to rate their mood.

The sum of money they'd found in the envelope made no difference to people's level of happiness. And the particular things bought weren't that important either. What mattered was *who* they spent their money on. The people who'd spent it on someone else felt significantly happier than those who treated themselves.[1]

This experiment was designed by the psychologist Elizabeth Dunn, who had also conducted a survey of a representative sample of people living in the United States, controlling for income, and found the happiest people are those who spend the highest proportion of their income on other people.

Interestingly, when Dunn's own students were asked whether people would get more joy out of spending $20 on themselves or $20 on others, they assumed most people would be selfish. And of course not everybody gets joy from giving. Studies from neuroscience have shown that some people experience greater activity in the ventral striatum area of the brain, part of the brain's reward system, when they get to keep money; while others experience it when they give money away.[2]

When you think about it, this is not very surprising. We don't need scans to tell us that attitudes to money vary. But what was interesting was that the brain activity detected by the scanners reflected people's different attitudes accurately, allowing researchers to distinguish between people they dubbed 'the altruists' – who in some quite fundamental sense were drawn to being generous – and those they called 'the egoists' – who were inclined to be more selfish.

When I mentioned this study to a friend, he suggested – half in jest – that perhaps governments could use brain scans to detect the egoists and therefore crack down on tax evasion. It's theoretically possible, I suppose, but it sounds rather Orwellian. After all, as one of the authors of the paper, economics professor William Harbaugh, explained, to carry out their experiment they needed 'a $3 million scanner, some liquid helium and a few weeks of computer time'. To scan the brains of all citizens to weed out tax dodgers would therefore cost hundreds of millions, require huge vats of liquid helium and years of time to analyse the results. And that's if you could persuade people to slide into the scanner in the first place.

So for the time being at least, those less generous souls need not worry that they will find themselves recorded on some official database as an egoist. It's not a very pleasant label to have after all; the label altruist has a much nicer ring to it.

Yet of course most altruists are not being entirely selfless. As we've already seen, at least part of the reason they give money away is because it gives them pleasure. And that warm glow of pleasure increases if others witness their generosity.

LOOK AT ME, I'M SOOO GENEROUS

I used to live quite near the small Tricycle Theatre in Kilburn, north-west London. As with other such independent theatres, it needs support from individuals to keep going, and it offers various tiers of membership to entice people to donate. Those who support get priority booking and the chance to mingle with directors and actors at back-stage events. But a large part of it is pure philanthropy. The cheapest tier of membership is 'Trailblazers', which costs a minimum of £125 a year. Then comes 'Innovators' (£500+), 'Pioneers' (£1,250), and finally 'Director's Circle', which will set you back £3,000.

I must confess that, though I love the place, I've never been a member so I don't want to downplay in any way the generosity of the various Trailblazers, Innovators, Pioneers and members of the Director's Circle. But that said, you'll find all their names listed on the Tricycle's website – which is doubtless part of the appeal of the scheme. Certainly research has found that donors enjoy the prestige of giving publicly in this way. But it's also shown that once donors have decided which tier they can afford, they don't tend to give more than the minimum amount required.[3] So I'd bet that the majority of Tricycle 'Pioneers' give almost exactly £1,250, and if they could afford nearer £2,500 they wouldn't just give that amount and stay a Pioneer, they'd find the extra £500 and trade up to the Director's Circle.

Which leads me to give this tip to fundraising managers: while there are clearly limits to the number of different tiers a patrons' scheme could have before it gets ridiculous, it would be a good idea to have as many as you can, particularly clustered at the lower end. This will encourage people to dig just a little deeper into their pockets so that they can get into the next category. So, at the Tricycle, they perhaps want to consider putting in 'Explorers' at £250 a year to lure a few Trailblazers up the giving scale.

There's nothing wrong with wanting recognition for your generosity. If you're going to give to charity, why shouldn't other people know about it? Whenever I'm asked to sponsor a friend who's running the marathon on JustGiving or an equivalent site I let them – and the world – know I've donated by recording my name alongside my 'Rather you than me' message. And I'm not alone. When I checked at random some JustGiving pages for various charities, on the two I found with the highest levels of donations – both coincidentally in aid of Leukaemia and Lymphoma Research – 94 per cent and 88 per cent of people had given their names. Only a small minority donated anonymously.

For charities themselves, the benefits of going public with people's level of donation are obvious. To use the French expression, it helps *pour encourager les autres*. We all know how this works. Your good friend is doing that triathlon for Breast Cancer Research, and you think £15 is a generous enough donation. But then you see that a mutual friend has given £30. How's it going to look if you only give half as much? When researchers from University College London analysed 2,500 online donation pages, they indeed found that after a higher-than-average donation, subsequent sponsors offered an extra £10 on average.[4] And if the fundraiser was an attractive woman and the bigger-than-average donor was a man, then subsequent men offered an average of £38 extra. So if you're trying to raise money online and you're a woman, the lesson from this is to get a male friend to make a large donation right at the start. Then watch the money flood in. But what about the attractiveness bit, I hear you say? That's something you don't get a choice about. Well, not necessarily. When the researchers had people rate the photos on attractiveness, the biggest factor affecting their ratings was whether or not the person was smiling. So say cheese for that photo and the charity will thank you.

Likewise, charity auctions work best when competition starts between two or three individuals, not so much to win the prize, but to display their wealth and to appear the most generous. I've seen this happen at charity dinners, and it can be quite tedious for the rest of us as the bidding for a week in a villa in Spain goes up and up and up – and on and on and on. But while we get fed up of seeing two rich boys in dinner jackets competing to show who is top dog in the richness stakes, the charity's fundraising staff are sitting there rubbing their hands with glee.

All of this might seem so obvious that there's no need for psychological research to prove it. But of course studies have been done.

One such study was carried out in Japan. People were told they'd repeatedly be given a small sum of money (the equivalent of three euros), and each time they had to decide whether to keep it or donate it to charity. The number of charities was large – 78 in total, ranging from UNICEF to the Sea Turtle Association of Japan to the Japan Spinal Cord Foundation – so there was something for everyone.

The names of the charities flashed up on a screen inside a brain scanner. Some of the participants were also able to see on their screen that they were being watched, while others were not observed.

In fact, to make the experiment easier to run, the first group were victims of an elaborate ruse. The room with two chairs and a video link they'd been shown before the experiment was empty and the people they saw on their screen in the scanner were actors who'd been filmed earlier. But it appeared these two people were carefully watching their decisions. And while they revealed no emotion, they moved and they blinked – and so surely they were making judgements?

So what happened?

On average all the participants donated to fewer than half the charities, and kept just over half the money for themselves. But people were significantly more likely to donate if they thought they were being watched.[5]

The intriguing thing about this study is that their brain activity revealed that donating money publicly was just as rewarding as keeping money for themselves while no one was watching. Both felt good. Yet being watched made all the difference to their behaviour.

TAINTED ALTRUISM

While we might think that charitable giving would be that much more laudable if we did it without fanfare, we're generally pretty forgiving of generosity being publicly recognised. The same isn't true though if people are seen to profit personally from charity.

Indeed this is known in psychology as the tainted altruism effect – and it can see people go from hero to zero almost overnight.

The researchers George Newman and Dalyian Cain from Yale University tell the story of an American fundraiser called

Daniel Pallotta.[6] In nine years his company raised more than $300 million for charities funding research into AIDS and breast cancer. You'd think he would be applauded, and for a time he was. But then it became clear that he was running a business and making a profit from his fundraising. He was also paying himself a big salary. A cool $400,000, no less. Suddenly his popularity collapsed and his company folded.

What this story shows is that really we want charities to run on a voluntary basis, despite the fact that the third sector is now a huge part of modern economies. It's why we tend to admire old soldiers out with their tins collecting for the Poppy Appeal, and to resent young chuggers who we know are paid commission if they sign people up to direct debits. One seems like a selfless act, the other like aggressive salesmanship.

And yet the charities persist with chugging despite its unpopularity, because it brings in larger and longer-lasting sums than street collections. And we don't expect employees of charities to do their jobs for free, or energy companies and stationery suppliers to provide their services to charities for nothing. So, our views on altruism and money are a curious mix.

Imagine there's an owner of a chain of shops who wants to drum up some more business. Is he a more ethical person if he donates £1 million to charity in order to get publicity, or if he spends the amount on advertising? This kind of scenario was put to people taking part in a study at Yale University, and respondents decided it was better for the businessman to pay for advertising rather than give money to charity, as in the latter case his intentions weren't pure. They preferred that no money went to charity than for the businessman to make a profit.

It's quite a remarkable finding and made more curious by the next stage of the study. Because when an additional sentence was added saying: 'He could have invested the money in advertising. This would have also increased the reputation of his company, but none of the money would have gone to charity', people changed their minds and no longer saw his altruism as tainted.[7] Again, we see how finely balanced our moral judgements about money are.

There are echoes of our disquiet at the idea of a friend offering to pay us for something which we think should be done as a favour (see Chapter 7). All of which is rather quaintly fastidious in a world where 'voluntary' organisations are contracted by governments to deliver essential services, and the bigger charities employ high-powered chief executives with MBAs, on large six-figure salaries, who run their organisations with ruthless business efficiency. Increasingly the boundaries between charitable activities, public services and business are blurred, with more and more organisations such as social enterprises and not-for-profits not fitting neatly into categories.

The moment money is considered in an interaction, our attitudes can change. Currently there is a movement in the UK against the practice of companies engaging unpaid interns because it means that valuable work experience can only be gained by those young people with parents rich enough to keep them. The companies are accused of exploitation. Yet when hundreds of so-called 'games-makers' worked for nothing at the London Olympics in 2012, no one suggested they were exploited. Very subtle differences in a situation can change our views on the intertwining of money and morality. If a young person volunteers for a charity and works abroad unpaid or even pays for the privilege, it is considered fair, but charities with unpaid interns in their offices at home are criticised.

In such a world, I'd suggest the key task for organisations working in areas which we generally associate with charity – international development, medical research, support groups and the like – is to be completely transparent about the way they operate, trusting that the public will understand that they need to run their affairs professionally, reward their staff, pay the market rate, etc., but making clear that they are not taking a profit and that as much money as possible raised from donors is going into front-line activities.

HOW WE MIGHT ENJOY PAYING TAX MORE THAN WE THINK WE DO

As we saw in the section before last, many of us get pleasure from giving money away to good causes – particularly if our charity is publicly recognised. But do we enjoy the same warm glow when we pay our taxes?

You can NOT be serious, I suspect many of you will be shouting, à la John McEnroe. But stop to think about it for a moment. The money you give to the taxman helps to fund some of the things we most value: hospitals, schools, the police, parks, care for the elderly. The list goes on and on. If these things weren't publicly funded through taxation, some of them would have to be supported by charity, as they were in the past or are in some countries now – or they wouldn't exist at all. So why should we take pleasure from giving money to charity, but so resent paying tax?

Well, perhaps we don't. Bear with me here. At the University of Oregon, each participant in one group was given $100 and forced to pay a certain proportion of the sum in tax to fund a local food bank. The rest of the money they could keep. By contrast, the other group of participants was allowed to choose whether they wanted to donate to the food bank and if so, how much. When the payment was voluntary, satisfaction with the transaction was 10 per cent higher.[8]

Which proves people prefer voluntary giving to being forced to pay tax, right? Well, yes. But there was an intriguing finding from inside the participants' brains. Yes, once again, the volunteers in this experiment were having their brain activity monitored in a scanner. And while it was true that the scans showed people who gave voluntarily to the food bank experienced a warm glow of giving (activity in the ventral striatum), so too did the people who had no choice but to pay their tax.

So it seems our brains may be showing something that we don't like to admit – that we actually quite *like* paying taxes. And this study was conducted in the US, where there's more of a culture than in some places that taxes must always be low, because paying tax is bad, while philanthropy is good.

Personally, I think this is a very encouraging finding, but before high-spending governments around the world cheer too much at this news, it's important to bear in mind one aspect of this experiment. The people were aware of exactly where the money was going. They knew it was going to a food bank – in other words, it was a hypothecated tax, which finance ministers tend to dislike. People might have reacted differently if they knew the money was just going into the general tax coffers.

Nonetheless, I do wonder if governments might think about including along with dull and arduous tax return forms a brochure showing where tax revenue has been spent in the previous year, in the same way that charities and some local councils in the UK do. Or would people just resent the cost of the brochure? 'More of my money being wasted by the government!' Maybe it depends on whether you're an altruist or an egoist.

Or does paying a lot of tax somehow need to be reframed – not as a penalty, but as a symbol of success? The more you pay, the more successful you are perceived to be and the more you are seen to be doing something positive for your country.

LET'S BE CHARITABLE – SOMETIMES THE RICH ARE GENEROUS

In the last chapter we saw how the work of Paul Piff, among others, seems to have demonstrated that the rich tend to be egoists. That's to say, the more money a person has, the meaner and more selfish with that money they seem to be. But even if that's true on average (and as we'll see it's by no means clear that it is), it doesn't mean that everyone who is rich is mean.

The financier Warren Buffett announced in 2006 that he was to give away 99 per cent of his fortune. The announcement attracted lots of publicity, and since then he's had some success exhorting others among the super-rich to give away more money too.

Of course the super-generous super-rich don't tell us any more about the rich in general than those who are extraordinarily mean and miserly. We might expect that everyone would gradually become more generous if their salaries slowly rise over time. But does this happen in reality?

Well, it depends on what you call 'rich'. The classic research on giving tends to suggest that the proportion of income that people give to charity is higher both among the poorest and the richest and lower among people somewhere in the middle. When this is shown in a graph you get a U-shaped curve.[9]

Recent research by Boston College has challenged this picture. For a start, the researchers point out that the figures are skewed because they don't include people who give no money away at all – typically, the very poor. This means those on very low incomes are not as generous as was assumed – which perhaps should come as no surprise. They can't afford to be.

What is so surprising from the Boston research, though, is how similar the level of giving is among other income groups. Their findings show that in income bands starting at $10,000 and going right up to $300,000 – which covers 98 per cent of the American population – the average percentage of income given to charity from band to band is remarkably constant at roughly 2.3 per cent. Now of course that doesn't mean 98 per cent of Americans *all* give away *exactly* the same proportion of their income. Within the income bands there is variation – from people who give almost nothing, to people who give a lot more than 2.3 per cent. But even so, averaging it out, there is astonishingly little variation between those on low, middle and high incomes. Far from a U-shaped curve, it's pretty much a flat line. It's almost as if some cultural norm is operating, as if Americans impose on themselves a flat-rate charity tax for all income levels of approximately 2.3 per cent.

So, on these findings, the people we might call the

'ordinary' rich don't appear to be particularly generous. Of course if you're earning around $300,000, you are giving a greater *amount* away than if your income's $30,000: almost $7,000 on average compared with $700. But at that high-income level, the larger amount of money should be easier to find. Having paid the basics, you should have more cash to spare.

But what about the very top earners, the 2 per cent earning more than $300,000? Well, people in this income band, a wide one inevitably, do give away more – on average 4.4 per cent of their income. So, as a group, the super-rich could lay claim to being more generous in their charitable giving. But again, for every Buffet there's a miserable miser, one hauling the average up and one dragging it down.[10]

All in all, the Boston research would appear to suggest that the rich are neither more generous nor stingier than the rest of us – except at the top end, where some remarkable philanthropists probably account for the super-rich as a group seeming rather more generous than everyone else.

And yet, of course, there's always another study that might suggest something different. Data collected by the newspaper *The Chronicle of Philanthropy* in 2014, for example. It seems to show that since the recession hit the United States, it was the rich, rather than the people on middle or low incomes, who stopped giving so much of their money away.[11]

Or this next study, which takes us back to the clumsy experimenters I described in Chapter 11. It was June 2010, and a group of researchers were walking up and down London streets dropping letters onto the pavement. In all, they dropped 15 in each of 20 different areas, each stamped and addressed by hand to a name that might be male or female, at an address which sounded residential. So how many got posted on and by whom?

Well, in this study the rich seem to have shown their more generous side. For 87 per cent of the letters dropped in richer areas, such as wealthy Wimbledon or posh Pinner, were picked up and put in post boxes, compared with just 37 per cent in poorer districts, like Limehouse and Shadwell.[12]

EXTRAORDINARY ALTRUISM

Another aspect of giving, in which the better-off appear to show their generous side, is with what are known as 'acts of extraordinary altruism'. These are actions that give very few extraneous benefits to the giver – this time there's no plaque with their name on, no one is applauding their generosity and there's no chance of someone doing the same for them in return.

Take living kidney donation to a stranger, for example. It involves pain, recovery time and numerous medical and psychological tests, all for no money and all to help someone you don't know and are never going to meet. So while surveys in the United States have suggested up to half of people would be prepared to donate a kidney to a stranger, the number who actually do is far lower. Indeed, between 1999 and 2010 fewer than a thousand donations took place in the US, with none happening at all in some states, such as Delaware and Mississippi.

By contrast, in Utah the number was 76.

So why was there such a difference between states? Kristin Brethel-Haurwitz and Abigail Marsh from Georgetown University tried to find out.[13] They looked at various factors including religiosity, which perhaps helps to explain why devoutly Mormon Utah came out top. But the strongest predictor was median income level. Simply put, states where people earned more money saw more kidney donations.

This doesn't of course mean that richer individuals are more likely to donate a kidney than poorer people. Too few donations have taken place to examine the characteristics of the individual donors. What it does suggest, however, is that higher altruism seems to be associated with increasing affluence in a population. And yet it's not affluence *per se* that's the key factor. Rather it's wellbeing. That's to say, the states with higher average incomes had higher rates of wellbeing, and it was this factor that seemed to lead people there to behave in a more altruistic way.

So if the United States wants to reduce the death rate among people waiting for kidney donations, which currently runs to 5,000 a year, it should be looking to raise the median income in all states, which in turn will raise wellbeing and therefore altruism. For if every American had an income and level of wellbeing on a par with Utah, there might be an extra 900 donations a year – almost the same number that took place in total during the 11 years covered by the study.

As generous as it is to donate a kidney, it is a relatively safe procedure for the donor. But what if death were a very real possibility? How do people behave in this situation, and does the amount of money they have make a difference?

Mitchell Hoffman from the University of California, Berkeley, has attempted an ambitious study to try to answer this question, using a complex methodology to examine what was, after all, a very complex real-life situation.[14]

During the Second World War, many thousands of people in Europe agreed to save the lives of Jews by hiding them in their homes, despite knowing that if they were ever caught they would themselves face execution. Here was a most truly extraordinary form of altruism. They couldn't even tell anyone else about their bravery, let alone gain any recognition for it. In fact, their friends and neighbours were likely to disapprove. Who, Hoffman wanted to know, would do such a thing?

First, he analysed a series of interviews with rescuers and non-rescuers, in which people had been asked whether or not they considered themselves well-off. He also examined the 'Yad Vashem Righteous among the Nations' list, compiled by the National Holocaust Museum in Israel, which recognises non-Jews who put their own life, freedom or position at risk in order to save Jews from the threat of death or deportation to a death camp.

Hoffman then looked at the 20 countries where the highest number of Jews were rescued and compared the average incomes in those countries, as well as taking lots of measures to reduce the risk of confounding his findings with other factors. And what he found was that in the countries with a higher GDP, where people were on average richer, such as Italy and the Netherlands, more people rescued Jews than in poorer countries such as Moldova and Romania. Indeed a 10 per cent rise in income was associated with a 20 per cent increase in the number of Jews rescued.

You're probably thinking that there could have been all sorts of differences between the political situations in those countries that would affect the decision to hide someone in your house or turn them away. Hoffman concedes that in

Poland, for example, people were living in a regime so repressive that people were frequently executed for something as small as owning a radio or breaking a curfew. The punishment for hiding someone in your home was not only your own execution, but that of your family as well. So it's not surprising that fewer people dared save Jews.

But when Hoffman redoes his calculations, excluding the figures for Poland, the results remain the same. But surely, you might think, if you have more money, it gives you more opportunities to save people. So he recalculates taking into account the number of rooms each person had in their home, in case this made it easier to help. Again the results were the same.

Of course it would be wise to be very cautious about these findings, particularly given the extremely sensitive subject matter, but even so Hoffman's models do show that better-off countries saved more Jews and that within a country the richer people tended to be more generous. Which if nothing else suggests that the widely held view that rich people are always more selfish is certainly not always true. Thankfully, people from all socio-economic groups are capable of great generosity and self-sacrifice, just as they're equally capable of horrific acts of selfishness and evil.

INDUCING PEOPLE TO GIVE AWAY THEIR MONEY

Whoever they get their money from, the rich or the poor, charities are always on the look-out for ways of attracting more donations. People are employed to work on charity appeals, crafting messages that emphasise the importance of the charity's work or pull on our heart strings. But what sort of language is the most effective in inducing people to give more?

A neat experiment in 14 bakeries in Brittany provides some clues. This was conducted by Nicolas Guéguen, the same psychologist who did the studies on waiters getting bigger tips when they presented the bill on a heart-shaped dish or touched customers lightly on the arm. This time his study wasn't about tips, but charitable donations. On the counter of each bakery, above the *tarte tatins*, the *pains au chocolate* and the *croissants*, a collecting tin was placed. On the label of every tin was identical information about the humanitarian work carried out by a charity in Togo in West Africa. But one single word was different. A third of the tins used the phrase 'donating = loving'; another third said 'donating = helping'; while the final third – the control tins – simply used the word 'donating'.

What we don't know is whether that word 'loving' induced more people to give or whether the same number of people donated, but gave more; but anyway, the tins with 'loving' on the label contained almost twice as much money as the 'helping' tins.[15]

The researchers speculated that once again the power of priming was at play, with the word 'loving' evoking feelings of compassion, solidarity and support, which led people to be more altruistic. I'd suggest 'loving' is an even more powerful primer than that, being such an emotional and personal word, drawing us to think of loved ones who we dearly want to protect. Anyway, it clearly worked wonders. By comparison, the researchers concluded that the word 'helping' was not just a bit redundant but was also an instrumental term, seeming to require something of people and stripping them of their freedom to donate. The fact that the word to donate in French, 'donner', is also used when you want to order someone to do something (*donnez-moi mon billet*) might also have had an impact.

All in all, love might seem a strong word to use in charitable appeals – after all we generally don't know the person we are helping with a donation, so how can we love them? But perhaps charities shouldn't be shy of using the word.

Charities could also turn to some other psychological studies that don't have the results we might expect. In a typical appeal after a cyclone, what could be more persuasive than a photograph of a family standing outside their flattened home, looking desperate, waiting for help to arrive, with one of the older children holding a beautiful baby with big eyes smiling up at you? Who could resist that?

A lot of people, it turns out. Various studies point to different problems with this classic image. First, we are more likely to give money if we see people as active participants, rather than passive victims, so a film of a family trying to build themselves a new shelter, however rudimentary, will make us more inclined to give them some money. Even when people have nothing left, it seems we still don't want them to look as though they're just standing around waiting for help.

But surely attractive children, smiling through adversity, would induce us to give? Again, not always.

Researchers at the University of Alberta asked people to visit made-up websites which described the options for sponsoring a child whose family had been caught up in a mudslide or a tsunami. On some of the sites, the photos showed very pretty children; on others, the children were less attractive.[16]

If the site said that the child had lost their parents and

their home as a result of the disaster, it made no difference how pretty the child was, but in less dire circumstances, people felt less empathy towards the pretty children and judged that they were less in need of help. Even though they were so young, people judged the prettiest children to be more intelligent, popular and more able to help themselves. Less photogenic children had the advantage here: they were viewed as more helpless. It led the authors of the study to go as far as suggesting that if charities want to raise as much money as possible they should deliberately use unflattering lighting to make sure the kids don't look too appealing.

The reason that charity appeals often focus on an individual story is that it's assumed that people are more likely to give away their money if they can identify with a particular person, and to try to imagine what it would be like to need help so desperately. But recent research shows that, in some circumstances, charities could fare better focusing on the organisation instead.[17] People hear so many individual stories that such tales can start to lose their impact. Individual campaigns also encourage donors to focus just on the people in the specific appeal, whereas what an NGO really needs is repeated donations from people who become committed to their organisation.

As members of the public, we're not even very good at judging how much need there is after a disaster. Donations tend to vary according to the number of deaths, not the number of survivors. So we're more likely to donate to a fund if an earthquake killed ten thousand people, leaving a thousand survivors in need of help, than if the death toll was a thousand, and ten thousand people were left in desperate need of food and shelter.[18]

And if there's any chance of finding a reason to blame

the victim, for example, where deforestation has led to mudslides, then stories of individuals can backfire. But there's another psychological reason why individual stories will work better in some situations than others.

Construal level theory explains how our thinking changes depending on how psychologically near an event feels. This can happen in all sorts of realms. So when it comes to time perception, for example, if an event is happening tomorrow we think about it in more concrete terms than if it's happening in six months' time, when we consider it more abstractly.[19] The same happens depending on how socially close we feel to someone. So if you're a farmer, you think more concretely about another farmer's experiences than you would about a doctor's, for example. And this can increase – or decrease – the likelihood that you will give to a particular charity.

In Israel psychologists recruited 300 people and told them about a rehabilitation centre for the survivors of road accidents. The centre was facing cuts. People were told that, if they chose to donate to the charity, their money would be used for one of four purposes. One group was told it would help an individual woman who had been in a serious car accident and needed help with her day-to-day activities. Another group that it would help an individual man, similarly injured. The remaining groups were told only that their money would help men or women at the centre. So, sometimes a specific person was mentioned and at other times it was more general. Sometimes the person giving was of the same gender as the victim, and sometimes they weren't. This gave the experimenters all the different options to be able to ascertain how effective individual stories are in eliciting donations in different circumstances.

And the results suggest that it's not always the case that charities should focus on individual stories. To take women's responses, on average they were prepared to donate \$35 to help the specific woman who had been injured, but just \$16 to help the women in general. But this pattern was reversed for men. In line with construal theory, they thought more abstractly about individuals with whom they didn't particularly identify, with the result that they gave \$39 to help the men in general, but only \$19 to help an individual man.[20]

The lesson for charities is that if potential donors can identify with the individuals they're being asked to help, then individual stories could work well. But if that's not true, then it might be better appealing to more abstract notions, such as changing the world or addressing issues of social justice.

Incidentally, while we're on the subject of different patterns of donation by men and women, the most recent global annual survey from the Charities Aid Foundation found that in high-income countries, women give more than men despite having lower average earnings, while in low-income countries, men give away more. And the same survey found that the top country for giving, measured by the percentage of people who'd given any money in the last month, is, wait for it . . . Myanmar. Surprising perhaps, but possibly explained by the tradition of giving to Theravada Buddhist monks in that part of the world. Thailand also scored highly. But it was beaten to third place by mainly Catholic Malta. Then came Ireland, and the largely secular UK.[21]

So when it comes to giving, our behaviour, as always, is complex, but it is clear that there are some patterns – patterns that charities could put to good use, if they want to garner more donations.

13

FOR A RAINY DAY

Why speaking German could help you to save more, what Odysseus can teach us about saving and how piggy banks are helping in the fight against malaria.

'THOSE WHO THRIVE exercise thrift.' It may sound like an old saying, but as far as I know I've just made it up. Not that this necessarily makes it less true. Of course, in the popular imagination, a person who thrives – in other words, who sees their material wealth increase – is often viewed as a risk taker, while thrift is a word generally associated with sparing expenditure, frugality even. Yet the two words have the same root for a reason. For most people who become prosperous – and more to the point, stay that way – do owe part of that prosperity to careful financial management as well as to bold entrepreneurialism or audacious speculations.

And we, in our small way, also appreciate that if we're to avoid hardship, we need to know not just how to earn sufficient money and to spend it sensibly, but also how to put enough aside for the future, to invest and save. Indeed there is probably no area in which asserting mind over money is more critical.

Yet many of us find saving very difficult. I certainly do. Ironically, it's a little easier if the thing we're saving for is not that important in the grand scheme of things. Putting money aside for a wedding or a holiday (or a lute) involves short-term sacrifices of course, but the reward is usually only months away – and we can enjoy imagining and anticipating it. By contrast, general, long-term saving for unforeseen circumstances, for old age or illness, is harder. We know it's sensible. It could be vital. But the thing we're saving for can be a long way off, indeed it might never happen – and it doesn't promise much in the way of pleasure. In the meantime, we are surrounded by immediate temptations.

In advanced economies, a bewildering variety of vehicles and schemes, of seemingly ever-greater complexity, have sprung up to 'help' us to save. But in order to make use of them, we need to recognise that a saving scheme that might work well for one type of person won't do the job for another. This is an area where the insights of psychological research can prove especially useful. Psychology shows that although sometimes we appear to make irrational choices about our money, in the longer term those decisions can turn out to be quite sensible. And the reason that's true is because we recognise that we are fallible human beings rather than rational actors and sometimes need to resort to devices that save us from the worst of ourselves.

So where to begin? Well, financial advisers often encourage us to spread whatever savings we have around. There's one indisputably good reason for this. It spreads risk. If a fund in which we have an investment goes belly up, that's always going to be bad news. But it's much worse of course if *all* our savings were in it. But this only really applies to the wealthy or to people who are speculating. Most people don't need to worry about this, because, for example in Europe, bank balances up to a certain amount are guaranteed in the event of a crisis. And it's not at all clear that putting your savings in lots of different pots is always sensible, even if you are wealthy.

Experiments in cognitive psychology have shown that when we're dealing with a lot of information, and the facts are fuzzy, we tend to make poor judgements. In particular, we tend to make judgements that are more favourable to us (and that's not always a good idea).

Let's take athletes as an example. Ask a sprinter to estimate their running speed, and generally they'll be spot on. But ask them to guess something less specific, with a number of variables, such as their mental toughness, and there's a strong likelihood they'll overestimate their abilities.[1]

Likewise, the rest of us tend to be far better at judging our skills at a particular aspect of driving, say parallel parking, than we are at estimating how good we are at driving in general.[2] In the latter case, we *all* think we're excellent drivers.

This tendency even happens with eating. I serve you a plate of food and then ask you how much you've eaten. Easy. But what about if you're at a party or a reception where plates of nibbles are being passed around? In this situation, you're much less likely to know the amount you've eaten and to wrongly assume it's not that much.

What's happening here is that when things are harder to measure, we give ourselves the benefit of the doubt.

But to get back to money. We've got our savings spread around in various accounts in order to exercise financial prudence. But because we have a pension scheme, and maybe an ISA, and that thing called a Savings Plus Account, and oh yes, we have some Premium Bonds, it's hard to keep track of how much we have in total. So we tend to guess. And we tend to overestimate how much we actually have and to use this (false) information to justify spending when we should be saving.

A series of experiments demonstrated this in laboratory conditions.

Students were randomly assigned either three accounts or a single account, which they were able to track on a screen throughout the experiment. Then they were given various tasks, such as maths problems, unscrambling anagrams of animal names, matching slogans to brands and guessing American states from their outline. If they could do all the tasks they'd earn $100, and whatever they earned could be assigned, in whichever way they wanted, to their accounts.

Next the students were asked to imagine what they'd like to buy from a list of various items. I say imagine, because as with the earned income, this was all a nominal exercise. Psychology projects don't generally have large budgets, so researchers have to ask participants to *pretend* that they're earning and spending. In this study however, the students were told that two out of every hundred participants would be able to complete an actual purchase. The idea was to make them take the exercise more seriously. The items they could buy included a university t-shirt, a photo album and a computer mouse.

Finally, the students were told that any 'money' left unspent in their nominal accounts at the end of the exercise would be put into a lottery that might result in them winning real money they could keep.

As ever with such experiments, its sounds quite complicated. But nonetheless I suspect you're ahead of me in guessing the results. The students with a single account were found to have 6 per cent more money left at the end of the exercise, compared with those who had three accounts.

Now, this might not sound like a lot, but trust me, behaviour change is very difficult to engineer, so for psychology this amounts to a difference worth having. And in later versions of the study, when the researchers asked students to justify their spending, a key finding for our purposes is that people suggested that if they had a single account it would be easier to keep track of their money, which would help them to save more.[3]

Personality played a part, too. The students who scored high on frugality in personality tests were not affected by having multiple bank accounts, so this study, and my musings above, shouldn't be taken as a blanket exhortation to bundle all of your savings into one account. After all, there are all those other things, such as ease of access, interest rate levels, and yes, spreading risk, to consider as well. Even so, if you're the type who finds saving difficult and may not be saving enough (that's to say, you're not the naturally frugal type) keeping it simple with one savings account could make a difference.

IGNORING FUNGIBLE THE BEAR

The economists in the room might be throwing their hands

up in horror at this point. You should be encouraging people to behave rationally, not to indulge their feelings. Placing your money in accounts that maximise your total returns is always the answer. And the number of those accounts doesn't matter, because in the end it's all the same money.

One of the reasons they think this way is because classical economics teaches them to see money as fungible. Now I adore the word fungible. It's so lovely you want to cuddle it. In fact, Fungible would be a good name for a Teddy Bear. But as for the concept, well, I have my doubts.

The word simply means every hundred pounds is the same as every other hundred pounds. Our sense of the value of our money should in no way be altered by how we earned it, how we account for it, or how we spend it. Yet as we saw in Chapter 3, we defy the fungible when it comes to spending, using quite sophisticated – if illogical – mental accounts, or psychological moneybags, to apportion money differently and to help us to make appropriate spending decisions. So, the £10 gin and tonic on the terrace of a romantic hotel is computed as justifiable, while we baulk at paying more than £20 for a whole bottle of gin in the supermarket.

The same happens with savings. Every pound is not the same as every other pound. For example, sometimes people choose to borrow money, even though they have some savings in another account. On the face of it, this is totally irrational, particularly as the interest you pay on the loan is bound to be far higher than the interest the bank pays on your savings. On the other hand, such borrowing can serve as a useful form of financial discipline. By taking out the loan, you're committing yourself to paying for something at a future date. No loan company, still less a loan shark, will allow you to miss payments. You have to make sure you have that money available. By contrast, if you'd paid for your purchase using savings there's no external pressure on you to restore the balance on your savings account.

Likewise most people take out a slightly bigger mortgage than they need instead of putting every penny of their savings towards the house in order to reduce the size of the loan they need. Of course other considerations come into this calculation, but one of the reasons why we do this is because we know we'll definitely make the effort to pay the mortgage (the building society will insist anyway), whereas we might not have the discipline to build up a savings pot again. As I've already said, offset mortgages, where your savings and your mortgage debt live in one account, have not been popular.

So while in the overall sense these sorts of strategies make little economic sense, they might be the best way for you to preserve your savings pot. But it's not just about self-control.

SAVING TIME

Another factor that can influence our propensity to save is the way we think about time. People vary a lot in how much they think about the past, the present and the future.[4] I'm sure it won't surprise you to hear that people who often think about the future, known as having a future time perspective, have been found to be more likely to save.[5]

That said, there are limits to the extent that thinking about the future inclines a person to save. Another study found this only happens if people have a reasonable level of financial knowledge about how to save.[6] All sorts of things increase or diminish our tendency to save, but being financially aware of the need to do so is the most important factor of all.

Yet even if we know we have to save, if only towards a pension, there's still the problem of when. For many of us, now never feels like a good time. At this point in our life we have all sorts of other financial pressures and commitments, and retirement feels a long way off. Yes, we will start saving, we tell ourselves, but not yet. There'll be plenty of time for that. And in the future we'll probably be richer anyway.

But is that true? Often it isn't. As I've demonstrated in my previous book *Time Warped*, we tend to overestimate how much time we'll have in the future. It's why we're more likely to agree to take part in a two-day conference or a weekend event if it's in six months' time rather than in two weeks. By then, we think falsely, we surely won't be as busy as we are now.

Likewise, we tend to believe that although we've not been good at saving up to now, we'll be better in the future. Surely in the future we'll earn more, spend less and save more. This is known as the budget fallacy. Unfortunately experiments show that we consistently underestimate how much we spent last week as well as underestimating how much we'll spend next week.[7]

Even the language we use to talk about the future can make a difference to when we think we should start doing something about it, such as saving. When we express a time-frame in smaller units, even though the numbers sound bigger, the future feels nearer. You might be ten years away from retirement, but expressed as 3,652 days, it suddenly doesn't seem so far away.[8]

Time plays some strange tricks on our minds when it comes to money. When people were asked to forecast how much they were likely to spend in the next month, they underestimated. No surprise there, perhaps. But if you ask people to forecast how much they will spend in the next year, they still underestimate a little, but get much closer to the correct figure.[9] The reason seems to be that because people are unsure, they factor in more room for error, adding on a bit, and in fact become more accurate.

With pensions, governments are increasingly taking the 'when to start' question out of our hands. In the UK, people already pay through general taxation towards the state pension that everyone receives, but as this provides only the most basic retirement income, the government has recently gone a step further. Everyone who is working and earns over a certain low amount, is now also 'auto-enrolled' into a company pension, with a personal contribution taken from monthly salaries along with a contribution from employers. People can opt out, but the hope is that inertia if nothing else will diminish the chances of that.

Such schemes might help when it comes to pensions, but of course there are other reasons to save. And another excuse we make for putting it off is that we believe we'll have more money in the future and so saving will be easier. What we don't take into account of course is that as we earn more, so we spend more. We eat out in slightly fancier restaurants, choose more expensive furniture, take more exotic holidays. Of course there's no doubt that it's much harder to save if you need almost every penny you earn for the basics, but that doesn't mean we get a huge amount better at saving if we start to earn more. We just think we will.

This is where Richard Thaler, author of the bestselling book *Nudge*, had a clever idea.[10] He devised a savings plan where people committed to save some of their income, not now, but in the future, if their salary went up. People committed to divert an extra 3 per cent of their salary into a savings plan every time they had a pay rise for the first four pay rises. It meant the decision to save was not deferred, but the pain was. It played neatly to loss aversion, among other things, for while any sacrifice of income straightaway is felt as a loss, committing to that sacrifice in the future, when you imagine yourself having more to spare, is much less difficult. They never saw the amount on their payslips drop.

Take up among those approached to take part in the Save More Tomorrow programme was an impressive 78 per cent. And it worked. After four pay rises, people were saving on average four times as much as they were initially. The thing I like about this idea is that it appeals to our optimistic side, that in the future we'll be better at all the things we find so hard today. We'll exercise. We'll eat healthily. And we'll spend sensibly.

There was a similar scheme running when I was at university. The idea was to raise money for Mandela scholarships for black students from South Africa. But rather than asking students who'd just arrived at university and were probably worrying about their own finances to give money immediately, the university authorities asked us to commit to donating money in the future. Specifically, we were asked if at the end of our three years of study we would give the money we'd paid as deposits for our accommodation. Optimistically we assumed that by then we'd be starting well-paid graduate jobs and wouldn't need the money, so we were happy to sign up to the scheme. For many of us, it wasn't quite like that of course, but for the scholarship fund it worked very well.

Another technique that people sometimes use to get themselves to save money is to start afresh. Ignore past mistakes, don't fret that you've been hopeless about saving up to now, just think about the future, set yourself some new goals, and strive towards those. It sounds like good advice. There's just one problem with this linear approach. It doesn't always work.

Consider this example. If someone says they're going to give up smoking in the future there's no reason why the future shouldn't start immediately. In fact, of course, when people make this pledge they tend to mean tomorrow, the next day, next week . . . and on it goes.

The future becomes abstract.[11] Which is the last thing you want when it comes to a thing like saving. You don't want abstract thoughts; you want concrete action, and you want to know why it didn't work last time you decided to start saving. Indeed researchers at Rice University in Houston have found that if people are told to ignore past mistakes with their money, they have a tendency to become over-optimistic about their behaviour in future, with the result that they allow themselves to put off that vital saving until later.

So rather than thinking of life as linear, it's better to think of it as cyclical. After all, much as we'd like to imagine otherwise, we don't really change much, do we? So another bit of advice I'd give if you find saving difficult is to learn to appreciate that you're likely to behave in a similar way from one year to the next. Be realistic about your ability to do better in the future.

When people were encouraged to think like this in a study

of savings behaviour, the results were striking. First, people were told to take into account their past successes and failures at saving, and then asked to estimate how much they thought they could save in the next two weeks. Rather surprisingly, those who took this approach made predictions 70 per cent higher than those in the control group who only looked forward into the future. But more impressive still, two weeks later the cyclical-thinking group had done even better than they had hoped, saving 80 per cent more than the others.

Now, of course, the amount anyone can save depends on their earnings and their outgoings, but in this study the researchers controlled both for current income and past savings and found that the people encouraged to think cyclically succeeded in saving significantly more money.[12]

WANT TO SAVE MORE? SPEAK GERMAN – OR OPEN AN ACCOUNT IN LOS ANGELES

You may not have heard of the Sapir-Whorf hypothesis, but you might be familiar with its central idea: that the language you use can influence the way you think. So, for example, if you speak Russian, you have specific words for light and dark blue and this influences your perception. You actually find it easier to distinguish between different shades of blue than English speakers do.[13]

In English, if you want to say tomorrow is going to be a cold day, you can either just say that, or you can say 'tomorrow will be cold'. The rules of the language require you to use a future tense. But in German, you can simply say, 'morgen ist kalt': literally, 'tomorrow is cold'. Although German does have a future tense, the Germans have sussed that there's no need to use it in this case, as in many others, as the word tomorrow implies the future anyway. Other languages that work something like this include Mandarin, Finnish and Estonian. Collectively they are known as 'weak future-time languages'. By contrast, English – and other languages, such as French – are called 'strong future-time languages'.

It's a fascinating area of study in all sorts of ways, but the important part for our purposes is that it's argued that people who speak languages where the future is emphasised tend to feel the future is further away. And we know what that can mean for saving.

Perhaps this seems a bit far-fetched, but the research has been done and the evidence has been gathered. UCLA economics professor Keith Chen compared saving rates in 76 different countries and, controlling for unemployment, growth, interest rates and level of development in each nation found that people who speak languages with weak future-time references, pay into their savings twice as often as people in countries speaking strong future-time reference languages, and partly as a result no doubt, when taken all together, people in those countries save 6 per cent more of their per capita GDP.[14]

As ever, there were some exceptions to the general findings. The Russian Federation, Ireland and the Czech Republic all speak languages where the future tense is emphasised, yet come quite close to the top of the savings chart. Meanwhile, in polyglot Ethiopia, where people speak three 'strong' languages and three 'weak' languages, there was a really fascinating statistical result, as it turned out that the language people spoke was a better predictor of how much they saved than the strength of their belief in the importance of saving.

Of course, since these kinds of studies only began towards the end of the twentieth century, we can't know which came first – the way that language is used or people's orientation towards the future. Perhaps it was future-mindedness that led to the use of such language in the first place, and so the language reflects rather than influences attitudes towards the future.

Nonetheless this research does highlight that our culture can have an impact on attitudes towards savings, even when other factors are taken into account. Which might lead you to think that I'm about to advise moving countries as a strategy for people who are bad at saving. But of course a spendthrift Brit would have to do more than move to Germany if he or she wanted to be more careful with money. They'd have to speak, and more importantly *think*, like a typical German. So taking this course is not very realistic.

Still, if emigrating is a bit of a stretch, how about moving your money instead of yourself? One curious study suggests there might be something in it.

In 2013 Sam Maglio, a social psychologist, set out to investigate whether people made different financial decisions depending on whether the money they were discussing was geographically near or far from them. This may sound odd, but bear with me.

As we already know, people tend not to be as interested in the promise of money in the future, as much as the promise of money right now, even when they can have more in the future. Maglio's hypothesis was that something similar might happen with locations near or far.

People living in New York were asked to fill in a survey in exchange for entry into a lottery. There was a one-in-a-hundred chance of winning, and the prize was $50, which would be deposited in a special account. Participants were told they wouldn't have to travel to get hold of these possible winnings, but half of them were told the account was based in New York, and the other half that it was based in Los Angeles, thousands of miles away. People then had to choose whether – in the event of winning – they would like to take their $50 straight away, or leave it in the account for three months and get $65 instead.

What the results showed was that when the New Yorkers were told that any money they might win in the lottery would be deposited in a New York account, just 49 per cent were prepared to wait to get the larger sum. But change the location of the account to Los Angeles, and the proportion of people saying they'd leave the money where it was and get the larger sum in three months' time went up to 71 per cent.[15] It was as though the geographical distance of the money, which was only hypothetical money after all, created a psychological barrier that meant leaving it there for a little longer was no great hardship.

So now that it's possible to choose online accounts nominally based all over the country, if not the world, you may want to think about opting for one that seems far away from where you live. It may just be that, if you live in Cornwall, you'll be less tempted to dip into your savings if they're deposited in the Yorkshire Building Society, for instance.

RESISTING THE SIREN CALL

Now, in the study I'm about to tell you about, time was a factor. Specifically, once the prospect of getting hold of their money in the immediate future was removed, the participants started to think more long term.

I'm sure you'll agree that sometimes there's no other way. Our money needs to be locked away, tied up somehow, kept from our immediate grasp. But this doesn't mean an outside authority has to confiscate it from us. One of the interesting things about people who are bad at saving is that they are often well aware of the fact. So the trick is to use that self-awareness to bring about the change in behaviour. In this study, a team of psychologists was on hand to help – but the lessons could apply to any of us.

The research took place in a rural area of the Philippines – a place where people are not very well off and struggle to save. The savings account they were offered had Homeric overtones. As the researchers themselves put it, the account was the equivalent of Odysseus tying himself to the mast and putting wax in the ears of his crew to avoid being lured onto the rocks by the songs of the Sirens.[16] Anyone who joined the scheme was told that they couldn't withdraw any of the money they'd put in until either a target amount or a specified date was reached.

Now, you're probably aware of similar savings vehicles available in the West. That's to say, once you've deposited money in the accounts you can't take any of it out, or not without stiff penalties, for a number of years. Part of the lure of these accounts is no doubt that they impose Odyssean discipline, though high interest is another attraction, and the catch is that you usually need to make a large initial deposit. This means that most people using such accounts can probably afford to have more easily accessible savings in other accounts. This wasn't the case with the people taking part in the Philippines – this was their only way of saving.

Despite these strict rules, just over 200 people (28 per cent of those approached, and more women than men) chose to open an account, with around two-thirds opting to save until a particular date – Christmas, a birthday, the large annual community party – and the rest choosing a particular sum of money they wanted to save.

Participants were also able to choose how they would physically deposit the money, the options being: travel to the bank, set up a regular transfer, or save the money at home in a locked moneybox known as a '*ganansiya*', to which the bank held the key. In focus groups beforehand, automatic transfers proved popular, but when it came to it, three-quarters of people went for the moneybox option (an interesting outcome given the success of an initiative in Kenya I'll consider below).

The accounts were a success. An 82 per cent increase in savings was recorded, far higher than among a control group who'd not been given restricted accounts, but instead were visited by a marketing person who emphasised the importance of saving. By Western standards, the average amount in accounts at the end of the study might seem low – just $8. But in this region of the Philippines that was enough to pay for two children to attend the local school for a year.

When the accounts matured, participants were free to withdraw their money. But in fact only one person did. Although people were informed they could earn higher interest in other, more accessible, accounts, they were not tempted. After two-and-a-half years, however, savings did drop, suggesting that schemes like this might be more effective in the short rather than the long term.[17]

So why did the scheme prove so popular for a while? Well, to answer the question we need to refer back to a concept I introduced in Chapter 10 called temporal discounting, when people would rather have £20 now, say, than £30 in a month's time. Some people are what are known as hyperbolic discounters. So although they choose to take the money immediately, when it's a choice between now and a month's time, when the temporal goalposts are shifted and the offer becomes £20 in six months or £30 in seven, they're more likely to hang on for the larger sum, on the basis that over the longer timeframe the extra month's wait seems neither here nor there.

I mention all this again because one of the issues that high-rate hyperbolic discounters particularly struggle with is saving, which of course is built on the notion that we should forgo instant gratification – or indeed immediate need – in order to reap larger benefits in the long run.

That said, such discounters often display a reasonable level of self-awareness about this issue. They know they *should* forgo some current spending in order to save for the future, they just find it very hard to actually do it. And they know that their decisions are inconsistent, that waiting a month now is really just as hard as waiting a month in the future, even though it doesn't feel like that.

These people – we (I include myself) – are called 'sophisticated hyperbolic discounters' – with the hyperbolic bit referring to our inability to think long term, and the sophisticated bit acknowledging that at least we're acutely conscious of our weakness.

This means us SHD-sufferers (I've invented the acronym myself, but why not) see the logic of savings vehicles that impose rigorous discipline on us, such as not allowing us access to our money or forcing us to commit to a scheme for a long period.

This was the reasoning of the group of Filipino villagers who took up the scheme. When they were given hypothetical questions that measured their hyperbolic preferences, those high on SHD were aware that this was a weakness they were prone to, and therefore welcomed the external discipline imposed on them by a particularly strict form of savings account.

BED NETS AND FLIP-FLOPS

In recent sections I've been suggesting that because saving is difficult for many of us, we need to adopt sophisticated strategies in order to help us do it. After all, we're complex psychological beings, and so it would seem to follow that we need smart ways of strengthening our good intentions and overcoming our weaknesses. In some cases, this is the right approach. But having started the chapter by saying that simplifying our approach to saving could be a help, I want to return to perhaps the simplest saving system of all, the one that we are first introduced to as children: piggy banks.

We all know how it works. You put any spare coins you have into a container which prevents you accessing your money once you've deposited it, with the result that you build up a fund for the future. As a little child perhaps the biggest incentive for sacrificing money you could spend on sweets is to see the coins drop through the slit in the pink piggy's back, all the while cheered on by your parents. And then eventually there's the fun to be had from emptying the pig when it's full and finding more coins than you ever imagined inside.

But of course, there's no additional financial return on the investment. And with no interest accruing, you might think we'd quickly lose interest (pun intended) in such crude forms of saving as we grow into adulthood. Yet in fact, if you go online you'll find many moneyboxes advertised for adults. Among the most popular are '*terramundi*' jars, which have to be smashed with a hammer when they are full. Some are even rather mystically dubbed as a 'Pot of Dreams', giving us the idea that they are an almost magical way to save up for holidays or Christmas.

Although as adults we could raid these jars any time we like, they do seem to cast a compelling spell over us. We don't like the idea of breaking them open even to get some money for an emergency. Surely ill-fortune will befall us. It's a case of money over mind perhaps, but at least it's helping us to save. A spell cast over us by a fairy godmother rather than a wicked witch.

Many people use these jars to save up for treats. And in their own way, they do work. This led some psychologists to wonder if an equivalent of a piggy bank could help the poorest of all to save a little money towards buying simple, but life-saving things.

In many parts of the world, malaria and other preventable diseases still cause widespread illness and death. Yet governments and aid agencies invest in information campaigns to tell people there are steps they can take to reduce the risk. As a result, even the poorest families generally know that chemically impregnated bed nets can help to prevent malaria, that filtering drinking water or using chlorine tablets prevents gut infections, that wearing flip-flops stops worms getting into their children's intestines via the soles of their feet and that newer cooking stoves ward off lung problems (as well as being cheaper to run).[18]

The problem is that people often don't act on this knowledge, for the simple reason that they cannot afford the upfront costs of such products.[19] This means that in the Western Province of Kenya, for instance, on average each family of five only has between one and two bed nets. People are literally dying because they have no savings.

Now, the villagers of Western Province have no access to savings banks or building societies. So was there an alternative way in which saving could be effectively encouraged? This is where the idea of using piggy banks came in.

Researchers arranged for a local artisan to make a simple green metal box for each family involved in the study. The box had uneven sides, a diagonal slit in the top and a padlock with a key. Families were also given a passbook in which they could keep a record of how much money they had saved as the study proceeded.

Three-quarters of the people who took part in the Kenyan experiment were so poor they had dirt floors in their homes. They were only able to put very small amounts of cash aside. And remember, they were not being incentivised to save by earning interest. The money they took out of their green metal boxes at the end of the study was the same money they put in. Even so, the results were dramatic. With the green moneyboxes, saving for bed nets went up by 66 per cent.[20]

This is a huge jump. Other savings initiatives, such as one that took place in three countries – Bolivia, Peru and the Philippines – tried sending regular text messages reminding people to save and saw savings rise by just 6 per cent.[21] That study was considered a success, and yet the Kenyan scheme performed ten times better. So why were the results so astonishing?

Perhaps it was simply that the notion of saving had been introduced into this society for the first time? It probably helped too that others were watching the results (as we saw in Chapter 6 this always helps people to achieve a goal). But it was also crucial that the method of saving was a simple and practical one – and directed toward a specific and important goal.

Having a clear target is one of the best ways of motivating us to save. It's the reason why churches put up giant thermometers on their gates. This way, the congregation can share in a collective sense of achievement as the red line rises towards the amount of money needed to restore the organ. You may also recall my lute fund, which I mentioned in Chapter 1. Looking back, I think I took greater satisfaction from meticulously colouring in my big picture of a thermometer every time I saved another pound than I'd ever have got from actually owning a lute.

Another important element was the discipline my saving method imposed on me. At least until my mid-teens, when I was done with the lute idea and blew the money on U2 albums, the lute fund was to my mind sacrosanct. Raiding it to buy something else was unthinkable – just as the Parish Council dipping into the Organ Restoration Fund to pay for a Christmas party would be in other circumstances. The weakness of my lute fund, though, was that the target was unachievable. If you recall, I set myself the task of saving £1,400, which realistically I was never going to reach. So another crucial factor in the Kenyan saving plan was probably that the villagers taking part had a good chance of saving enough to buy the bed nets with the saving plan to help them.

The lesson we can all draw if we find saving difficult, or think we simply can't afford to put any money aside, is to start small and stay simple. As our financial system becomes ever more complex and sophisticated, the danger is that people who aren't especially numerate, and can't afford financial advisors and all the rest of it, reject the thought of saving even a small amount. This is where 'Christmas club' schemes and *terramundi* jars have their place. They won't transform people's finances, but they do help people who may have turned away from saving to learn again the disciplines and, yes, the joys of saving.

14

THE JOY OF SPENDING

Why, if you want the good life, you should spend your money on experiences not things (while allowing yourself a bit of retail therapy), why buying high-quality prosciutto that you don't need might not be extravagant and why it's better not to know your hourly rate.

OF COURSE, THERE'S more to money than saving. Sometimes you want to spend, and not just on life's necessities. We've seen that it's good to save and it's good to give, but I want to reassure you that it's also good to *spend*. Though having said that, it depends what you spend your money on.

The wealth of research in this area (another intended pun) points to a number of different ways in which a person might spend to increase happiness.

One tip is to buy experiences instead of material goods. For instance, those who are lucky enough to have a lot of money would be much better advised to spend it on a cruise to the Antarctic or a gorilla-watching trip in Rwanda (both expensive trips – I know; I've looked them up and can't possibly afford either of them) than buying yet more fancy clothes or furniture. The experience will live with them and give them more pleasure.

If you think about it, that is exactly what some of the super-rich do. Richard Branson splurges on attempts at hot-air ballooning records or on grand projects like building space rockets. Even Donald Trump presumably entered the race for president of the United States not because he initially expected to win, but for the fun of the ride. Regardless of the annoyance he might have induced in other people, for him as an individual, it could be argued it was a good use of his billions. It's bought him extraordinary experiences. Some rich people, of course, do exactly the opposite and will even live in a country they don't really want to live in, to avoid paying so much tax, then complain that they're 'not allowed' to visit their home country very often. Then you begin to wonder what the point of having so much money is, if you can't even live where you want to.

What about the rest of us? You might think that the problem with spending on experiences is that they are over so quickly (bungee jumping) while material goods (a £500 leather jacket) last a long time. It doesn't quite work like that, however.

When I was left a small amount of money by my great aunt, I spent it on two things: a weekend away with my partner in Dublin and a fax machine. At the time I was very pleased with the fax machine. It seemed like a good way to spend the money. As now, I worked from home quite a bit in those days, and having my own machine meant I no longer needed to go to the newsagents to send and receive faxes (this shows how long ago it was). Within a couple of years, though, along came the internet and my fax machine was quickly rendered redundant. And even without the march of technology, I'd have got used to my fax machine, and the pleasure I took from it would have worn off. (Yes, I do realise it's a bit sad to get pleasure from a fax machine, but I liked it.) By contrast, the weekend in Dublin, though long in the past, is an experience I still remember well and look back on fondly. Now, whenever I hear about Dublin, I always think of my great aunt in a way that I don't when I see a picture of a fax machine.

Research backs up my anecdote, showing that usually the extra happiness you get from a material purchase tends to wear off quickly.[1] After all, a new car isn't new for long. And people who choose to move further away from work in order to buy a bigger house soon become accustomed to having an extra bedroom, while the delays they experience during their longer commute continue to annoy them.[2] Research has even shown that the extra pleasure brought by experiences begins way before they actually take place. In an experiment rather nicely entitled 'Waiting for Merlot', psychologists from Cornell University demonstrated that the joy of anticipation was higher for people looking forward to experiences. Whereas when people considered a material purchase in advance, they felt no happier.[3]

Spending your money on material goods can work though, if it leads to pleasurable experiences. So, that new car could prompt you to go to places you've never been before, visit friends further afield, or enjoy experiences you wouldn't have tried otherwise. Or moving to a larger flat with a spare room and access to a garden in a friendly street might seem like a material purchase, but could lead you to make new friends, to see your family more often because there's somewhere for them to sleep and to experience the joys of gardening.

CLEVER SPENDING

'I want every single mouthful to be good. It's a knife in the belly every time I have to eat a sub-standard meal.'

So says Tony Holmes. Which is all very well, you might think, if you have plenty of money, as Tony once did – before things went wrong.

> Charmed life • cool job • Platinum Amex • business class • turbo-charged coupé • Prada/Agnès B/Nicole Farhi • Nobu/Racine/Club Gascon • life-changing shit-storm • alcoholism • depression • breakdown • pills/vodka/ Stanley knife • closed curtains/bailiffs • home repossession • bankruptcy • homeless hostel • community mental health team • temporary council flat • housing association flat • voluntary work • hope • relapse • try again

This list comes from the 'About' section of Tony's website. It chronicles his spiral down from being an organiser of corporate events, travelling all over the world for product launches, earning well in excess of £100,000 a year, to the life he leads now. Which is one without a lot of money, but with good food still at its heart. Tony's chronicled this latter period of his life, to some acclaim, on his blog The Skint Foodie.[4]

I met him in a café in south-east London. It serves excellent coffee – Tony wouldn't put up with anything less – and now he's got some paid work again, he sometimes allows himself little luxuries like this.

'When I first got into financial trouble I couldn't envisage how I'd live without the trappings of wealth,' Tony told me. 'But having reached rock bottom, I realised I could do without almost everything except eating well.' Out of that conviction, and with great single-mindedness (along with some advantages that come from not always having been poor), Tony has fashioned an admirable strategy for coping with his poverty, and not letting it define all aspects of his life.

So how does he do it? Well, he doesn't have much money, but he does have quite a bit of time. And he devotes that time to buying good food judiciously and cooking it imaginatively. 'It's not about eating as cheaply as possible, but eating the best I can,' Tony explains. Which doesn't just mean eating healthily. Tony calculates he could have done that for £20 a week. Instead he was spending up to twice that during the time he was living on benefits, which meant a large proportion of his income was going on food.

But for that, Tony says, a man can eat 'like a king. Or at least, a prince.' As well as having a lot of free time, he had a Freedom Pass, which meant he could travel quite widely on tubes and buses to find bargains. It also helped that cooking was a passion for him, and he was good at it. Some of his ethical convictions, buying organic or free-range produce, had to be ditched. But not his insistence – at least for crucial ingredients – on quality. Indeed that insistence was integral to his desire to eat well. Each Sunday afternoon, he'd plan very carefully how much of the basics he'd need for the coming week's meals – two onions, three carrots, 300g of potatoes (he only bought exactly what he needed and leftovers from meals were always used: vegetables for minestrone soup or stock; fruit for smoothies). But during the week he would also seek out some products that might appear like luxuries even to people who are affluent. 75p for a tin of tomatoes might seem steep, but they were San Marzano tomatoes, and for Tony that made a real difference to a dish. Most of the time he was shopping in the cheaper supermarkets on the Old Kent Road or from some of the market stalls on Peckham Rye, but he'd make forays to fancy Borough Market to buy 50g of highest quality prosciutto or skirt steak. These were expensive items in themselves but Tony dotted them through meals in small amounts throughout a week, adding a touch of top-end taste to dishes. He also knew where the good stuff could be found at the bargain stores. He'd go to Lidl just for their aged parmesan, for instance. He also made his own sourdough bread and cakes.

So Tony had to put in quite a lot of hard work to eat so well for so little. But then food wasn't just fuel, or even a nice diversion from a difficult life. It was his life. He recognised that a way of coping with having hardly any money (particularly after having had so much before) was to simplify his life radically, to cut out other pleasures and concentrate on one. In this way, he wasn't defined by his poverty, but by his singular and successful way of conquering it, using it to his advantage, and eventually – the ultimate irony – getting offers to monetise it. The recipes and tips he posted on his blog and Twitter feed attracted a large number of followers and offers of publishing deals followed. His method of coping with poverty helped to lift him out of its darkest depths.

Despite the offers Tony hasn't written a book, but he does have a job working in mental health and is not such a skint foodie as he was, although he earns nothing like the amount he used to in his former life. His is not a classic story of poverty of course, and he's the first to acknowledge it. But his story does show that there are strategies that can mitigate the effects of poverty in a money obsessed world. In many ways, Tony had to act like all people on low or no incomes have had to do down the ages. Doing without, cutting down on things, being very careful about what he bought, budgeting, budgeting, budgeting . . . But he managed to combine these sacrifices with some indulgences. Indeed, the former allowed for the latter.

Of course it's nothing new to work out a way of being able to afford the small pleasures in life, whether it's getting a nice TV, or buying lottery tickets. Typically these acts are seen by some middle-class moralisers as signs of fecklessness. But while there are negative health consequences in some cases, and – as we've seen – it is easy to make money worries worse through such things as gambling, in other ways perhaps we should not only understand, but applaud people for keeping some money back in order to enjoy the things that give them pleasure.

Tony Holmes told me that being poor was hard work. He told me he understood why the research shows poverty can affect your thinking, as we saw in Chapter 10. His way of dealing with it was to channel some of that work towards an end that he found particularly satisfying. For him, it was good food. For others, it might mean growing a lot of plants from seed and spending all hours weeding and digging so that you can have a nice garden. One thing we can all learn perhaps is that we can't have it all, however well off we are, so we're more likely to enjoy life if we concentrate on those things that bring us most pleasure.

FORGET ABOUT THE COST!

But sometimes we can't enjoy even simple everyday experiences, because we know that time is money. And free time is not actually free time for most of us. We have to earn it.

After conducting dozens of studies on money and happiness, the psychologists Elizabeth Dunn (who we met earlier) and Michael Norton have shown that this knowledge can spoil our enjoyment of simple pleasures. In their experiments, listening to 2 minutes of music that you like is rendered less pleasurable if you've just calculated your hourly rate at work.[5] You can't help but work out how much that 2 minutes is 'costing' you.

Workers paid by the hour know exactly what their time is worth in monetary terms and are less willing to engage in activities that they enjoy or even to do volunteer work. People paid this way are of course generally on lower incomes, and they have to spend more of their time making money for the essentials of life. But when people were asked in an American survey if they'd give up some spare time in exchange for more money, 32 per cent of hourly-paid workers said they would, compared with only 17 per cent of people paid monthly. The explanation was that the latter group tend not to have a sense of exactly what an hour of their time is worth, while the former group generally do.[6]

It might sound perfectly rational to think about whether a certain hour could be better spent earning money than doing something you can't even guarantee that you will enjoy, but the evidence shows that thinking in this way is not going to make you feel happier.[7] You need to take time out more freely than that.

It's a problem that afflicts the better off as well as poorer people of course. True, people on higher incomes should in theory have to work fewer hours to get what they need, and therefore have more time for pursuing leisure activities. But few people in well-paid jobs are able to work less than full-time – either because their employers demand it or because they've got used to a certain, more costly, lifestyle. And of course, many high earners are chronic workaholics. They work endless hours, making more and more money. Sometimes this makes them happier. They really do 'love' their jobs. But in these cases, it's usually the mental stimulation, the buzz, the challenge, the status, and not the money they're making, which is increasing their happiness levels.

Another tip for maximising happiness from spending is to pay well in advance. This divorces the pain of paying from the joy of possession or doing. It also means you get to enjoy the pleasure of anticipation. Be warned, though. This strategy could cost you. In a study from 1987, students were asked how much they would be prepared to pay to kiss their favourite celebrity either immediately, in 24 hours' time or in three days' time. Students knew that delaying the pleasure would increase the pleasure. And they were prepared to pay for it. Most chose to enjoy the kiss three days later, but in exchange for three days of anticipation, they were prepared to pay 75 per cent more than for an instant kiss.[8]

THE JOY OF THRIFT – AND WHY RETAIL THERAPY IN MODERATION IS A GOOD THING

So spending on other people and on experiences rather than material goods can make you happier. But there are also ways of deliberately *not* spending that can work. The psychologist Sonya Lyubomirsky, who has spent her career studying happiness, is convinced that thrift is a forgotten virtue. Vintage shops might be in fashion, but even so, what many of us want to do is to buy new things. Thriftiness might sound miserly, but as I mentioned right back at the beginning of Chapter 13, it shares the same root as the word 'thrive'.

How then, to use the evidence from researchers such as Lyubomirsky, to be thrifty and yet thriving? She suggests paying more attention to the things we own, thinking actively about the benefits and pleasures they've brought us, so that our joy in them doesn't wear off. You should be constantly reminding yourself how much more comfortable your present car is compared with your old one, for example.[9] Another trick, Lyubomirsky suggests, is to recycle the initial pleasure you used to get from your old possessions by bringing them back into service. Or my favourite, renting happiness. So instead of splashing out on a better car, you make do with the perfectly serviceable one you have, but treat yourself by renting a fancy sports car for a weekend. This might feel extravagant in some ways, but in fact it's much cheaper than buying a new car, and it will give you the pleasure of a memorable experience, which won't wear off.

But, I hear you cry, what if you enjoy shopping? What if it makes you feel better to save up your money and reward yourself with something nice, with something that will give you pleasure every time you look at it, like a lovely pair of shoes? Although spending on material goods that don't bring new experiences might be a short-lived pleasure, it's pleasurable all the same. There's a reason they call it retail therapy.

US researchers found that small treats can temporarily improve your mood and that, as we've probably all observed, people are more likely to buy themselves a gift when they're feeling miserable.[10] In fact the American study, conducted at a shopping centre, implied that people often spend money strategically, knowing full well that their purchase would only cheer them up temporarily, but they chose to do it anyway. Clever marketing people trade on our insecurities and low mood by trying to convince us this or that purchase will somehow transform our lives, but most of the time we don't buy it. The marketing, that is.

Which feels like an appropriate note on which to end this chapter. Yes, money in all sorts of ways is a power for good. If we exert mind over money, we can use it to make our lives, but also other people's lives, better. But for all its pervasiveness and power in our world, money isn't going to transform us. We can spend as much as we like, donate as much we like, win as much as like and save as much as we like, but money will only help us to live a more fulfilled life if we know what to do with it – and, crucially, we know it won't solve all our problems. Still, we need to be in control. So in my final chapter, I draw on all the research I've been summarising in this book in order to give you a short, handy guide to maximising your chances of achieving *Mind Over Money*.

15

MONEY TIPS

BY MY COUNT I've mentioned 263 experiments in this book. Between them, psychologists have spent many years devising these studies, recruiting participants, collecting data and analysing the results. So what can the rest of us learn from their endeavours? Here are some tips, every one of which is based on evidence from research. I'm not promising these tips will turn your life around, but if you employ them appropriately, you could find your relationship with money is both healthier and, in the widest sense, wealthier.

1. Always pay for snacks in cash if you're trying to eat healthily.
2. When you are about to buy something on a credit card, imagine taking the equivalent money out of a cash machine. Would you still want to spend it? Only if you would, should you go ahead and buy the item.
3. Don't choose the same lottery numbers every week or you will never be able to stop playing.
4. Don't go on a wine course. If you learn too much about expensive wines, you'll start caring about

what you're drinking. If you don't, cheap wine will carry on tasting good, especially if your friends lie to you about the price.

5. If your headache is really bad, buy the more expensive branded pain relief, even though you know it contains the same ingredients as the cheap stuff. It really might reduce the pain more quickly.

6. Choose an expensive all-you-can-eat buffet rather than a cheap one, if you want to enjoy the food more and not feel overly full.

7. The next time you find yourself running a market stall of some kind, write on the sign, 'spend a little time' and more people will stop.

8. If you are buying a product and the shop gives you a choice of three, don't let the expensive one sway you towards the middle one. Ignore anything big and shiny. Before you buy anything, imagine it in your own home.

9. When a discount in a shop is expressed as a percentage, always do the calculation and work out the actual price. The offer might not be as good as you think.

10. Never tell an estate agent who comes to value your house the valuations the other agents gave you, until they've given you theirs.

11. In negotiations, always name your price before the other person does, unless you really have absolutely no idea what price is appropriate.

12. Think carefully about when to buy insurance. Are you insuring against possible regret in the future or because you really can't afford to pay if the worst happens?

13. If you want to bribe schoolchildren to do better, pay them to do specific tasks and tell them how to do it. Don't just pay them for better grades.

14. If you're offering a bribe, make sure it's large enough and choose your circumstances carefully.

15. Never offer to pay friends for favours.

16. Only introduce an incentive scheme if you can afford to keep paying for it in the long term.

17. If you want to build a nuclear waste dump, don't try to bribe the nearby residents with money.

18. Don't tell your children their drawing is the best you've ever seen. Instead praise the effort and the way they went about the task.

19. If you are setting an asking price for something you want to sell, try to imagine you don't own it.

20. If you are bidding at an auction, beware bidding more that you intended just because the previous (entirely different) item sold for a lot of money.

21. Beware of wine traders who buy vintage bottles in restaurants and then ask if they can take the empty bottles home.

22. In the event that you unexpectedly find yourself becoming a millionaire, don't go immediately for the best that money can buy. If you do, everyday pleasures will start to pale in comparison. Instead buy yourself lots of little pleasures.

23. If you are lonely, turning to materialism and pursuing money in compensation won't make you any happier, but enjoying little luxuries might.

24. When looking to raise money from rich people ask for a straight donation. Don't imply it is some kind

of investment for them. If you do they will give you less money.

25. If you want to get better at saving, it's no good just trying to turn over a new leaf. Appreciate that the same patterns repeat themselves and find a new way of doing it instead.

26. When you go to a restaurant with a group of friends, don't agree to sharing the bill equally until everyone has ordered.

27. Open a savings account at the other end of the country. The money will feel further away even if it's instantly accessible online. You'll be less likely to dip into your savings.

28. If you're planning a charity fundraising campaign, choose pictures of less pretty children and make sure the families look as though they are actively helping themselves, rather than waiting passively for someone else to do it.

29. If you want to spend your money on making yourself happier, buy experiences rather than material goods (or if you want to buy material goods make sure that they lead to good experiences).

30. Buy yourself treats that are memorable.

31. If you are paid by the hour, don't calculate how much money you've lost if someone invites you to go and do something that's more fun instead of working. If you think you'd enjoy it, then just do it.

32. Before you focus too much effort on trying to get a promotion to a job that's less fun than the one you do now, remember that making more money might, but won't necessarily, make you any happier.

NOTES

With apologies to second, third and fourth authors – who no doubt did a lot of the work – to save space, where there are multiple authors, I've only listed the first. I hope I have included every study mentioned. Sorry if I've missed you out. All links were accessed on 13 December 2015. If link rot stops them working, there should be enough information here for you to search online for the source.

INTRODUCTION

1 You can see this interview from RTÉ's *The Late Late Show* online at Ironmantetsuo, K Foundation Burn a Million Quid, YouTube video uploaded 6 September 2007: https://www.youtube.com/watch?v=i6q4n5TQnpA

2 For the history of the band and their other projects, see Higgs, J. (2013) *The KLF: Chaos, Magic and the Band Who Burned a Million Pounds*. London: Weidenfeld & Nicolson.

3 See Evans, D. (2015) *The Utopia Experiment*. London: Picador. This is an extraordinary tale.

4 Polanyi, K. (2014) *For a New West. Essays, 1919–1958*. London: Polity.

5 James, W. (1983, originally published in 1890) *The Principles of Psychology*. Cambridge, Massachusetts: Harvard University Press.

6   See Chapter 10, Harari, Y.N. (2014) Sapiens: A Brief History of Humankind. Harvill Secker.

7   Lea, S. & Webley, P. (2006) Money as Tool, Money as Drug: The Biological Psychology of a Strong Incentive. *Behavioral & Brain Sciences*, 29, 161–209.

CHAPTER 1

1   Breiter, H.C. et al (2001) Functional Imaging of Neural Responses to Expectancy and Experience of Monetary Gains and Losses. *Neuron*, 30, 619–639.

2   Kim, H. et al (2011) Overlapping Responses for the Expectation of Juice and Money Rewards in Human Ventromedial Prefrontal Cortex. *Cerebral Cortex*, 21(4), 769–776.

3   McClure, S.M. (2004) Separate Neural Systems Value Immediate and Delayed Monetary Rewards. *Science*, 306(5695), 503–507.

4   Becchio, C. et al (2011) How the Brain Responds to the Destruction of Money. *Journal of Neuroscience, Psychology & Economics*, 4 (1), 1–10.

5   Reserve Bank of Australia, Banknotes – Deliberate Damage: http://banknotes.rba.gov.au/legal/deliberate-damage/

6   Zuel, N. (1992) PM's Signature May be Illegal. *Sydney Morning Herald*, 17 November, 4.

7   Gould, J. (17 November 2011) Funny Money Has Phillip Seeing Red: http://www.sunshinecoastdaily.com.au/news/not-so-funny-money-has-bloke-seeing-red/1176472/

8   See the suffragette-defaced penny in the British Museum: http://www.britishmuseum.org/explore/a_history_of_the_world/objects.aspx#95

9   European Commission recommendation on the legal tender of the euro, ESTA Conference, Bratislava, 2012: http://www.esta-cash.eu/documents/bratislava-presentations-2012/9.-the-ec-recommendation-on-legal-tender-implementation-in-the-member-states-and-next-step-ra-diger-voss-ec.pdf

10 De Martino, B. et al (2010) Amygdala Damage Eliminates

Monetary Loss Aversion. *Proceedings of the National Academy of Sciences*, 107, 3788–3792.

11   Miller, H. (1946) *Money And How It Gets That Way*. This book is out of print, but there's an excellent summary including extensive quotes on Maria Popova's Brain Pickings blog. http://www.brainpickings.org/2014/08/04/henry-miller-on-money/

12   Stolp, M. (2011) Children's Art: Work or Play? Preschoolers Considering the Economic Questions of their Theatre Performance. *Childhood*, 19(2), 251–265.

13   Lau, S. (1998) Money: What It Means to Children and Adults. *Social Behavior and Personality*, 26(3), 297–306.

14   Webley, P. et al (1991) A Study in Economic Psychology: Children's Savings in a Play Economy. *Human Relations*, 44, 127–146.

15   Mischel, W. (2014) *The Marshmallow Test: Mastering Self-Control*. London: Little Brown & Company.

16   Berti, A.E. & Bombi, A.S. (1981) The Development of the Concept of Money and Its Value: A Longitudinal Study. *Child Development*, 52(4), 1179–1182. See also their 1988 book *The Child's Construction of Economics*. Cambridge: Cambridge University Press.

17   Flight of the Conchords (27 August 2012) Feel Inside (And Stuff Like That). YouTube video: https://www.youtube.com/watch?v=gnO75DHfxTA

18   These four stages were outlined by Berti, A.E. & Bombi, A.S. in 1988, in their book *The Child's Construction of Economics*. Cambridge: Cambridge University Press.

19   Ruckenstein, M. (2010) Time Scales of Consumption: Children, Money and Transactional Orders. *Journal of Consumer Culture*, 10(3), 383–404.

20   Atwood, J.D. (2012) Couples and Money: The Last Taboo. *American Journal of Family Therapy*, 40(1), 1–19.

21   Furnham, A. (1999) Economic Socialisation. *British Journal of Developmental Psychology*, 17, 585–604.

22   Kim, J. et al (2011) Family Processes and Adolescents'

Financial Behaviors. *Journal of Family & Economic Issues*, 32, 668–679.

23 Zaleskiewicz, T. et al (2013) Money and the Fear of Death: The Symbolic Power of Money as an Existential Anxiety Buffer. *Journal of Economic Psychology*, 36C, 55–67.

24 Zaleskiewicz T. et al (2013) Saving Can Save from Death Anxiety: Mortality Salience and Financial Decision-Making. *PLoS ONE*, 8(11): e79407. doi:10.1371/journal.pone.0079407

CHAPTER 2

1 Graeber, D. (2014) *Debt: The First 5000 Years*. Brooklyn, New York: Melville House Publishing.

2 Friedman, M. (1991) The Island of Stone Money. *Working Papers in Economics E–91–3*. The Hoover Institution: Stanford University.

3 See this blog for an interesting discussion on the way that stories of the Yap money are told and retold by economists: http://jpkoning.blogspot.co.uk/2013/01/yap-stones-and-myth-of-fiat-money.html

4 See Bank of England. Banknotes – Frequently Asked Questions – Questions about the Banknote Character Selection – £20 Nominations: http://www.bankofengland.co.uk/banknotes/Pages/about/faqs.aspx

5 Lea, S.E.G. et al (1987) *The Individual in the Economy*. Cambridge: Cambridge University Press.

6 Di Muro, F. & Noseworthy, T. (2012) Money Isn't Everything, But It Helps If It Doesn't Look Used. *Journal of Consumer Research*, 39, 1330–1341.

7 Lea, S.E.G. (1981) Inflation, Decimalization and the Estimated Sizes of Coins. *Journal of Economic Psychology*, 1, 79–81.

8 Bruner, J.S. & Goodman, C.G. (1947) Value and Need as Organizing Factors in Perception. *Journal of Abnormal and Social Psychology*, 42, 33–34.

9 Burgoyne C.B. et al (1999) The Transition to the Euro: Some Perspectives from Economic Psychology. *Journal of Consumer Policy*, 22, 91–116.

10   Hussein, G. et al (1987) A Characteristics Approach to Money and the Changeover from the £1 Note to the £1 Coin. *Exeter University Technical Report*, no. 87/1.

11   Webley, P. (2010) Foreword: Inertia and Innovation in Inter-disciplinary Social Science. *Anthropology Matters Journal*, 2010, 12(1).

12   Sparshott, J. Should US Replace $1 Bills With Coins? Fed to Weigh In, 11 December 2013: http://blogs.wsj.com/economics/2013/12/11/should-u-s-replace-1-bills-with-coins-fed-to-weigh-in/

13   Dollar Coin Alliance, Facts About the Dollar Coin: http://www.dollarcoinalliance.org/facts-about-the-dollar-coin/
Ahlers, M.M. $1 Coins – Unwanted, Unloved and Out of Currency, 30 November 2013: http://edition.cnn.com/2013/11/28/us/one-dollar-coins/

14   Lambert, M. et al Costs and Benefits of Replacing the $1 Federal Reserve Note with a $1 US Coin, December 2013 [Staff Working Paper]: http://www.federalreserve.gov/payment-systems/staff-working-paper-20131211.pdf

15   Reuters, Americans Prefer Dollar Bill to Coin – Poll, 14 April 2008: http://www.reuters.com/article/2008/04/14/us-money-penny-idUSN1435329120080414

16   Eur-Lex, Review of the Introduction of Euro Notes and Coins: http://europa.eu/legislation_summaries/economic_and_monetary_affairs/introducing_euro_practical_aspects/l25064_en.htm

17   Berezin, M. (2000) The Euro is More than Money. *Center for Society & Economy Policy Newsletter – The Euro*, 1(1).

18   Eur-Lex, Review of the Introduction of Euro Notes and Coins: http://europa.eu/legislation_summaries/economic_and_monetary_affairs/introducing_euro_practical_aspects/l25064_en.htm

19   Berezin, M. (2000) The Euro is More than Money. *Center for Society & Economy Policy Newsletter – The Euro*, 1(1).

20   Eur-Lex. Communication from the Commission to the

European Council – Review of the Introduction of Euro Notes and Coins: http://eur-lex.europa.eu/legal-content/EN/TXT/?uri=CELEX:52002DC0124

21 Ranyard, R. et al (2005) A Qualitative Study of Adaptation to the Euro in the Republic of Ireland: I. Attitudes, the 'Euro Illusion' and the Perception of Prices. *Journal of Community & Applied Social Psychology*, 15, 95–107.

22 Reuters, Recession-weary Italians Catch Nostalgia for Lira, 15 January 2014: http://www.reuters.com/article/2014/01/15/italy-lira-nostalgia-idUSL6N0KN38V20140115

23 Gamble, A. et al (2002) Euro Illusion: Psychological Insights into Price Evaluations with a Unitary Currency. *European Psychologist*, 7(4), 302–311.

24 Gamble, A. et al (2002) Euro-illusion: Psychological Insights into Price Evaluations with a Unitary Currency. *European Psychologist*, 7(4), 302–311.

25 Eur-Lex. Communication from the Commission to the European Council – Review of the Introduction of Euro Notes and Coins: http://eur-lex.europa.eu/legal-content/EN/TXT/?uri=CELEX:52002DC0124

26 Kooreman, P. et al (2004) Charity Donations and the Euro Introduction: Some Quasi-Experimental Evidence on Money Illusion. *Journal of Money, Credit, and Banking*, 36(6).

27 For more on the impact of happiness on cognitive skills, see my 2011 book *Emotional Rollercoaster*, London: Harper Perennial, and also these two papers: Isen, A.M. et al (1987) Positive Affect Facilitates Creative Problem Solving. *Journal of Personality and Social Psychology*, 52, 1122–1131; and Fredrickson, B.L. & Losada, M.F. (2005) Positive Affect and the Complex Dynamics of Human Flourishing. *American Psychologist*, 60(7), 678–686.

28 Thomas, M. et al (2011) How Credit Card Payments Increase Unhealthy Food Purchases: Visceral Regulation of Vice. *Journal of Consumer Research*, 38(1), 126–139.

29 See Soman (1999) cited in Prelec & Simester (2001) Always

Leave Home Without It: A Further Investigation of the Credit-card Effect on Willingness to Pay. *Marketing Letters*, 12, 5–12.

30 Prelec, D. & Simester, D. (2001) Always Leave Home Without It: A Further Investigation of the Credit-card Effect on Willingness to Pay. *Marketing Letters*, 12, 5–12.

31 *Verum* Consumer Trends Report (May 2014). London: Verum Research.

CHAPTER 3

1 Kahneman, D. (2012) *Thinking, Fast and Slow.* London: Penguin.

2 Mullainathan, S. & Shafir, E. (2013) *Scarcity: Why Having Too Little Means So Much.* London: Allen Lane.

3 Tversky, A. & Kahneman, D. (1981) The Framing of Decisions and the Psychology of Choice, *Science*, 211, 453–458.

4 Dolphin, T. & Silim, A. (2014) *Purchasing Power: Making Consumer Markets Work for Everyone.* London: IPPR.

5 You can listen to the interview with Daniel Kahneman on 'Health Check' on the BBC World Service. The theatre ticket story is from the full, unedited version of this interview: http://www.bbc.co.uk/programmes/p00mmnj2

6 Kahneman, D. & Tversky, A. (1984) Choices, Values and Frames. *American Psychologist*, 39, 209–215.

7 Thaler, R.H. & Sunstein, C.R. (2008) *Nudge.* London: Yale University Press.

8 Kojima, S. & Hama, Y. (1982) Aspects of the Psychology of Spending. *Japanese Psychological Research*, 24(1), 29–38.

9 Shefrin, H.M. & Thaler, R. (1988) The Behavioural Life-cycle Hypothesis. *Economic Inquiry*, 26, 609–643.

10 Council of Mortgage Lenders, 2015.

CHAPTER 4

1 For an extremely comprehensive description of Kahneman's own work, as well as that of many others in the field, see the

best-selling Kahneman, D. (2012) *Thinking, Fast and Slow*. London: Penguin.

2 Loewenstein, G.F. (1988) Frames of Mind in Intertemporal Choice. *Management Science*, 35, 200–214.

3 Chen, M.K. et al (2006) The Evolution of Our Preferences: Evidence from Capuchin Monkey Trading Behavior. *Journal of Political Economy*, 114(2006), 517–537.

4 Buonomano, D. (2011) *Brain Bugs: How the Brain's Flaws Shape Our Lives*. London: W.W. Norton & Co.

5 Van de Ven, N. & Zeelenberg, M. (2011) Regret Aversion and the Reluctance to Exchange Lottery Tickets. *Journal of Economic Psychology*, 32, 194–200.

6 Zeelenberg, M. & Pieters, R. (2004) Consequences of Regret Aversion in Real Life: The Case of the Dutch National Lottery. *Organizational Behaviour and Human Decision Processes*, 93, 155–168.

7 Kahneman, D. et al (1990) Experimental Tests of the Endowment Effect and the Coase Theorem. *Journal of Political Economy*, 98(6), 1325–1348.

8 Harbaugh, W.T. et al (2001) Are Adults Better Behaved Than Children? Age, Experience, and the Endowment Effect. *Economics Letters*, 70(2001), 175–181.

9 Purhoit, D. (1995) Playing the Role of Buyer and Seller: The Mental Accounting of Trade-ins. *Marketing Letters*, 6, 101–110.

10 Santos, L.R. (2008) *Endowment Effect in Capuchin Monkeys*. BPhil, Trans. R. Soc. B 363, 3837–3844.

CHAPTER 5

1 Journalist Corie Brown's telling of this story contains some fascinating details – Brown, C. $75,000 a Case? He's Buying. *Los Angeles Times*, December 2006: http://articles.latimes.com/2006/dec/01/entertainment/et-rudy1

2 Wallace, B. (13 May 2012) Château Sucker, *New York Magazine*: http://nymag.com/news/features/rudy-kurniawan-wine-fraud-2012-5/

3   Wallace, B. (13 May 2012) Château Sucker, *New York Magazine*: http://nymag.com/news/features/rudy-kurniawan-wine-fraud-2012-5/

4   Secret, M. A. (13 December 2013) Kock Brother, on a Crusade Against Counterfeit Rare Wines, Takes the Stand, *New York Times*: http://www.nytimes.com/2013/12/14/nyregion/william-koch-on-counterfeit-wine-crusade-testifies-against-rudy-kurniawan.html?_r=0

5   Wallace, B. (13 May 2012) Château Sucker, *New York Magazine*: http://nymag.com/news/features/rudy-kurniawan-wine-fraud-2012-5/

6   FBI (18 December 2013) Wine Dealer Rudy Kurniawan Convicted in Manhattan Federal Court of Creating and Selling Millions of Dollars in Counterfeit Wine [Press Release]: http://www.fbi.gov/newyork/press-releases/2013/wine-dealer-rudy-kurniawan-convicted-in-manhattan-federal-court-of-creating-and-selling-millions-of-dollars-in-counterfeit-wine

7   Plassmann, H. et al (2008) Marketing Actions Can Modulate Neural Representations of Experienced Pleasantness. *PNAS*, 105(3), 1050–1054.

8   Goldstein, R. et al (2008) Do More Expensive Wines Taste Better? Evidence from a Large Sample of Blind Tastings. *AAWE Working Paper*, No. 16 April.

9   Shiv, B. et al (2005) Placebo Effects of Marketing Actions: Consumers Get What They Pay For. *Journal of Marketing Research*, XLII, 383–393.

10 Branthwaite, A. & Cooper. P. (1981) Analgesic Effects of Branding in Treatment of Headaches. *British Medical Journal*, 282, 1576–1578.

11 Shiv, B. et al (2005) Placebo Effects of Marketing Actions: Consumers Get What They Pay For. *Journal of Marketing Research*, XLII, 383–393.

12 Just, D. et al (2014) Lower Buffet Prices Lead to Less Taste Satisfaction. *Journal of Sensory Studies*, 29(5), 362–370.

13 Mogilner, C. & Aaker, J. (2009) 'The Time vs. Money Effect':

Shifting Product Attitudes and Decisions through Personal Connection. *Journal of Consumer Research*, 36(2), 277–291.

14 Simonson, I. (1989) Choice Based on Reasons: The Case of Attraction and Compromise Effects. *Journal of Consumer Research*, 16, 158–174.

15 Tversky, A. & Simonson, I. (1992) Choice in Context: Tradeoff Contrast and Extremeness Aversion. *Journal of Marketing Research*, XXIX, 281–295.

16 Hsee, C.K. & Zhang, J. (2010) General Evaluability Theory. *Perspectives on Psychological Science*, 5(4), 343–355.

17 Knutson, B. et al (2007) Neural Predictors of Price. *Neuron*. 53, 147–156.

18 Furnham, A. (2014) *The Psychology of Money*. London: Routledge. This book contains many such examples, as well as a useful review of all the different types of pricing companies apply.

19 Winer, R.S. (1986) A Reference Price Model of Brand Choice for Frequently Purchased Products. *Journal of Consumer Research*, 13, 250–256.

20 Saini, R. et al (2010) Is That Deal Worth My Time? The Interactive Effect of Relative and Referent Thinking on Willingness to Seek a Bargain. *Journal of Marketing*, 74, 34–48.

21 Navarro-Martinez, D. et al (2011) Minimum Required Payment and Supplemental Information Disclosure Effects on Consumer Debt Repayment Decisions. *Journal of Marketing Research*, 48, S60–S77.

22 McHugh, S. & Ranyard, R. (2013) The Effects of Alternative Anchors on Credit Card Repayment Decisions. Paper presented at British Psychological Society Annual Conference in Harrogate.

23 Furnham, A. & Boo, H.C. (2011) A Literature Review of the Anchoring Effect. *Journal of Socio-economics*, 40(1), 35–42.

24 Critcher, C.R. & Gilovich, T. (2008) Incidental Environmental Anchors. *Journal of Behavioral Decision Making*, 21, 241–251.

25 Oppenheimer, D.M. et al (2008) Anchors Aweigh: A Demonstration of Cross-modality Anchoring and Magnitude Priming. *Cognition,* 106, 13–26.

26 Epley, N. & Gilovich, T. (2010) Anchoring Unbound. *Journal of Consumer Psychology,* 20, 20–24. And also Furnham, A. & Boo, H.C. (2011) A Literature Review of the Anchoring Effect. *Journal of Socio-economics.* 40, 35–42. Both provide excellent reviews of some of the classic work on anchoring.

27 Strack, F. & Mussweiler, T. (1997) Explaining the Enigmatic Anchoring Effect: Mechanisms of Selective Accessibility. *Journal of Personality & Social Psychology,* 73, 437–446.

28 Nunes, J.C. & Boatwright, P. (2004) Incidental Prices and Their Effect on Willingness to Pay. *Journal of Marketing Research,* XLI, 457–466.

29 Nunes, J.C. & Boatwright, P. (2004) Incidental Prices and Their Effect on Willingness to Pay. *Journal of Marketing Research,* XLI, 457–466.

30 Englich, B. et al (2006) Playing Dice with Criminal Sentences: The Influence of Irrelevant Anchors on Experts' Judicial Decision Making. *Personality & Social Psychology Bulletin,* 32(2), 188–200.

31 Kahneman, D. (2012) *Thinking, Fast and Slow.* London: Penguin.

32 Galinsky, A.D et al (2009) To Start Low or To Start High?: The Case of Auctions Versus Negotiations. *Current Directions in Psychological Science,* 18, 357–361.

33 Kristensen, H. & Garlin, T. (1997) The Effects of Anchor Points and Reference Points on Negotiation Process and Outcome. *Organizational Behavior and Human Decision Processes,* 71(1), 85–94.

34 Galinsky, A.D et al (2009) To Start Low or To Start High?: The Case of Auctions Versus Negotiations. *Current Directions in Psychological Science,* 18, 357–361.

35 Furnham, A. & Boo, H.C. (2011) A Literature Review of the Anchoring Effect. *Journal of Socio-economics,* 40, 35–42.

Both provide excellent reviews of the classic work on anchoring.

CHAPTER 5½

1 See the philosopher Julian Baggini's feature on tipping around the world. Baggini, J. (10 March 2015) To Tip or Not to Tip?: http://aeon.co/magazine/culture/tipping-polite-gift-or-demeaning-hand-out/

2 Feinberg, R.A. (1986) Credit Cards as Spending Facilitating Stimuli: A Conditioning Interpretation. *Journal of Consumer Research*, 13(3), 348–356.

3 Guéguen, N. (2002) The Effects of a Joke on Tipping When It Is Delivered at the Same Time as the Bill. *Journal of Applied Social Psychology*, 32(9), 1955–1963.

4 Smith, D.E. et al (1982) Interpersonal Touch and Compliance with a Marketing Request. *Basic & Applied Social Psychology*, 3(1), 35–38.

5 Ereceau, D. & Guéguen, N. (2007) The Effect of Touch on the Evaluation of the 'Toucher'. *Journal of Social Psychology*, 147(4), 441–444.

6 Guéguen, N. & Jacob, C. (2005) The Effect of Touch on Tipping: An Evaluation in a French Bar. *International Journal of Hospitality Management*, 24(2), 295–299.

7 Guéguen, N. & Jacob, C. (2014) Clothing Color and Tipping: Gentlemen Patrons Give More Tips to Waitresses With Red Clothes. *Journal of Hospitality & Tourism Research*, 38(2), 275–280.

8 Guéguen, N. (2013) Helping With All Your Heart: The Effect of Cardioid Dishes on Tipping Behavior. *Journal of Applied Social Psychology*, 43, 1745–1749.

9 Lynn, M. & Latané, B. (1984) The Psychology of Restaurant Tipping. *Journal of Applied Social Psychology*, 14, 551–563.

10 Gneezy, U. et al (2004) The Inefficiency of Splitting the Bill. *The Economic Journal*, 114(495), 265–280.

CHAPTER 6

1 *Inside the Bonus Culture*, BBC Radio 4, 25 March 2013: http://www.bbc.co.uk/programmes/b01rg1h8. Also, in 1979 the top paid manager at Barclays earned 14.5 times more than the average employee. Assessed 30 years later, the difference was 75 times more, with a lead executive's salary being more than £4.3 million a year. See The High Pay Commission, Cheques With Balances: Why Tackling High Pay is in the National Interest: http://highpaycentre.org/files/Cheques_with_Balances.pdf

2 Schwab, R.S. (1953) Motivation in Measurements of Fatigue. In Floyd, W.F & Welford, A.T. (Eds) *The Ergonomics Research Society Symposium on Fatigue*. London: H.K. Lewis & Co. Ltd.

3 Deci, E. (1999) A Meta-Analytic Review of Experiments Examining the Effects of Extrinsic Rewards on Intrinsic Motivation. *Psychological Bulletin*, 125 (6), 627–668.

4 Schwab, R.S. (1953) Motivation in Measurements of Fatigue. In Floyd, W.F & Welford, A.T. (Eds) *The Ergonomics Research Society Symposium on Fatigue*. London: H.K. Lewis & Co. Ltd.

5 *Time* magazine article by Amanda Ripley – Ripley, A. (8 April 2010) Should Kids Be Bribed to Do Well in School?: http://content.time.com/time/magazine/article/0,9171,1978758,00.html

6 Fryer, R.G. (2011) Financial Incentives and Student Achievement: Evidence from Randomised Trials. *Quarterly Journal of Economics*, 126, 1755–1798.

7 See Cowen, T. (2008) *Discover Your Inner Economist*. London: Penguin.

8 Slavin, R.E. (2010) Can Financial Incentives Enhance Educational Outcomes? Evidence from International Experiments. *Educational Research Review*, 5 (1), 68–80. A really useful review of schemes that have been tried out across the world.

9 Gneezy, U. et al (2011) When and Why Incentives (Don't) Work to Modify Behaviour. *Journal of Economic Perspectives*, 25(4), 191–209.

10 Skoufia, E. & McClafferty, B. (2001) Is Progresa working? A Summary of the Results of an Evaluation by IFPRI. *IFPRI Discussion Paper*, 118.

11 For details of this scheme and those in other countries see Slavin, R.E. (2010) Can Financial Incentives Enhance Educational Outcomes? Evidence from International Experiments. *Educational Research Review*, 5(1), 68–80.

12 Slavin, R.E. (2010) Can Financial Incentives Enhance Educational Outcomes? Evidence from International Experiments. *Educational Research Review*, 5(1), 68–80.
   There's also an excellent summary of what works and what doesn't from the economist Uri Gneezy. Gneezy, U. et al (2011) When and Why Incentives (Don't) Work to Modify Behaviour. *Journal of Economic Perspectives*, 25(4), 191–209.

13 Abolghasemi, N.S. et al (2010) Blood Donor Incentives: A Step Forward or Backward. *Asian Journal of Transfusion Science*, 4(1), 9–13.

14 Dhingra. N. (2013) In Defense of WHO's Blood Donation Policy. *Science*, 342, 691.

15 See Lacetera, N. et al (2013) Economic Rewards to Motivate Blood Donations, *Science*, 340, 927–928, for a review of the studies that have been done on blood donation.

16 Iajya, V. et al (2012) The Effects of Information, Social and Economic Incentives on Voluntary Undirected Blood Donations. *NBER Working Paper 18630*, NBER: Cambridge, MA.

17 See Lacetera, N. et al (2013) Economic Rewards to Motivate Blood Donations, *Science*, 340, 927–928.

18 Mellstrom, C. & Johannesson, M. (2008) Crowding Out in Blood Donation: Was Titmuss Right? *Journal of the European Economic Association*, 6(4), 845–863.

19 Reich, P. et al (2006) A Randomized Trial of Blood Donation Recruitment Strategies. *Transfusion*, 46, 1090–1096.

20 Gollan, J. (2008) Offenders Given Choice: Pay Fine or Donate Blood. *Sun Sentinel*, Florida.

21   Abolghasemi, N.S. et al (2010) Blood Donor Incentives: A Step Forward or Backward. *Asian Journal of Transfusion Science*, 4(1), 9–13.

22   Machado, S. (2014) Loss Aversion and Altruism in Repeated Blood Donation. Conference paper presented at American Society of Health Economics, Los Angeles: https://ashecon. confex.com/ashecon/2014/webprogram/Paper2366.html

23   Lumley, J. et al (2009) Interventions for Promoting Smoking Cessation during Pregnancy. *Cochrane Database Systematic Reviews*, 8(3): CD001055.

24   There are various schemes like this. This one was 'Smoke Free, Save Big' run by Birmingham East and North Primary Care Trust.

25   Mantazari, E. et al (2012) The Effectiveness of Financial Incentives for Smoking Cessation During Pregnancy: Is It From Being Paid or from the Extra Aid? *BMC Pregnancy Childbirth*, 12:24.

26   Giles, E. et al (2014) The Effectiveness of Financial Incentives for Health Behaviour Change: Systematic Review and Meta-Analysis. *PLoS ONE*, 9(3).

27   Lumley, J. et al (2009) Interventions for Promoting Smoking Cessation During Pregnancy. *Cochrane Database Systematic Reviews*, 8(3): CD001055.

28   Ierfino, D. et al. (2015) Financial Incentives for Smoking Cessation in Pregnancy: A Single-arm Intervention Study Assessing Cessation and Gaming. *Addiction*, 110(4), 680–688.

29   In a south London scheme not dissimilar to Tom's, drug users are given vouchers if they stay clean, but also have to take part in eight group sessions, as well as attend a weekly drop-in. Again, participants told me they find the moment of the drug test inspirational. Some even bring family members, who are often weary of repeated broken promises, to witness the clean test results.

30   Lussier, J.P. et al (2006) A Meta-analysis of Voucher-based

Reinforcement Therapy for Substance Use Disorders. *Addiction*, 101, 192–203.

31 Petry, N.M. (2009) Contingency Management Treatments: Controversies and Challenges. *Addiction*, 105, 1507–1509.

32 Weaver, T. et al (2014) Use of Contingency Management Incentives to Improve Completion of Hepatitis B Vaccination in People Undergoing Treatment for Heroin Dependence: A Cluster Randomised Trial. *The Lancet*, 384(9938), 153–163.

33 Ierfino, D. et al (2015) Financial Incentives for Smoking Cessation in Pregnancy: A Single-arm Intervention Study Assessing Cessation and Gaming. *Addiction*, 110(4), 680–688.

34 Petry, N.M. (2009) Contingency Management Treatments: Controversies and Challenges. *Addiction*, 105, 1507–1509.

35 Petry, N.M. (2009) Contingency Management Treatments: Controversies and Challenges. *Addiction*, 105, 1507–1509.

CHAPTER 7

1 Deci, E. (1971) Effects of Externally Mediated Rewards on Intrinsic Motivation. *Journal of Personality & Social Psychology*, 18(1), 105–115.

2 Henderlong, J. & Lepper, M.R. (2002) The Effects of Praise on Children's Intrinsic Motivation: A Review and Synthesis. *Psychological Bulletin*, 128(5), 774–795.

3 Brummelman, E. et al (2014) "That's Not Just Beautiful— That's Incredibly Beautiful!" The Adverse Impact of Inflated Praise on Children With Low Self-esteem. *Psychological Science*, 25(3), 728–735.

4 Mueller, C.M. & Dweck, C.S. (1998) Praise for Intelligence Can Undermine Children's Motivation and Performance. *Journal of Personality & Social Psychology*, 75(1), 33–52.

5 Gneezy, U. & Rustichini, A. (2000) Pay Enough or Don't Pay at All. *The Quarterly Journal of Economics*, 115 (3), 791–810.

6 You can hear my BBC Radio 4 documentary *Mind Changers*,

where I visit Skinner's study, at http://www.bbc.co.uk/
programmes/bo639gxq

7 Cameron, J. & Pierce, W.D. (1994) Reinforcement, Reward
and Intrinsic Motivation: A Meta-analysis. *Review of Educational
Research*, 64(3), 363–423.

8 Ariely, D. (2008) *Predictably Irrational*. New York: Harper
Collins.

9 Ariely, D. (2008) *Predictably Irrational*. New York: Harper
Collins.

10 See Webley, P. et al (2001) *The Economic Psychology of Everyday
Life*. Sussex: Psychology Press. See p.155 for some interesting
discussion on this topic.

11 Ariely, D. (2008) *Predictably Irrational*. New York: Harper
Collins.

12 Jordet, G. et al (2012) Team History and Choking under
Pressure in Major Soccer Penalty Shootouts. *British Journal
of Psychology*, 103(2), 149–292.

13 For an explanation of this theory, see Baumeister, R.F. (1984)
Choking under Pressure: Self-consciousness and Paradoxical
Effects of Incentives on Skillful Performance. *Journal of
Personality & Social Psychology*, 46(3), 610–620.

14 Mobbs, D. et al (2011) Choking on the Money: Reward-Based
Performance Decrements Are Associated With Midbrain
Activity. *Psychological Science*, 20(8), 955–962.

15 Aarts, E. et al (2014) Dopamine and the Cognitive Downside
of a Promised Bonus. *Psychological Science*, 25, 1003.

16 Frey, B.S. & Oberholzer-Gee, F. (1997) The Cost of Price
Incentives: An Empirical Analysis of Motivation Crowding-Out.
American Economic Review, 87(4), 746–755.

17 Gneezy, U. & Rustichini, A. (2000) A Fine is a Price. *Journal
of Legal Studies*, 29(1), 1–17.

CHAPTER 8

1 Fraser, G. (17 January 2014) The Wolf of Wall Street Sexes
Up Greed, but Systemic Immorality Does More Damage:

http://www.theguardian.com/commentisfree/belief/2014/jan/17/
wolf-wall-street-sexes-greed-immorality

2 Griffiths, M.D. (2013) Financial Trading as a Form of
   Gambling. *i-Gaming Business Affiliate*, April/May, 40.

3 Gregg, P. et al (2012) Executive Pay and Performance: Did
   Bankers' Bonuses Cause the Crisis? *International Review of
   Finance*, 12(1), 89–122.

4 CIPD (2015) Show Me the Money! The Behavioural Science
   of Reward. This is a very comprehensive report that brings
   together masses of research on the use of rewards with adults
   at work and makes concrete recommendations.

5 Osterloh, M. (2014) Viewpoint: Why Variable Pay-for-
   performance in Healthcare Can Backfire: Evidence from
   Psychological Economics. *Evidence-based HRM: A Global
   Forum for Empirical Scholarship*, 2(1), 120–123.

6 Larkin, I. et al (2012) The Psychological Costs of Pay-for-
   performance: Implications for the Strategic Compensation of
   Employees. *Strategic Management Journal*, 33, 1194–1214.

7 Speech by Adair Turner, Chairman, Financial Services Authority
   at the City Banquet, Mansion House, London, 22 September
   2009: http://www.fsa.gov.uk/pages/Library/Communication/
   Speeches/2009/0922_at.shtml

8 CIPD (2015) Show Me the Money! The Behavioural Science
   of Reward.

CHAPTER 9

1 For a comprehensive explanation of the typologies proposed
   by different authors see Adrian's Furnham's 2006 book, *The
   New Psychology of Money*. London: Routledge.

2 These headings are from a typology outlined by Goldberg,
   H. & Lewis, R.E. (1978) *Money Madness: The Psychology of
   Saving, Spending, Loving, and Hating Money*. (Los Angeles:
   Wellness Institute Ltd.) I have summarised the characteristics
   they give here in my own words, but this book outlines the
   types in full.

3 See Keller and Siegrist on p.97 of Furnham, A. (2006) *The New Psychology of Money*. London: Routledge.

4 See Paul Webley et al's excellent textbook *The Economic Psychology of Everyday Life* for a summary of the research in this area, beginning on p.107.

5 Engleberg, E. & Sjoberg, L. (2006) Money Attitudes and Emotional Intelligence. *Journal of Applied Social Psychology*, 36(8), 2027–2047.

6 See Adrian Furnham's *The New Psychology of Money*, Chapter 5, for a comprehensive summary of this field of study.

7 *The Big Money Test – Results*, BBC Science, 14 March 2013: http://www.bbc.co.uk/science/0/21360144

8 Dew, J. et al (2012) Examining the Relationship Between Financial Issues and Divorce. *Family Relations*, 61(4), 615–628.

9 Burgoyne, C. (2004) Heartstrings and Purse Strings: Money in Heterosexual Marriage. *Feminism & Psychology*, 14(1), 165–172.

10 Prince, M. (1993) Women, Men, and Money Styles. *Journal of Economic Psychology*, 14, 175–182.

11 Mitchell, T.R. & Mickel, A.E. (1999) The Meaning of Money: An Individual Difference Perspective. *Academy of Management Review*, 24(3), 568–578.

12 For more of Elaine's story see *Making Slough Happy*, BBC2, 6 December 2005.

13 Sullivan, P. (20 January 2006) William 'Bud' Post III; Unhappy Lottery Winner: http://www.washingtonpost.com/wp-dyn/content/article/2006/01/19/AR2006011903124.html

14 Runion, R. (1 May 2007) Lawsuit: Millionaire Stole Lotto Ticket: http://www.theledger.com/article/20070501/NEWS/705010406

15 *BBC News* (11 August 2004) Rapist Scoops £7m on Lotto Extra: http://news.bbc.co.uk/1/hi/uk/3554008.stm

16 Hedenus, A. (2011) Finding Prosperity as a Lottery Winner: Presentations of Self after Acquisition of Sudden Wealth, *Sociology*, 45(1), 22–37.

17 Brickman, P. et al (1978) Lottery Winners and Accident Victims: Is Happiness Relative? *Journal of Personality and Social Psychology*, 36(8), 917–927.

18 Armenta, C.N. et al (2014) Is Lasting Change Possible? Lessons from the Hedonic Adaptation Prevention Model. In Sheldon, K.M. & Lucas, R.E. (Eds) *Stability of Happiness*. New York: Elsevier.

19 Quoidbach, J. et al (2010) Money Giveth, Money Taketh Away: The Dual Effect of Wealth on Happiness. *Psychological Science*, 21(6), 759–763.

20 *Happy Money* by Elizabeth Dunn & Michael Norton (2013) gives an excellent account of how to use the evidence on spending to use money to make yourself happier. London: One World.

21 Thaler, R.H. (1999) Mental Accounting Matters. *Journal of Behavioral Decision-making*, 12(3), 183–206.

22 Haushofer, J. & Shapiro, J. (2013) Household Response to Income Changes: Evidence from an Unconditional Cash Transfer Program in Kenya. Massachusetts Institute of Technology Working Paper.

23 Stevenson, B. & Wolfes, J. (2013) Subjective Well-Being and Income: Is There Any Evidence of Satiation? *American Economic Review*, 103(3), 598–604.

24 Deaton, A. (27 February 2008) Worldwide, Residents of Richer Nations More Satisfied. Gallup: http://www.gallup.com/poll/104608/worldwide-residents-richer-nations-more-satisfied.aspx

25 Aknin, L.B. et al (2009) From Wealth to Well-being? Money Matters, but Less Than People Think. *The Journal of Positive Psychology*, 4(6), 523–527.

26 Helga Dittmar's book *Consumer Culture, Identity & Well-Being*. (Hove: Psychology Press) contains a chapter 'Is This as Good as it Gets?' on the consequences of materialism, containing this data and many other studies.

27 Csikszentmihalyi, M. (2002) *Flow: The Psychology of Happiness*. London: Rider.

28 Locke, E.A. et al (2001) Money and Subjective Well-being: It's Not the Money, It's the Motives. *Journal of Personality and Social Psychology*, 80(6), 959–971.

29 For details of this study, see Helga Dittmar's 2008 book *Consumer Culture, Identity and Well-being*, pp.85–94 Hove: Psychology Press.

30 Pieters, R. (2013) Bidirectional Dynamics of Materialism and Loneliness: Not Just a Vicious Cycle. *Journal of Consumer Research*, 40, 615–631.

CHAPTER 10

1 Harris, L.T. & Fiske, S.T. (2006) Dehumanizing the Lowest of the Low: Neuroimaging Responses to Extreme Out-Groups. *Psychological Science*, 17, 847–853.

2 Levi, P. (1988) *The Drowned and the Saved*. London: Abacus.

3 Bamfield, L. & Horton, T. (22 June 2009) Understanding Attitudes to Tackling Economic Inequality: http://www.jrf.org.uk/publications/attitudes-economic-inequality

4 Clery, E., et al (April 2013) Prepared for the Joseph Rowntree Foundation – Public Attitudes to Poverty and Welfare, 1983–2011. Analysis Using British Social Attitudes Data: http://www.natcen.ac.uk/media/137637/poverty-and-welfare.pdf

5 Hall, S. et al (2014) *Public Attitudes to Poverty*. Joseph Rowntree Foundation.

6 Heberle, A. & Carter, A. (2015) Cognitive Aspects of Young Children's Experience of Economic Disadvantage. *Psychological Bulletin*, 141(4), 723–746.

7 Weinger, S. (2000) Economic Status: Middle Class and Poor Children's View. *Children & Society*, 14, 135–146.

8 Heberle, A. & Carter, A. (2015) Cognitive Aspects of Young Children's Experience of Economic Disadvantage. *Psychological Bulletin*, 141(4), 723–746.

9 Cozzarelli, C. et al (2001) Attitudes Toward the Poor and Attributions for Poverty. *Journal of Social Issues*, 57, 207–227. Also for a useful summary of many studies of attitudes towards

the poor see Lott, B. (2002) Cognitive and Behavioural Distancing from the Poor. *American Psychologist*, 57(2), 100–110.

10 Crandall S.J. et al (1993) Medical Students' Attitudes Toward Providing Care for the Underserved: Are We Training Socially Responsible Physicians? *JAMA*, 269, 2519–2523.

11 Lerner, M.J. (1980) *The Belief in a Just World: A Fundamental Delusion*. New York: Plenum Press.

12 Weiner, D.O. et al (2011) An Attributional Analysis of Reactions to Poverty: The Political Ideology of the Giver and the Perceived Morality of the Receiver. *Personality & Social Psychology Review*, 15(2), 199–213.

13 Guzewicz, T. & Takooshian, H. (1992) Development of a Short-form Scale of Public Attitudes Toward Homelessness. *Journal of Social Distress & the Homeless*, 1(1), 67–79.

14 Horwitz, S. & Dovidio, J.F. (2015) The Rich – Love Them or Hate Them? Divergent Implicit and Explicit Attitudes Toward the Wealthy. *Group Processes & Intergroup Relations*, doi: 10.1177/1368430215596075

15 Mani, A. et al (2013) Poverty Impedes Cognitive Function. *Science*, 341(6149), 976–980.

16 Mullainathan, S. & Shafir, E. (2013) *Scarcity: Why Having Too Little Means So Much*. London: Allen Lane. 12.

17 Mani, A. et al (2013) Poverty Impedes Cognitive Function. *Science*, 341(6149), 976–980.

18 Pew Charitable Trust (2013) Payday Lending in America: Report 2 – How Borrowers Choose and Repay Payday Loans.

19 Prelec, G. & Loewenstein, D. (1998) The Red and the Black. *Marketing Science*, 17(1), 4–28.

20 Nickerson, R.S. (1984) Retrieval Inhibition from Part-set Cuing: A Persisting Enigma in Memory Research. *Memory & Cognition*, 12(6), 531–552.

21 Mullainathan, S. & Shafir, E. (2013) *Scarcity: Why Having Too Little Means So Much*. London: Allen Lane. 107.

22 Shah, A. et al (2013) Some Consequences of Having Too Little. *Science*, 338, 682–685.

23 Von Stumm, S. et al (2013) Financial Capability, Money Attitudes and Socioeconomic Status. *Personality and Individual Differences*, 54, 344–349.

24 Haushofer, J. (2011) Neurobiological Poverty Traps. Working paper: University of Zurich. This paper is an excellent and very honest summary of the state of the field.

25 Haushofer, J. (2011) Neurobiological Poverty Traps. Working paper: University of Zurich.

26 Luby, J. et al (2013) The Effects of Poverty on Childhood Brain Development. *JAMA Pediatrics*, 167(12), 1135–1142.

27 Piketty, T. (2014) *Capital in the Twenty-first Century*. Cambridge, Massachusetts: Harvard University Press.

CHAPTER 11

1 Vohs, K.D. et al (2006) The Psychological Consequences of Money. *Science*, 314, 1154–1156.

2 Bargh, J.A. et al (1996) Automaticity of Social Behavior: Direct Effects of Trait Construct and Stereotype Activation on Action. *Journal of Personality and Social Psychology*, 71(2), 230–244.

3 Grenier, M. et al (2012) Money Priming Did Not Cause Reduced Helpfulness: http://www.psychfiledrawer.org/replication.php?attempt=MTQ2

4 Vohs, K.D. (2015) Money Priming Can Change People's Thoughts, Feelings, Motivations, and Behaviors: An Update on 10 Years of Experiments. *Journal of Experimental Psychology*, 144(4), e86–e93.

5 Kouchaki, M. (2013) Seeing Green. Mere Exposure to Money Triggers a Business Decision Frame and Unethical Outcomes. *Organizational Behavior and Human Decision Processes*, 121(1), 53–61.

6 Campbell, W.K. (2004) Psychological Entitlement: Interpersonal Consequences and Validation of a Self-report Measure. *Journal of Personality Assessment*, 83(1), 29–45.

7 Piff, P.K. (2014) Wealth and the Inflated Self: Class, Entitlement, and Narcissism. *Personality and Social Psychology Bulletin*, 40(1), 34–43.

8 Piff, P.K. (October 2013) Does Money Make You Mean? TED Talk. https://www.ted.com/talks/paul_piff_does_money_make_you_mean?language=en

9 Brickman, P. et al (1978) Lottery Winners and Accident Victims: Is Happiness Relative? *Journal of Personality and Social Psychology*, 36(8), 917–927.

10 Piff, P.K. et al (2012) Higher Social Class Predicts Increased Unethical Behaviour. *PNAS*, 109(11), 4086–4091.

11 Trautmann, S.T. et al (2013) Social Class and (Un)Ethical Behavior: A Framework, With Evidence From a Large Population Sample. *Perspectives on Psychological Science*, 8(5), 487–497.

12 Bauer, R. et al (2014) Donation and Strategic Behavior of Millionaires. Working Paper, Rotterdam Behavioral Finance Conference.

13 Cikara, M. & Fiske, S.T. (2012) Stereotypes and Schadenfreude. Affective and Physiological Markers of Pleasure at Outgroup Misfortunes. *Social Psychological and Personality Science*, 3(1), 63–71.

14 Belk, R. & Wallendorf, S. (1990) The Sacred Meanings of Money. *Journal of Economic Psychology*, 11, 35–67.

15 Zizzo, D.J. & Oswald, A. (2000) Are People Willing to Pay to Reduce Others' Incomes? Working Paper. *Warwick Economic Research Papers*, No. 568.

16 Van de Ven, N. et al (2010) The Envy Premium in Product Evaluation. *Journal of Consumer Research*, 37(6), 984–998.

17 Jealousy and envy aren't strictly speaking the same thing. For jealousy, think love triangle: three people, with one person fearing the loss of another to the third. Envy, by contrast, involves just the two of us. You have something I want, whether that's a particular skill, success in life or, yes, a lot more money. In this case, Pieters and his team used the word

jealousy because they thought it sounded less negative than envy and because it's often used colloquially to mean the same thing.

18 Festinger, L. (1957) *A Theory of Cognitive Dissonance*. Stanford: Stanford University Press.

19 Xie, W. et al (2014) Money, Moral Transgressions, and Blame. *Journal of Consumer Psychology*, 24 (3), 299–306.

20 Lewis, A. et al (2012). Drawing the Line Somewhere: An Experimental Study of Moral Compromise. *Journal of Economic Psychology*, 33(4), 718–725.

21 Marwell, G. & Ames, R. (1981) Economists Free Ride. Does Anyone Else? *Journal of Public Economics*, 15(3), 295–310.

22 Frank, R.H. et al (1993) The Evolution of One-shot Cooperation: An Experiment. *Ethology and Sociobiology*, 14(4), 247–256.

23 Goldberg, H. & Lewis, R.E. (1978) *Money Madness: The Psychology of Saving, Spending, Loving, and Hating Money*. Los Angeles: Wellness Institute Ltd.

24 Hanley, A. & Wilhelm, M.S. (1992) Compulsive Buying: An Exploration into Self-esteem and Money Attitudes. *Journal of Economic Psychology*, 13, 5–18.

25 Pascal, B. (1660, 1958) *Pascal's Pensées*. New York: Dutton.

26 For a good review of the studies, see Hahn, C. et al (2013) 'Show Me the Money': Vulnerability to Gambling Moderates the Attractiveness of Money Versus Suspense. *Personality and Social Psychology Bulletin*, 39(10), 1259–1267.

27 Hahn, C. et al (2013) 'Show Me the Money': Vulnerability to Gambling Moderates the Attractiveness of Money Versus Suspense. *Personality and Social Psychology Bulletin*, 39(10), 1259–1267.

28 Chen, E.Z. et al (2012) An Examination of Gambling Behaviour in Relation to Financial Management Behaviour, Financial Attitudes, and Money Attitudes. *International Journal of Mental Health Addiction*, 10, 231–242.

29 Slutske, W.S. et al (2005) Personality and Problem Gambling.

A Prospective Study of a Birth Cohort of Young Adults. *Archives of General Psychiatry*, 62(7), 769–775.

30 Michalczuk, R. et al (2011) Impulsivity and Cognitive Distortions in Pathological Gamblers Attending the UK National Problem Gambling Clinic: A Preliminary Report. *Psychological Medicine*, 41(12), 2625–2635.

31 Clark, L. (2010) Decision-making during Gambling: An Integration of Cognitive and Psychobiological Approaches. *Philosophical Transactions: Biological Sciences*, 365, 319–330.

32 Cocker, P.J. et al (2013) A Selective Role for Dopamine D_4 Receptors in Modulating Reward Expectancy in a Rodent Slot Machine Task. *Biological Psychiatry*, 75(10), 817–824.

33 Clark, L. (2010) Decision-making during Gambling: An Integration of Cognitive and Psychobiological Approaches. *Philosophical Transactions: Biological Sciences*, 365, 319–330.

34 Clark, L. (2010) Decision-making during Gambling: An Integration of Cognitive and Psychobiological Approaches. *Philosophical Transactions: Biological Sciences*, 365, 319–330.

35 Michalczuk, R. et al (2011) Impulsivity and Cognitive Distortions in Pathological Gamblers Attending the UK National Problem Gambling Clinic: A Preliminary Report. *Psychological Medicine*, 41(12): 2625–2635.

CHAPTER 12

1 Dunn, E.W. et al (2008) Spending Money on Others Promotes Happiness. *Science*, 319(5870), 1687–1688.

2 Harbaugh, W.T. et al (2007) Neural Responses to Taxation and Voluntary Giving Reveal Motives for Charitable Donations. *Science*, 316(5831),1622–1625. Quote is from: EurekAlert! Paying Taxes, According to the Brain, Can Bring Satisfaction (14 June 2007): http://www.eurekalert.org/pub_releases/2007-06/uoo-pta061107.php

3 Harbaugh, W.T. (1998) What Do Donations Buy? A Model of Philanthropy Based on Prestige and Warm Glow. *Journal of Public Economics*, 67, 269–284.

4   Raihani, N.J. & Smith, S. (2015) Competitive Helping in Online Giving. *Current Biology*, 25(9), 1183–1186.

5   Izuma, K. (2009) Processing of the Incentive for Social Approval in the Ventral Striatum during Charitable Donation. *Journal of Cognitive Neuroscience*, 22(4), 621–631.

6   Newman, G.E. & Cain, D.M. (2014) Tainted Altruism: When Doing Some Good Is Evaluated as Worse Than Doing No Good at All. *Psychological Science*, 25(3), 648–655.

7   Newman, G.E. & Cain, D.M. (2014) Tainted Altruism: When Doing Some Good Is Evaluated as Worse Than Doing No Good at All. *Psychological Science*, 25(3), 648–655.

8   Harbaugh, W.T. et al (2007) Neural Responses to Taxation and Voluntary Giving Reveal Motives for Charitable Donations. *Science*, 316, 1622–1625.

9   Andreoni, J. (2006) 'Philanthropy' in Serge-Christophe Kolm and Jean Mercier Ythier (Eds) *Handbook of Giving, Reciprocity, and Altruism*. Amsterdam: Elsevier/North-Holland.

10 Schervish, P.G. et al (2006) 'Charitable Giving: How Much, By Whom, To What, and Why' in Powell, W.W. & Steinberg, R. *The Nonprofit Sector: A Research Handbook*. Connecticut: Yale University Press.

11 *The Chronicle of Philanthropy* (2014) – How America Gives: https://philanthropy.com/specialreport/how-america-gives-2014/1

12 Holland, J. et al (2012) Lost Letter Measure of Variation in Altruistic Behaviour in 20 Neighbourhoods, *PLoS ONE*, 7(8): e43294.

13 Brethel-Haurwitz, K. & Marsh, A. (2014) Geographical Differences In Subjective Well-Being Predict Extraordinary Altruism. *Psychological Science*, 25(3), 762–771.

14 Hoffman, M. (2011) Does Higher Income Make You More Altruistic? Evidence from the Holocaust. *The Review of Economics and Statistics*, 93(3), 876–887.

15 Guéguen, N. & Lamy, L. (2011) The Effect of the Word 'love' on Compliance to a Request for Humanitarian Aid: An Evaluation in a Field Setting. *Social Influence*, 6 (4), 249–258.

16 Fisher, R.J. & Ma, Y. (2014) The Price of Being Beautiful: Negative Effects of Attractiveness on Empathy for Children in Need. *Journal of Consumer Research*, 41(2), 436–450.

17 Ein-Gar, D. & Levontin, L. (2013) Giving From a Distance: Putting the Charitable Organization at the Center of the Donation Appeal. *Journal of Consumer Psychology*, 23, 197–211.

18 Evangelidis, I. & Van den Bergh, B. (2013) The Number of Fatalities Drives Disaster Aid. Increasing Sensitivity to People in Need. *Psychological Science*, 24(11), 2226–2234.

19 See my 2013 book *Time Warped* for more details of this research pioneered by Yaacov Trope and Nira Liberman.

20 Ein-Gar, D. & Levontin, L. (2013) Giving From a Distance: Putting the Charitable Organization at the Center of the Donation Appeal, *Journal of Consumer Psychology*, 23, 197–211

21 Charities Aid Foundation World Giving Index, 2014: https://www.cafonline.org/about-us/publications/2014-publications/world-giving-index-2014

CHAPTER 13

1 Felson, R.B. (1981) Ambiguity and Bias in the Self-concept. *Social Psychology Quarterly*, 44, 64–69.

2 Dunning, D. et al (1989) Ambiguity and Self-Evaluation: The Role of Idiosyncratic Trait Definitions in Self-serving Assessments of Ability. *Journal of Personality and Social Psychology*, 57, 1082–1090.

3 Himanshu M. et al (2013) Influence of Motivated Reasoning on Saving and Spending Decisions. *Organizational Behavior and Human Decision Processes*, 121(1), 13–23.

4 See my book *Time Warped* (2013) published by Canongate for a whole book's worth of discussion on this.

5 Warneryd, K.E. (2000) Future-orientation, Self-control and Saving. Paper presented at XXVII International Congress of Psychology, Stockholm.

6   Howlett. E. et al (2008) The Role of Self-Regulation, Future Orientation, and Financial Knowledge in Long-Term Financial Decisions. *Journal of Consumer Affairs*, 42(2), 223–242.

7   Peetz, J. & Buehler, R. (2009) Is There a Budget Fallacy? The Role of Savings Goals in the Prediction of Personal Spending. *Personality & Social Psychology Bulletin*, 35(12), 1579–1591.

8   Lewis, N.A. & Oyserman, D. (2015) When Does the Future Begin? Time Metrics Matter, Connecting Present and Future Selves. *Psychological Science*, 26(6), 816–825.

9   Ulkumen, G. et al (2008) Will I Spend More in 12 Months or a Year? The Effect of Ease of Estimation and Confidence on Budget Estimates. *Journal of Consumer Research*, 35(2), 245–256.

10 Thaler, R.H. & Sunstein, C.R. (2008) *Nudge*. London: Yale University Press.

11 Trope, Y. & Liberman, N. (2003) Temporal Construal. *Psychological Review*, 110(3), 403–421.

12 Tam, L. & Dholakia, U. (2014) Saving in Cycles. How to Get People to Save More Money. *Psychological Science*, 25(2), 531–537.

13 Chen, K. (2013) The Effect of Language on Economic Behavior: Evidence from Savings Rates, Health Behaviors, and Retirement Assets. *American Economic Review*, 103(2), 690–731.

14 Chen, K. (2013) The Effect of Language on Economic Behavior: Evidence from Savings Rates, Health Behaviors, and Retirement Assets. *American Economic Review*, 103(2), 690–731.

15 Maglio, S. J. et al (2013) Distance From a Distance: Psychological Distance Reduces Sensitivity to Any Further Psychological Distance. *Journal of Experimental Psychology: General*, 142(3): 644–657.

16 Ashraf, N. et al (2006) Tying Odysseus to the Mast: Evidence from a Commitment Savings Product in the Philippines. *The Quarterly Journal of Economics*, 121(2), 635–672.

17 Ashraf, N. et al (2006) Household Decision Making and Savings Impacts: Further Evidence from a Commitment

Savings Product in the Philippines. Yale University Economic Growth Center Discussion Paper No. 939.

18 Meredith, J. et al (2013) Keeping the Doctor Away: Experimental Evidence on Investment in Preventative Health Products. *Journal of Development Economics*, 105, 196–210.

19 Bench, G. et al (2014) Why Do Households Forgo High Returns from Technology Adoption: Evidence from Improved Cook Stoves in Burkina Faso, Ruhr Economic Papers.

20 Dupas, P. & Robinson, J. (2013) Why Don't the Poor Save More? Evidence from Health Savings Experiments. *American Economic Review*, 103(4), 1138–1171.

21 Karlan, D. et al (2014) Getting to the Top of Mind: How Reminders Increase Saving. *National Bureau of Economic Research Working Paper*, 16205: http://karlan.yale.edu/sites/default/files/top-of-mind-oct2014.pdf

CHAPTER 14

1 Dunn, E.W. et al (2011) If Money Doesn't Make You Happy, Then You Probably Aren't Spending it Right. *Journal of Consumer Psychology*, 21, 115–125.

2 Paul Dolan's book *Happiness by Design* (London: Penguin) explains how to work out what gives you real pleasure in life, and how to make the decisions that can make you happier.

3 Kumar, A. et al (2014) Waiting for Merlot. Anticipatory Consumption of Experiential and Material Purchases. *Psychological Science*, 25(10), 1924–1931.

4 The Skint Foodie – Food + Recovery + Peckham (With Added Employment), online blog: http://www.theskintfoodie.com/

5 Dunn, E. & Norton, M. (2013) *Happy Money: The New Science of Smarter Spending*. London: One World.

6 DeVoe, S.E. & Pfeffer, J. (2008) When Time is Money: The Effect of Hourly Payment on the Evaluation of Time. *Organizational Behaviour and Human Decision Processes*, 104(1), 1–13.

7 Dunn, E. & Norton, M. (2013) *Happy Money: The New Science of Smarter Spending*. London: One World.

8 Loewenstein, G. (1987) Anticipation and the Value of Delayed Consumption. *The Economic Journal*, 97(387), 666–684.

9 Chancellor, J. & Lyubomirsky, S. (2011) Happiness and Thrift: When (Spending) Less is (Hedonically) More. *Journal of Consumer Psychology*, 21, 131–138.

10 Atalay, A. & Meloy, M. (2011). Retail Therapy: A Strategic Effort to Improve Mood. *Psychology and Marketing*, 28(6), 638–659.

RECOMMENDATIONS FOR ADDITIONAL READING

The endnotes contain detailed references, but if you are simply looking for some more books to read on the topic of money these are my favourites, listed alphabetically.

Ariely, D. (2008) *Predictably Irrational*. London: HarperCollins

De Cremer, D et al (2006) *Social Psychology and Economics*. London: Lawrence Erlbaum Associates.

Dunn, E. & Norton, M. (2013) *Happy Money: The New Science of Smarter Spending*. London: Oneworld.

Earl, P.E. & Kemp, S. (Eds) (1999) *Consumer Research and Economic Psychology*. Cheltenham: Elgar.

Furnham, A. (2008) *The Econonic Socialisation of Young People*. London: The Social Affairs Unit.

Furnham, A. (2014) *The Psychology of Money*. London: Routledge.

Kahneman, D. (2012) *Thinking Fast and Slow*. London: Penguin.

Lewis, A. (Ed) (2012) *Psychology and Economic Behaviour*. Cambridge: Cambridge University Press.

Mullainathan, S. & Shafir, E. (2013) *Scarcity: Why Having So Little Means So Much*. London: Allen Lane.

Sandel, M.J. (2013) *What Money Can't Buy: The Moral Limits of Markets*. London: Penguin.

Thaler, R.H. & Sunstein, C.R. (2008) *Nudge*. London: Yale University Press.

Webley, P. et al (2001) *The Economic Psychology of Everyday Life*. Sussex: Psychology Press.

INDEX

ACKNOWLEDGEMENTS

In this book, I've scoured the global literature for the most interesting studies on the psychology of money, and of course that wouldn't be possible without the many psychologists, historians, sociologists and economists who have spent years working on these topics and designing the studies that I describe. Running experiments requires a level of patience that I don't have. There are too many to list individually here, but I am in debt to the author of every paper and book you'll find in the endnotes.

If I were to name a few of those who have particularly influenced my thinking, I would have to include Paul Webley, Adrian Furnham, Daniel Kahneman, Stephen Lea, Elizabeth Dunn, Uri Gneezy, Dan Ariely, Sendhil Mullainathan and Carole Burgoyne. I'm grateful to Herb Goldberg and Robert T. Lewis for their typology.

And thank you to those who were kind enough to answer my email queries, often on the same day – Paul Webley, Pascaline Dupas, Robert Frank, Paul Piff, Nicola Phillips, Penny Fielding, David Shanks, Irene Tracey, Stuart Kelly, Sophie Scott and Helga Dittmar.

Several people have been kind enough to let me interview them – Tony Holmes, Mike Redd, Paul Buck, Robert Farago, James Hulse, Stan Parks and Stian Reimers. Thank you also to the others I've interviewed whose names I've changed in order to protect their privacy. I interviewed some of them for BBC Radio 4 programmes, and I'm grateful to the producers in the BBC Radio Science unit for their work on those interviews and for putting up with me endlessly talking about how hard I'm working on my book.

My friends Jo, Becca, Grant, Paula, Andrew, Chris, Philippa and Jim were all generous enough to provide me with some peace to write in France, by allowing me to make their kitchens, living rooms and bedrooms into make-shift offices at various times. Somehow they always seemed to know when I wanted to get on undisturbed and when I would welcome distraction. And all this accompanied by their amazing meals. You couldn't ask for more.

Special thanks go to Lorna Stewart for her research on the book. She is not only brilliant at research, but a lovely person to work with.

Canongate are the friendliest, most efficient publishers you could wish for. My editor Jenny Lord has improved the book immeasurably with her thoughtful suggestions, always so tactfully made. Copy editor Octavia Reeve has both an extraordinary eye for detail and for spotting mistakes. Will Francis, who is my agent at Janklow & Nesbit, was enthusiastic from the moment I called him to suggest the idea for his book, and he's been great throughout.

Finally, my husband Tim spent weeks going through the entire manuscript line by line, telling me when it didn't make sense and suggesting many, many improvements. He has made it a much better book. I'm lucky to have him.